diakonia

DEVOTED TO PROMOTING EASTERN CHRISTIANITY IN THE WEST

UME XVII
MBER 1
1982

H— 11/yr 3 issues

DIAKONIA   Volume XVII   Issue I
                      1982

EDITORIAL

ARTICLES

ORTHODOX AND CATHOLICISM:
A NEW ATTEMPT AT DIALOGUE
   Rev. Theodore Stylianopoulos 4

REFLECTIONS ON THE ORTHODOX-
CATHOLIC DIALOGUE
   John F. Long, S.J. 21

THE HOLY SPIRIT IN THE CHURCH
   Metropolitan Damaskinos of Tranoupoleos 40

COMMENT
MARY AND THE CHRISTIAN IN THE MYSTICAL
POETRY OF ST. EPHREM
   Stephen Bonian, S.J. 46

KHOMIAKOV AND HIS THEORY OF SOBORNOST
   Mary Grace Ritchey 53

CHRONICLE OF EVENTS FOR THE YEAR 1981
IN EASTERN CHRISTIAN JURISDICTIONS
AND ASSOCIATED ORGANIZATIONS
   Thomas F. Sable, S.J. 63

DOCUMENTATION
RUSSIAN ORTHODOX ROMAN CATHOLIC
CONVERSATIONS AT ODESSA 80

VISIT TO ROME OF HIS HOLINESS, ILIA II 83

BOOKS RECEIVED 87

JOHN XXIII INSTITUTE FOR EASTERN CHRISTIAN STUDIES
(Summer Courses) 1981 88

ANNOUNCING A NEW BOOK 89

DIAKONIA INDEX 90

EDITORIAL

The names of two old men have recently been in the news again. In various parts of the world celebrations have taken place for the one hundredth anniversary of the births of Angelo Giuseppi Roncalli and Augustin Bea. Each of them, when almost seventy eight years of age, had been launched into new careers which were to enable them to leave lasting marks on the history of Christianity in the twentieth century.

As Pope John XXIII, Roncalli was to open the door to a movement of updating and renewal which is still affecting the Roman Catholic Church and many other people and institutions. His simple confidence in God who was still guiding the world of His creation, his fidelity to Christ revealing Himself in and through the Church, his willingness to open his heart and mind to the needs and aspirations of people all over the world, his openness to dialogue with all people of good will, whatever their condition or ideology, helped to give new understanding to millions of people of the office of Peter in the Church. In a particular way he has become an inspiration for the Roman Catholic-Orthodox dialogue for he had developed a love for the Christian East which was genuine and deep. This love was translated into words and actions which were to serve as the foundation for a remarkably new development in the relations between Catholics and Orthodox during the past two decades. Totally dedicated to the truth, Pope John XXIII became a symbol of all that is best in what has come to be known as the dialogue of love.

Augustin Bea was a scholar, a student of Holy Scripture who spent long years in scrutinizing the word of God so as to better understand and transmit it. This had taught him to respect and love others, especially those who were working diligently to search out the saving truth which God had revealed. His nomination as cardinal was considered by many as a worthy crown of his past achievements. Instead, he was to use the last nine years of his life in a new and bold effort towards sensitizing the Catholic Church to the demands which the growing ecumenical movement was making on that church and its people. It was not easy. At the beginning he had

1

little acquaintance with or knowledge of the Christian East. By the time he died he had earned the respect and confidence of many Orthodox and had become a symbol of how best one could carry on with them the dialogue of truth, in love.

We are reminded of these two great pioneers as we look forward to the continuation of the dialogue between the Christian East and West. There is a tendency in some circles to down play this dialogue. It moves so slowly, its results are meagre, its promises are uncertain. Powerful voices have been raised in opposition to it; the majority of Christians are indifferent to it. And yet it goes on, impelled by the dynamic of Christ's efficacious prayer "that all may be one." The foundations laid by people such as Pope John XXIII and Cardinal Bea remain strong and deep; they only need builders to construct something upon them.

DIAKONIA seeks to contribute to this work of construction. For that reason, and in consideration of the fact that the Roman Catholic-Orthodox International Theological Commission will hold its second meeting in July of this year, the major part of this issue is devoted to Catholic-Orthodox dialogue. If the spirit of this dialogue and the results it achieves are to make any impact on the Christian people, they must know what is going on. They must be made aware of the problems and prospects of the dialogue. It must be something they make their own. This dialogue is too important to be left merely to a small group of experts. For that reason this review will seek to present as much information and interpretation as possible about the dialogue. It repeats the request already made in the past that the church authorities and those participating in official dialogue provide the widest possible information about its progress so that the Church as a whole may be conscious of its own involvement in it and be able to react sanely to, and profit from what is being achieved.

There is a tendency on the part of some to be discouraged by the negative reactions to the dialogue which are expressed by important persons and groups within the Catholic and Orthodox Churches. The words and actions of Church leaders may sometimes be quite contrary to what has been accomplished—sometimes painfully—through the dialogue. However regretable this may be, it must be understood in the context of the history of the relations between the two Churches. It will take the wisdom and intellectual courage—and the love rooted in dedication to truth—of people like Pope John XXIII and Cardinal Augustin Bea to overcome the prejudices and the fears of the past and open the minds and hearts of people to what the future promises.

Perhaps full communion in faith and in love which will be expressed in full Eucharistic communion will not be achieved in a short time. Still there is no reason to be pessimistic about the ultimate results as long as the spirit of the ecumenical pioneers of both churches remains strong and their dedication to doing the truth in love remains the guiding star of their successors.

John F. Long, S.J.

ARTICLES

ORTHODOXY AND CATHOLICISM: A NEW ATTEMPT AT DIALOGUE

by Theodore Stylianopoulos

The Very Reverend Dr. Theodore Stylia-nopoulos is professor of New Testament and Orthodox Spirituality, Hellenic College/Holy Cross Greek Orthodox School of Theology, Brookline, Massachusetts. This article is the text of a keynote address delivered at a meeting of the National Association of Diocesan Ecumenical Officers of the Roman Catholic Church in the U.S.A., 5 May 1981, in Boston, Ma. It first appeared in The Greek Orthodox Theological Review, vol. XXVI, Number 3, 1981. We thank the author and editor of the Review for their kind permission to reprint it here.

The New Dialogue

A new attempt at official dialogue between the Orthodox and Roman Catholic Churches began last year with a meeting of a special theological commission at Patmos and Rhodes. After a millenium of cultural and theological alienation, the first meeting of the Orthodox-Roman Catholic Theological Commission, 29 May-4 June 1980, which dealt with procedural issues and selected the theme of the mysteries or sacraments, seemed to many like a miracle.

In less than two decades four protagonists, Popes Paul VI and John Paul II on the one hand, and Ecumenical Patriarchs Athenagoras I and Demetrios I on the other, prepared the ground through what they called a "dialogue of love . . . in complete fidelity to the one Lord Jesus Christ."[1] These leaders, through mutual visits, exchange of letters, symbolic gestures, ecclesiastical initiatives, and joint statements seem to have reversed, at least officially, centuries of strife and polemics in two traditions in which people faced one another more frequently as rivals and enemies rather than friends and brothers.

The climax of the preparatory period came when Pope John Paul II and Ecumenical Patriarch Demetrios I met in Constantinople, 29-30 November 1979, to announce a new phase of what may be called a "dialogue of truth"—formal theological dialogue through a mixed theological commission. In their joint statement the two church leaders announced the decision to begin formal dialogue the main purpose of which is "the re-establishment of full communion between the Catholic and Orthodox sister churches."[2] In unprecedented liturgical gestures Demetrios I was present when John Paul II celebrated Mass in the Roman Catholic Cathedral of the Holy Spirit in Constantinople and on the following day John Paul II was present when Demetrior I celebrated the Eucharist in the Patriarchal Church of Saint George. In both instances Pope and Patriarch exchanged the kiss of peace but did not, of course, share in the Lord's Supper because of the existing division between the two Churches.

The Orthodox-Roman Catholic Theological Commission is comprised of some sixty top ecumenical officers and theological experts on both sides, including cardinals, metropolitans, bishops, and lay theologians. The Catholic membership is led by Cardinal Willebrands, head of the Vatican's Secretariat for Promoting Christian Unity. The Orthodox membership is led by Archbishop Stylianos of Australia who represents the Church of Constantinople. According to Archbishop Stylianos, who spoke to a Greek Orthodox Conference in the United States in July 1980,[3] this special commission created a sixteen-member coordinating committee which will meet annually and three working committees which will also meet annually. The entire commission will meet bi-annually. Cast in somewhat technical terms, the exact formulation of the commission's first theme according to Archbishop Stylianos is: "The mystery of the Church and the Eucharist in the light of the Blessed Trinity." The choice to discuss the Eucharist and the nature of the Church signals a prevalent desire among leaders on both sides to begin the dialogue by concentrating on areas of greatest agreement.

Prior to taking up its work, the new commission went on a spiritual pilgrimage to Patmos and then moved on to Rhodes for its working session due to the need for sufficient accommodations and for other technical reasons. Starting with Patmos, where according to tradition John the Disciple of Love and herald of Christ's truth composed the Book of Revelation, the commission underscored the basic presuppositions of the dialogue which is to be guided by an ecumenism of love and an ecumenism of truth. It also raised eschatological hopes concerning the future of this new dialogue which has tremendous implications not only for the Catholic and Orthodox Churches but also for all Christianity and perhaps as well for the entire human family.

Future Prospects

What are the hopes for the future? For all who take seriously Christ's will for Christian unity the hopes are for more miracles through fervent prayer and hard work. However, a realistic Orthodox view is to expect not so much a dramatic breakthrough especially in doctrinal matters but rather happy surprises about the extent of agreement in both theology and practice, while the two sides pray and search for ways to grapple with the central divisive issues. That this new modern dialogue has begun, and has begun in a spirit of mutual love and respect and largely free of political pressures—factors never before present in the past millenium—is truly a miracle of God. But we are only at the beginning of an era which may take many decades, yes even many generations, for the fulfillment of the final goal of eucharistic communion as another miracle of God.

Not only for pastoral but also for theological reasons, it is wise to remember that there is a dialogue between officials and a dialogue between the people at large nurtured in the two traditions. This point is particularly sobering for the Orthodox who theologically hold to the primacy of the life of the Church. The failed attempts at reunion in Lyons (1274) and Florence (1438-1439) poignantly showed that official signatures by bishops to a formula of reunion mean little in the Orthodox world if the agreement is not perceived by the universal conscience of the Orthodox Church to be an authentic expression of Christian truth.

The deep historical consciousness of estrangement between Orthodoxy and Catholicism will not be healed in one or two decades no matter how quickly Church leaders and theologians may wish to move in the dialogue. It was just six years ago that the Orthodox Churches agreed to begin preparing for a formal dialogue with Rome and only seventeen years ago at the Pan-Orthodox Conference in Rhodes that they had officially refused to send observers to the third and final session of Vatican II.[4] These past two decades of preparation for the dialogue were not without grave cautions, disagreements, and even opposition within the Orthodox world. The relations between the Church of Greece and Rome have been strained in recent years.[5] Two of the representatives of the Church of Greece to the Orthodox-Roman Catholic Theological Commission have resigned, one of them reportedly giving as reasons "inadequate preparation on the Orthodox side, disagreement over the subject to be initially discussed, and the unresolved problem of Uniatism."[6] The last point is a reference to Eastern Churches in communion with Rome, a sensitive issue between the Catholic and Orthodox Churches.

Another significant objection to the new dialogue on the Orthodox side came from the twenty monastic communities of Mount Athos which are influential in the Orthodox world. In an extraordinary double assembly,[7] the representatives of the monasteries issued a sharply worded statement warning the Orthodox that the "Roman Catholics are preparing a union of a Uniate type" and proclaiming to the Orthodox that "the Holy Mountain . . . is not going to accept a *fait accompli*." Rigorous in spirit, this statement upholds the Orthodox Church as the only true Church, denies ecclesial reality to all other Christian bodies which are viewed as heretical, objects to 'Uniates' in the Roman Catholic membership of the new theological commission as an affront to the Orthodox, and even cautions the Orthodox about participation in common prayer and liturgical assemblies with other Christians prior to doctrinal agreement.

I have accented the above difficulties and objections in order to provide a balanced view of present attitudes to the dialogue in the Orthodox world. Despite these problems the new ecumenism of love is indeed viable because it has at least the cautious support of most Orthodox bishops, priests, theologians, and faithful and it will continue to grow in influence among the Orthodox barring any unwise acts by Church leaders. But the road ahead will be a long one: a millenial pattern of mistrust, misconceptions, and theological differences will not be unravelled and re-woven in a new pattern of love, understanding, and theological agreement in one decade or even in one generation. The period of dialogue will be a period of mutual growth. Metropolitan Meliton of Chalcedon well remarked at the Pan-Orthodox Conference of 1968 that unity is not a "mechanical event accomplished at a certain moment at the conclusion of specialized negotiations" but rather "unity appears in front of us as a profound, vital state that is gradually developed until it reaches its completion, that is, the confession of a common faith."[8]

The Role of Leadership

What are we to expect from our leadership? Given a wholistic and dynamic rather than static and formal view of the process of dialogue, we can expect our leadership to continue with persistent and courageous efforts at responsible dialogue in obedience to Christ's will. A top priority is the building up of trust on all sides. To many watching eyes the dialogue would be discredited unless the dialogue of love and the dialogue of truth are intimately connected so that, as Archbishop Stylianos has stated, "neither truth may offend love, nor love may offend truth."[9]

Thus far popes, patriarchs, and other prelates have shown both inspirational and effective leadership gaining widespread support. At times Patriarch Athenagoras I of blessed memory, moved by Christian love, risked bold statements[10] for the cause of unity which created apprehensions among other Orthodox church leaders, theologians, and faithful. In their joint statement of 1979, Pope

John Paul II and Patriarch Demetrios I also spoke of their firm will "to hasten the day" of union, an expression which is premature for the Orthodox because it reminds them of failed "hasty" attempts at reunion in the past which the Orthodox perceived as detrimental to Christian truth and to their ecclesial freedom. It is best to proceed with and to use the language of balanced pace, and at the same time to be as open as possible in the dialogue, so that anxieties about something "being secretly planned" or something "being forced" are alleviated.

The Orthodox leadership in particular must continue to work toward a true consensus between the Orthodox Churches and Orthodox Christians themselves, such as in the instance of the composition of the Orthodox membership in the new theological commission, the expected position papers, and future new decisions or new steps regarding the dialogue. I do not see how a genuine Orthodox consensus can hold if representatives of the monastic communities of Mount Athos are not eventually invited to participate in the work of the theological commission. Consensus has for the Orthodox an indispensable theological value and is consequently extremely important because all the family members of the Orthodox Church participate in the dialogue by free conciliar choice and any one or more of the Orthodox Churches can pull out of it at any time the consensus seriously fails. When the Orthodox speak of official dialogue they mean exactly a dialogue officially approved by a consensus of the Orthodox Churches. The forthcoming Great and Holy Synod of the Orthodox Church,[11] now in a gradual process of preparation, will certainly help the strengthening of an Orthodox consensus, but it is not decisive to the ecumenical dialogue, at least not in the present, because the Pan-Orthodox conferences well serve the purpose of discussion of intra-Orthodox concerns on ecumenical matters.

Other helpful initiatives by our leaders among the prelates and participants in the new dialogue include various efforts within our churches to heighten our consciousness to two truths. First, the truth that division for a Christian is unacceptable because it is a tragedy, yes a sin against Christ, and that both sides bear responsibility for the existing deep separation. This is particularly needed among the Orthodox who do not readily acknowledge that they can be faulted in any way, if not for the historical causes of the separation, notably the schism of 1054 and the sack of Constantinople in 1204, at least for the deepening and widening of the rift through subsequent hatred and polemics. Secondly, the church leaders must also heighten our consciousness to the truth of not to expect any sudden capitulations or humiliations on one side or the other. Authentic dialogue, a dialogue of love, cannot be fostered by attitudes of rivalry, argument winning, confusing the other side, imposing demands and the like, but by attitudes of prayerful listening to one another, sensitive understanding of one another's true position, and willingness to break out of defensive positions to common ground insofar as truth allows. At the heart, then, what must be removed is the proselytizing intent of one side trying to convert the other by arguments or strategems. Rather, what is needed, together with honest and thorough discussion of the issues, is the spirit of prayer, patient love, and deep humility so that the truth itself may convert all to a common vision regarding essentials. That truth for Christians is Jesus Christ himself.

Key Challenges

What are the key challenges in this dialogue? As an Orthodox I perceive three kinds of challenges. The first is our profound estrangement which has both in the distant past and in more recent times, not without encouragement from episcopal leaders, theologians, and teachers themselves, been expressed through words and acts of hatred, prejudice, misconception, trivialization, and even derision of each other's theology, practice, and piety. This challenge is already being met by the ecumenism of love. It is true that we have a long way to go. But I trust that the Lord will deliver us from this darkness of soul which permits Christians to quote Jesus' teaching on loving one's enemy and doing good to him, yet blinds them to their hostility for or indifference to their separated Christian brothers. He will deliver us, that is, if church leaders never cease proclaiming Christ's love, which alone can free Christians, so that they may respect each other's ways of thinking and traditions while honestly disagreeing with some of them.

The second kind of challenge involving several points is more intractable but not insurmountable. For an Orthodox viewpoint, this kind of challenge has to do with basic spiritual attitudes toward Western Christianity in general and Roman Catholicism in particular, attitudes which have long been fostered among Orthodox Christians partly because of sensitivity to the importance of doctrine, partly because of devotion to the principle of tradition, and partly because of experience of ecclesiastical hurts in the past—and I am here thinking of Eastern Europe and the Middle East—which still hurt. For example there is an almost natural Orthodox triumphalism which holds that because Orthodoxy alone has maintained the fullness of Christian truth, the Orthodox are consequently right about everything and have essentially nothing to learn from westerners who are "innovators."[12] This attitude can hopefully be cured by a more realistic view of history, by an appreciation of the fact that in the Orthodox tradition itself many non-dogmatic developments and changes have occurred and that not all change is in principle negative, and by taking seriously the fact of *legitimate* variety in the Christian tradition as regards liturgy, practice, art, piety, theological motifs, and other matters outside of the content of dogma.

Another example of this second kind of challenge is a rigorous interpretation of Western Churches in terms of the classic model of heresy which denies all ecclesial reality to Christian communions outside of the Orthodox Church which is, to use the words of the Creed, the "one, holy, catholic and apostolic Church." This is a matter which Orthodox clerics and theologians understandably find difficult to discuss in formal meetings or in print, yet one which powerfully informs traditional Orthodoxy and, consequently, explains why a traditional Orthodox Christian is fearful of contact especially in common prayer and worship with 'Roman Catholics' and 'Protestants.' I suspect that this will quickly surface as a significant question for clarification in the Orthodox-Roman Catholic Theological Commission and among the Orthodox faithful, especially in traditional Orthodox lands, as soon as attention is drawn to it through scrutiny of commission statements.

In the absence of a formal ecumenical statement by the

Orthodox Churches similar to the Decree on Ecumenism by Vatican II, the Orthodox may well find it extremely difficult, without risking a break up of their own consensus and their own unity, to clarify the above question even with regard to the Roman Catholic Church. Statements by Orthodox leaders which recognize the Roman Catholic sacraments are regarded by many Orthodox as individual opinions not necessarily reflecting the true position of Orthodoxy. Thus it may be possible that during the first phase of the actual dialogue substantial agreement may be reached on the sacraments in formal theological terms, and yet still be followed by an actual reluctance on the part of the Orthodox officially to recognize ecclesial reality in Roman Catholicism. The reason for this is that the Orthodox have traditionally worked out no positive theology concerning Christian bodies canonically separated from the Orthodox Church. No satisfactory solution has been offered to this problem on the grounds of Orthodox ecclesiology which intimately connects the Eucharist, right doctrine, and canonical bishop.[13] However, such a solution or at least formal clarification is needed if the dialogue of love and the dialogue of truth are taken seriously. The Orthodox need to find a way to accept the principle that officially recognizing ecclesial reality in other Christian bodies neither is an affront to the Orthodox Church as the one, holy, catholic, and apostolic Church, nor necessitates sacramental communion with them. Acceptance of this principle would then relieve the Orthodox position from the heavy burden of virtually denying that other people in this world are Christians.[14]

A final profoundly sensitive issue in this second kind of challenge is that of the Eastern Churches in communion with Rome or, to use traditional Orthodox language, the 'Uniate Churches.' These churches are a constant reminder of the painful experience of the whole spector of proselytism[15] by Western missionaries in Orthodox Eastern Europe and the Orthodox Middle East during long periods of politico-cultural weakness when most of the Orthodox peoples there were under Islamic or Western subjugation. It is not meaningful to say that the Orthodox should not feel so deeply about this issue because they do feel deeply about it, not least for the reason that they are still suffering from the consequences of Western proselytism. At the same time, it is unrealistic for the Orthodox to expect that the Roman Catholic Church should suddenly dismantle these churches in the East for the sake of the new dialogue. Can a solution be found? It would at least be helpful to many Orthodox if during the first phase of the dialogue Roman Catholic representatives from these churches do not officially participate in the work of the theological commission.

The above two kinds of challenges involving a variety of issues are fairly formidable but not insurmountable because they are attitudinal and ecclesiastical rather than purely doctrinal. Yet considerable progress in meeting the above kinds of challenges is probably necessary before trying to tackle the third kind of challenge involving the central divisive issues or even before other dramatic ecumenical acts or steps are taken such as on 7 December 1965 when Pope Paul VI and Patriarch Athenagoras I lifted the formal mutual anathemas of 1054 pertaining to their Sees.[16] A similar future act, after sufficient preparation, might be the celebration of Easter on a common date, a matter of tremendous implications for the Orthodox world,[17] which would also require consultation with the other Western Churches.

The third and seemingly insurmountable kind of challenge involves the core divisive issues, namely, the *filioque* and the place of the pope in a reunited Christianity. These two issues loom so large in the historical and theological horizon of the Orthodox consciousness that an immediate resolution of them by a miracle of God would bring down all the other barriers. These are the issues which according to the Orthodox ultimately caused the schism and gradually separated the one faith community into two faith communities which, in their mutual relationships, came to regard construction of litanies of differences and complaints against one another as a high virtue. Would that these core issues be immediately approachable! In human terms they are insurmountable. Only God can make what is impossible possible when His Catholic and Orthodox peoples build up enormous trust between them on other issues.

The issue of the *filioque,* one would daringly say, may be the easier of the two to tackle because this formula was after all not part of the ancient Ecumenical Creed, but was offered by Augustine as a kind of theological speculation on the Creed,[18] and the Orthodox have an acceptable interpretation of it. At heart the *filique* need not be a decisive difference in dogma, because Western and Eastern Christians commonly confess the dogma of the Holy Trinity, but it is an important difference in the interpretation of the trinitarian dogma.[19] What is decisive for Orthodox theology derived primarily from Athanasios and the Cappadocian Fathers is not the formula itself, which can be interpreted in an Orthodox manner, but the underlying doctrinal teaching about the living God in His eternal mode of being and in His revelation in creation, history, church, sacraments, and each Christian's personal communion with Him. Applied to God's revelation in time, the *filioque* can be interpreted in an Orthodox manner, but applied to God's eternal mode of existence—as the relevant articles of the Creed would clearly have it,[20] the *filioque* contradicts the intent of the Creed. But the intent of the Creed can 'exegetically' be derived only from the theological controversies of that time and the theological writings of the Church Fathers mentioned above who were immediately involved with them. Therefore, if Catholic and Orthodox theologians can agree on the patristic theology behind the First and Second Ecumenical Synods, it might be possible for them to find a new formula consistent both with the intent of the Creed and with the intent of the *filioque* in the context in which it later prevailed in the Western Church.

The place of the pope in a reunited Catholic Christianity is the most difficult of all issues because the role of the pope is definitive for Roman Catholicism. Whereas the Orthodox speak about the primacy of the life of the Church, to which even bishops and Ecumenical Synods are accountable,[21] the Roman Catholics speak of the primacy of the pope whose authority is viewed to extend not only over bishops but also over entire Ecumenical Synods. In similar fashion, whereas Roman Catholics fundamentally conceive of unity as communion with a particular see, the Orthodox conceive of unity as communion not with a particular see, but with the full catholic consensus of the ancient undivided Church, doctrinally, sacramentally, and canonically as represented by the family of Orthodox Churches today in its conciliar unity and diversity.

14

If the issue of the role of the pope is viewed as a canonical matter, which is most proper according to Orthodox thinking, Orthodoxy based on legitimate ancient traditions could indeed accept a weighty interpretation of the primacy of the see of Rome as the leading and central see in word and teaching, a unifying center, and even an important, although not absolute, court of appeals for all Christendom.[22] However, if the issue is viewed as a dogma, that is, in terms of a universal and infallible authority over and constitutive to the entire Church, then the Orthodox Churches have neither theological nor canonical categories to deal with such an absolute Roman primacy. Acceptance of it would simply mean the surrender of their apostolic and conciliar independence, as well as a fundamental redefinition of their theology of the episcopate, which are constitutive elements of Orthodoxy. Eventual discussion of this issue will require the presence of angles in the midst of the participants.

As a final word to the above issues it may be noted that on the basis of Vatican II's Decree on Ecumenism and Decree on the Eastern Churches in communion with Rome, the Catholic position toward Orthodoxy is enormously conducive to quick and immediate progress in the dialogue, the only thing lacking in the Orthodox Churches being communion with Rome. If the Orthodox Churches would be prepared to accept the primacy of the pope as presently interpreted by Rome, then they could retain everything else and even the power to govern themselves. From such a perspective Orthodox bishops and theologians can be made to feel a lot of brotherly pressure by their Roman Catholic counterparts, or can be made unwittingly to appear as inflexible, if the journey of reconciliation is not hastened. Already in Roman Catholic theology a tendency exists to co-opt Orthodox theologians into positions quite legitimate for Roman Catholic theologians and in the process to hug Orthodoxy into oblivion. However, the Orthodox Church has its own theology on the Trinity, church, episcopate, sacraments, and conciliar unity which can neither be co-opted nor allow differences on essentials as alternative interpretations to be accepted by the Roman Catholics but not necessarily by the Orthodox. To accept the latter as a working principle would imply a trivialization of the dialogue. Rather, the promise of the new attempt at dialogue lies in honoring these fundamental differences in theological positions and prayerfully grappling with them toward the mutual discovery of a consensus expressing the fullness of Christian truth, as the two sides maintain their deep commitment to a dialogue of love and truth.

Local Ecumenism

What is needed on the part of each Christian and local ecumenical officer to further dialogue and cooperation between Orthodox and Roman Catholic believers locally? The first need on each Christian's part is a growing new life in Christ. Believe in the power of God, in the power of prayer, and in the power of conversion of the heart to Jesus Christ. The formidable obstacles that lie ahead in the international Catholic-Orthodox dialogue will not simply be resolved by experts in theological tournaments or by prelates through ecclesiastical agreements. The most urgent and continuous need for all of us is to view and to interpret the work of responsible ecumenism as the work of Christ in our midst. It is His "to equip the saints for the work of ministry, for building up the body of Christ, until we all attain to the unity of the faith" (Eph 4.12-13).

The goal set before us is best served when Orthodox and Catholic believers deepen their life of faith within their own local parishes and when they respect the ecumenical guidelines formulated by one another's churches. United with Christ and prayerfully sustaining the fresh edge of a personal life with Him, Catholic and Orthodox Christians will be given by the Lord both the genuine concern and enabling power to seek one another out properly, to create Christian fellowship with each other, and to build up a common life in Christ. It has been my experience, too, that without authentic spiritual renewal the sacred challenge of Christian unity is but another obligation or a once-a-year meeting. The words of First Peter call out to all of us: "Come to him, to that living stone ... and like living stones be yourselves built into a spiritual house" (1 Pet 2.4-5)

With this faith vision Christians can foster a true ecumenical spirit first of all in the concrete setting of their own parishes by making sure that their ways of speaking about other Christians, as well as their teaching aids, are not only informed and fair but also brotherly and caring. In the local Orthodox parishes there is a petition heard in Eucharist after Eucharist: "Let us pray to the Lord for the peace of the world, the stability of the holy churches of God and for the union of all!" Surely this petition can apply locally to our dialogue and cooperation. Through prayer we must re-examine our attitudes toward one another and make the necessary changes at all levels of parish life.

Secondly, in order to become knowledgeable and truly caring about each other, ecumenical officers and other motivated Christians in local parishes must reach out for contact and fellowship with Christians of other churches. According to my limited experience, mixed Bible study groups, timely ecumenical prayer services, together with effective talks, parish conferences or seminars, occasional participation in Catholic marriage encounters by Orthodox Christians, various shared ministries to others, and the like, are extremely valuable. In such cases Catholic and Orthodox Christians may come together not to debate one another's positions or try to resolve the differences between their churches, but rather to build up their faith and life in Christ, to share what can be shared, to learn more about the views and traditions of one another, and together to serve cases of urgent need.

In the United States the task is to overcome indifference and to discover spiritual motivation for local ecumenical sharing. With regard to earnest ecumenical work, Orthodox Christians have much to learn from the example of Roman Catholic Christians. In other parts of the world, where Orthodox and Roman Catholics have long encountered one another as rivals and competitors, feelings of mistrust and prejudice run high. We need to pray for them and also to ask them to pray for us. According to the call of our church leaders, Catholic and Orthodox Christians everywhere in their local parishes must in their own way contribute to the dialogue of love and truth in obedience to Christ.

In an unusually irenic disputation between Anselm of Havelberg and Niketas of Nicomedia in 1136, Anselm "compared himself and Niketas with the two disciples walking along the road to Emmaus. Just as those first disciples recognized the Lord in the

17

breaking of bread, so he and Niketas would recognize the truth in their analysis of Scripture."[23] The renewed journey of Catholicism and Orthodoxy in our times may be a long one as well. But let our hearts unceasingly burn with the love of the Lord who accompanies us so that our journey together, however long, may not again be interrupted.

NOTES

1. The 'Joint Statement' in the *Orthodox Observer,* 19 December 1979, p. 3, issued on the occasion of the 1979 visit of John Paul II to Constantinople. See also *Tomos Agapis: Vatican-Phanar (1958-1970)* (Rome, 1971), published in Greek and French. For a complete bibliography on this preparatory period for the dialogue, see Michael A. Fahey, "Orthodox Ecumenism and Theology: 1970-78," *Theological Studies* 39 (1978) 454-59. For an account that includes the Orthodox-Roman Catholic Dialogue in the U.S.A., see Edward J. Kilmartin, *Toward Reunion: The Orthodox and Roman Catholic Churches* (New York, 1979).

2. *Orthodox Observer,* p. 3. For an account of the visit, see Thomas Fitzgerald, "A New Phase in Orthodox-Roman Catholic Relations," *Greek Orthodox Theological Review* 25 (1980) 119-30, and *Origins* 9:26, 13 December 1979.

3. The writer was present and took notes. For Archbishop Stylianos' published text in Greek, see *Orthodox Observer,* 16 July 1980, pp. 17 and 19.

4. Fahey, p. 455, interprets the action a bit too strongly as a "boycott." Perhaps the attitude of the Orthodox can be expressed with these words: "We are not ready for official contacts; let's wait and see." Fahey also makes reference to a somewhat aloof comment on the Orthodox official absence from Vatican II by Yves Congar stating that Orthodoxy missed a unique opportunity of ecumenism and charging that Orthodoxy "bears a very serious responsibility for that." Many Orthodox would take exception to this statement. After all, why should the Orthodox Churches have at that time expected anything new from or have been eager for official contacts with Rome when pressure-filled attempts at dialogue and reconciliation long ago virtually meant their being swallowed up by Rome?

5. For ecclesiastical and political reasons, the Church of Greece asked the Vatican not to appoint a successor to the Bishop for the Catholics of the Byzantine rite in Athens and was not heeded. Also, the Greek government and the Vatican recently established diplomatic relations, which the Church of Greece regards as an affront to the Orthodox Church.

6. John S. Romanides, "The Theologian in the Service of the Church in Ecumenical Dialogue," *Greek Orthodox Theological Review* 25 (1980), 145. For some of the inner dynamics of the Orthodox-Roman Catholic preparatory committee which disbanded in 1978, see ibid. pp. 143-45.

7. Comprised of the regular representatives, together with a special delegate from each monastery, usually the abbot. An English translation of the statement appeared in the *Orthodox Observer*, 8 October 1980.

8. *Proche Orient Chrétien*, 18 (1968) 361, cited by Cardinal Willebrands in his commentary on an exchange of letters between Paul VI and Athenagoras I in a release from Information Service (SPCU), August 1971, entitled *Relations with the Orthodox Churches*, p. 6.

9. *Orthodox Observer*, 16 July 1980, p. 19, translated from the published Greek text.

10. In his published official correspondence with Paul VI, as for example, in his 21 March 1971 letter: "Actually, even if the Eastern Church and the Western Church are separated, for causes known to the Lord, they are not divided, however, in the substance of communion in the mystery of Jesus, God made man, and of his divine-human Church," Information Service release, p. 4.

11. *Towards the Great Council: Introductory Reports* (London, 1972); Fahey, pp. 451-54; Metropolitan Damaskinos of Tranoupolis, "Towards the Great and Holy Council: Part II," *Eastern Churches News Letter*, New Series 11 (Autumn, 1980) 37-46 and Stanley S. Harakas, *Something Stirring in World Orthodoxy* (Minneapolis, 1978).

12. And yet the Orthodox have learned and are learning much from Western Christians and scholars such as in the areas of patristic studies, biblical studies, church and society, and others, aside from many technical and methodological matters.

13. See, for example, Kallistos Ware, "Church and Eucharist, Communion and Intercommunion," *Sobernost* 7 (1978) 550-67. An interesting precedent is the case of the Oriental Churches separated from the Orthodox Church and regarded as heretical since the Fourth Ecumenical Synod (451) but now no longer regarded as heretical by some Orthodox theologians, although canonically still separated from Orthodoxy. Yet the crucial change of attitude among these theologians has occurred because, so they are convinced, the disputed difference over a christological formula is a matter of terminology rather than of substance. For the dialogue of the Orthodox and Oriental Churches, see *Greek Orthodox Theological Review* 3 (1968) 125-320 and 16 (1971) 1-259.

14. The occasional Orthodox opinion that persons outside of the Orthodox Church are saved individually by God's choice and not by virtue of their ecclesial membership sounds sophistical because such persons come to know Christ through their community of faith, that is, through baptism, the Lord's Supper, and nurture in that community, and through no other means.

15. For periods of peace and periods of hardening of the lines, and the dynamics involved, see for example K. T. Ware, "Orthodox and Catholics in the Seventeenth Century: Schism or Intercommunion?" in *Studies in Church History, Volume 9, Schism, Heresy and Religious Protest*, ed. D. Baker (Cambridge, 1972), pp. 259-76.

19

16. For the texts, see *Tomos Agapis* and *Be Reconciled to Your Brother: The Lifting of the Anathema of 1054 as a Step Toward Reconciliation* (New York, 1966). In a communiqué on the lifting of the anathemas, the Patriarchate of Constantinople has interpretted the action as "an affair between the two Churches of Rome and Constantinople" and that "now the schism has been abolished" and that "things thus [have] returned automatically to the state prior to 1054," although the two Churches have not yet come back to the common cup which "constitutes the final stage," Information Service release, p. 4. The prevailing view among the Orthodox is that the anathemas have been lifted but the state of division still exists.

17. Because the Orthodox Churches, aside from theological reasons, see their common celebration of Easter as a sign of their own unity. Further on this, see T. K. Ware, "A Common Easter—How Soon?" *Eastern Churches Review* 8 (1976) 79-81.

18. *De Trin.* 15.2, 5, 22-24 and 28.

19. This is my conclusion in a position paper on the issue in *Concilium: Conflicts About the Holy Spirit,* ed. H. Küng and J. Moltmann (New York, 1979), pp. 23-30.

20. So also according to more and more Western scholars. See Dietrich Ritschl, "The History of the Filioque Controversy," in *Concilium: Conflicts About the Holy Spirit,* pp. 9-12 and K. Ware and C. Davey, eds., *Anglican-Orthodox Dialogue: The Moscow Agreed Statement* (London, 1977). In the latter dialogue, as it is known, the Anglicans agreed to drop the *filioque* clause from the universal creed for theological and canonical reasons, a decision that is extremely important to the Orthodox, but the Anglican Church has not acted firmly on the recommendation. A Roman Catholic theologian, Terrence R. O'Connor, "*Homoousios* and *Filioque*: An Ecumenical Analogy," *Downside Review,* 83 (1965) 18-19, suggests the elimination of the *filioque* because it is not urgently necessary to the Creed as an expression of the catholic faith, as it was necessary in the context in which it originated, and also because it would be a significant ecumenical gesture toward the Orthodox.

21. See the excellent article by Kallistos Ware, "The Ecumenical Councils and the Conscience of the Church." in *Kanon: Jahrbuch der Gesellschaft für das Recht der Ostkirchen,* 2 (Vienna, 1974) pp. 217-33.

22. See again Kallistos Ware, "Primacy, Collegiality, and the People of God," in *Orthodoxy: Life and Freedom,* ed., A. J. Philippou (Oxford, 1973), pp. 116-29 and Demetrios Constantelos, "*Lumen Gentium*: Concern Over Collegiality: An Eastern Orthodox Theologian's Assessment," *Emmanuel* 85 (1979) 533-37.

23. Norman Russell, "Anselm of Havelberg and the Union of Churches," *Sobernost* 1 (1979) 25.

REFLEXIONS ON THE
ORTHODOX-CATHOLIC DIALOGUE

by *John F. Long, S.J.*

Rev. John F. Long, S.J. was a staff member for seventeen years at the Vatican Secretariat for Promoting Christian Unity. At present he is Director of the John XXIII Ecumenical Center and a member of the International Orthodox-Roman Catholic Theological Commission. This article is the substance of his remarks in response to the address of Fr. Stylianopolis at the meeting of NADEO in Boston, 5 May 1981.

The Developing Dialogue

The opening of the official dialogue between the Roman Catholic and the Eastern Orthodox Churches, which took place in Patmos and Rhodes in June, 1980 was the result of a development which had taken place over a period of eighteen years. If the Popes Paul VI and John Paul II and the Ecumenical Patriarchs Athenagoras I and Demetrios I were the protagonists most in view during this development, it is well to recall some of the other persons and groups who made significant contributions to it.

The exchanges of visits between qualified delegations of the Roman Catholic Church and the various Autocephalous Orthodox Churches were frequent and fruitful. It is possible to enumerate only a few of them: the yearly visits between Rome and Constantinople on the patronal feasts of each Church; the participation of Catholic prelates at significant events of the Orthodox Churches, e.g. the election and installation of the Patriarchs of Moscow, of Romania and the jubilee celebrations of the Church of Bulgaria; the prayerful and heartfelt participation of so many Orthodox in the events of 1978, the year of the three Popes; the return of the relics of St. Andrew, of St. Titus, of St. Isidoros of Chios to their original resting places, accompanied by a large participation of the Orthodox faithful.

One recalls with gratitude the persistence and dedication to deepening Catholic-Orthodox relations shown by such persons as Augustin Cardinal Bea and the Metropolitan Nikodim of Leningrad and Novgorod—among those who have passed to the Lord—and the Metropolitan Meliton of Chalcedon, Cardinal John Willebrands, and Archbishop Iakovos—among those who are still actively engaged in this work.

During this same period, theologians and pastors have been actively engaged in reflecting together on the great truths of faith which Catholics and Orthodox share in common and on those points of difference which still prevent full communion among them. Again, it is possible to mention only a few: the conferences and symposia sponsored by the *Pro Oriente* foundation of Vienna; the yearly consultations in Reginsburg, Germany, which have resulted in some excellent publications on our common faith; the regular conferences of the International Society for Eastern Canon Law which brings together Orthodox scholars as well as those of the various Catholic traditions of East and West.

Between 1967 and 1980, five sets of theological consultations between representatives of the Roman Catholic and Russian Orthodox Churches have taken place on subjects connected with the nature of the Church and her role in the modern world. At the last meeting in Odessa, Metropolitan Filaret of Kiev could state with justification that these meetings provided substantial help in preparing for the general Catholic-Orthodox dialogue which was about to begin.[1]

Finally, due attention should be given to the official dialogue begun in America in 1966 under the sponsorship of the National Conference of Catholic Bishops and the Standing Conference of Canonical Orthodox Bishops in America. This dialogue has combined serious theological reflection with pastoral concern and has produced a series of statements which deserve greater attention on the part of Catholics and Orthodox alike. One particular merit of this dialogue is that it has been able to combine rigor of theological thinking and concern for tradition with an openness to new questions, free of the polemics and prejudices which sometimes still exist in the "old" countries.

This general overview is sufficient to show that serious work is already being done towards preparing the official dialogue between Catholicism and Orthodoxy. All recognize that there is still a great deal of work ahead to overcome what are real differences between the two Churches. However, what has already been achieved should not be ignored. It provides a base for the ongoing dialogue and merits serious attention so that its results are integrated into the developments that are hoped for in the future. It would be unfortunate if the newly formed theological commission found it necessary to go over old ground because it did not give enough serious attention to what has already been going on in the two churches.

Dialogue of Love: Its Significance

Certain people have seen in the developments of the last years only sentimental manifestations of good will and spectacular efforts at overcoming hatred and animosity. Somehow, the dialogue of love spoken of by Catholic and Orthodox leaders is seen as in contradistinction to the dialogue of truth, which is the only real dialogue. Such an attitude betrays a narrow understanding of what has been going on in these past years.

Church historians agree that it is very difficult to pin-point the exact time of the separation between the Churches of East and West. The division which actually exists is rather the result of a long estrangement which slowly took possession of the Churches. A breakdown in mutual respect and love was an essential ingredient in this process. The rebuilding of this respect and love must also be an integral part of the reverse process. Growing in love is not an alternative to growing into truth; it is an essential part of it, which must permeate it and guide it.

Through the dialogue of love there is developing a renewed consciousness of the identity of both Churches in their sacramental structures. This dialogue is informed with the sentiment so clearly expressed in the Orthodox Divine Liturgy, just before the recitation of the profession of faith: "Let us love one another *so that* we may, with one heart, confess the Father, Son and Holy Spirit, Trinity one in substance and undivided." A common recitation of the formulas of Christian faith would be a sterile exercise unless it were infused by that love which is God's gift to His people.

It is well to reflect on the theological significance of some of the gestures which have taken place over the years of the dialogue of love. In Jerusalem, in 1964, Pope Paul VI presented to the Ecumenical Patriarch, Athenagoras I a chalice for the celebration of the Divine Liturgy. One must remember how strict Roman Catholic theologians were against offering the vessels for the celebration of the Eucharist to non-Catholics except under very rigid conditions. The Pope went beyond the quarrels of the schools to say, by his gesture, that he recognized in the Eucharist celebrated in the Orthodox Church, not something other, but rather the Eucharist of the one Church of Jesus Christ. The Patriarch used a similar gesture to express a profound truth: in July 1967, during the Pope's visit to the Phanar, Athenagoras presented him with a priestly stole as a sign of the priesthood of Christ which they shared in common.

The return of relics to their original resting places and the veneration shown them must not be considered as mere colorful folklore. They are a testimony of a common love and reverence for the apostles, martyrs and holy persons who are the sources of a common faith and authentic witnesses of genuine Christian life and spirituality.

The dialogue of love has also had its effect in the canonical field. In the minds of the protagonists, the exchange of letters on great feast days and church occasions have been more than gestures of protocol or courtesy. They are a recognition of the pastoral office shared by Catholic and Orthodox Prelates as they seek to serve their people. Latin Canon Law, in its simplistic division between "Catholics" and "non-Catholics" frequently joined together Orthodox Christians, Hindus and African animists into a single category. Paul VI, writing to Patriarch Alexis of Moscow at Easter in 1966, and referring to "that part of the flock of Christ of which you are the Pastor", or speaking later of Catholic and Orthodox hierarchies who should recognize each other and respect each other as "pastors of the part of the flock of Christ which is entrusted to

them",[2] spoke from a completely different canonical and ecclesiological context which is that of the second Vatican Council.

The unexpected and moving act of Pope Paul VI in kneeling
and kissing the feet of the representative of the Ecumenical Patriarch at the end of a service in the Sistine Chapel was also more than
an isolated gesture. Through it he wished to demonstrate his understanding of the papacy as an office of service to the Church and not
of domination. It is quite possible that he had in mind some historical events when the pope or his representatives did not have this
concept of their office so clearly in their minds. One thinks, for
example of the arrival of the Ecumenical patriarch in Ferrara in
1438 when he was not given a solemn and official welcome because
he would not follow Roman protocol and kiss the pope's feet.[3] Pope
Paul's gesture effectively erases from our minds the memory of that
earlier lack of fraternal love.

The dialogue of love has never been conceived of as a flashy
display of good will or reformed intentions. It is founded on a
recognition of what we share in common with regard to the funda-
mentals of the Christian faith, sacramental life and a hierarchical
priesthood based on the apostolic succession. It is meant to animate
and accompany a sincere theological dialogue which does not try to
gloss over the real differences which still exist between the two
churches, but seeks to put these differences in proper perspective
and to shed new light which would help resolve them in complete
fidelity to God's revelation in Christ.[4] This is clearly underlined in
the common declaration of the pope and patriarch signed on
October 27, 1967: "They recognize that the true dialogue of charity
which should be at the basis of all relations between themselves and
between their churches, must be rooted in total fidelity to the one
Lord Jesus Christ and in mutual respect for each one's traditions."
The two leaders continued:

"In order to prepare fruitful contacts between the Roman Catholic
Church and the Orthodox Church, the Pope and the Patriarch give
their blessing and pastoral support to all efforts for cooperation
between catholic and orthodox scholars in the field of historical
studies, of studies in the traditions of the Churches, of patristics, of

liturgy and of a presentation of the Gospel which corresponds at one and the same time with the authentic message of the Lord and with the needs and hopes of today's world. The spirit which should inspire these efforts is one of loyalty to truth and of mutual understanding, with an effective desire to avoid the bitterness of the past and every kind of spiritual or intellectual domination."[5]

It would seem that avoiding the bitterness of the past and every effort of *spiritual or intellectual domination* is the most authentic way to remain loyal to the truth received from apostles and fathers of the church and lived by the Catholic and Orthodox faithful over almost two thousand years.

Previous Efforts at Reunion

There is an old adage that "those who do not know history are condemned to relive it." That is why it is so important to reflect on previous efforts made to reestablish full communion between the Roman Catholic and Orthodox Churches. This should not be so much a judgement of the people involved in these efforts as an attempt to understand why, despite good intentions, they failed. Father Stylianopolis has correctly stated that the Orthodox faithful did not understand these efforts, were not ready to accept the results and finally refused the communion their hierarchical and theological leaders had thought they had achieved.

Pope Paul VI, in his letter for the seventh centenary of the Council of Lyons (October, 1974) has some trenchant remarks to make on this subject:

"Even the peace restored between the Latin and Greek Churches—a peace already heavily influenced by the historical situation mentioned above—rested on uncertain and shifting foundations. The reconciliation between the two Churches was brought about by the supreme authorities. It was ratified by the Emperor Michael VIII Palaeologus without giving the possibility to the Greek Church of expressing itself freely in this matter. On the other hand, the Latins chose texts and formulae expressing an ecclesiology that had been conceived and developed in the West. These were proposed to the Emperor and the Greek Church to be accepted simply without discussion. It is understandable then that, no matter what may have been the sincerity of its authors, a unity achieved in this way could not be accepted completely by the mentality of the eastern Christians, and therefore, when the first difficulties arose, it was unhappily broken again."[6]

The circumstances of the Council of Florence were somewhat different. There was ample time for discussion and the main differences between the churches received thorough treatment. However, as one reads the various accounts of the Council, the question can be asked as to how effective these discussions were. Certainly there were indications on both sides of those efforts for spiritual and intellectual domination, mentioned above. Devotion to truth was sometimes equated with truth as perceived by a single individual or a small group. No thought was given as to how the highly intellectual contents of the debates could be translated into expressions understandable by the body of the Church. Monks and educated Greek lay people were not prepared for decisions toward which they had made no contribution and in which they seemed to see a betrayal of their traditional faith. The Latins still were heretics to them.

On the Latin side things were not much better. Ordinary preachers and teachers had not had the special training in trinitarian theology that participation in the Council would have given them. Union for many meant submission and when it wasn't given forthwith, the Greeks continued to be treated as heretics and schismatics. The ecclesiological presuppositions of the agreement were not clear nor were they developed in the concrete relations between the two communities after the Council. Just one indication of a much larger problem can be given: despite the fact that full communion between the churches had been proclaimed, the Latin patriarchate of Constantinople continued to exist and that situation prevailed concerning many episcopal sees in the East.

In the minds of the majority of Latin and Greek faithful, the reunion was still-born. Many learned studies have been made of the various factors which contributed to making the Council of Florence a "success that failed." Among these the fact that the Church at large was not involved in the process is very significant. Hence the importance of Father Stylianopolis' insistence on engaging the people not only in the dialogue of love but also in the dialogue of truth. The Church as a whole must be able to see in any full communion achieved the realization not only of its deepest yearnings but also of its fidelity to the truth committed by Christ to His Church and lived out through the operation of the Holy Spirit.

Theological Expression of Faith

The necessity of engaging the people in the dialogue also points to the question of leadership by Church hierarchs and theologians. Here we enter upon something which is complex and important for it involves the relationship between faith and the theological expression of that faith.

In many parts of the Church and across the ages pastors and teachers have sought to penetrate more deeply into the mystery of faith. This is due to the insatiable human thirst for knowledge but also to the desire to feed the spiritual life of individuals and the community. Sometimes whole systems have been elaborated to bring about this deeper understanding of the faith. The effort is both necessary and difficult for in the final analysis attempts to express the infinite truth are made in finite forms. No matter how developed the systems are, they can never express ultimate reality in a complete way.

This does not mean that the human mind cannot achieve the truth or that all truth is relative. The theologians and the Church herself, acting under the Spirit, has understood and proclaimed the great truths of God revealed in Jesus Christ. At the same time, there is need for a great humility which has not always characterized theological reflection and debate. As one rereads the sad history of Catholic-Orthodox estrangement one is struck by the amount of effort put into stressing the differences existing between us. The polemical language of Cardinal Humbert and Michael Caerularius have had, unfortunately, too many imitators. One erects one's own system into the only legitimate statement of faith. This is one more reason why the theological dialogue must be informed by the dialogue of love. Otherwise we risk perpetuating the sterile quarrels which mark the past history of the two churches.

The Second Vatican Council, in its Decree on Ecumenism (n.17) has indicated a fruitful approach to this question.

"In the study of revealed truth, East and West have used different methods and approaches in understanding and confessing divine things. It is hardly surprising then, if sometimes one tradition has come nearer to a full appreciation of some aspects of a mystery of revelation than another, or has expressed them in a better way. In such cases, these various theological formulations are to be considered often as complementary rather than conflicting."[7]

Theologians in dialogue, therefore, must search out the authentic theological tradition and be able to distinguish them from individual theories or even aberrations. Here the question of language is very important. In the search for truth and the effort to combat error the Church has found formulations for expressing her basic faith which have served generations of Christians. Each generation, however, must search into these formulations and make them a living part of the proclamation of faith. It is particularly important that Catholics and Orthodox develop a hermeneutic of the dogmatic declarations of Church Councils and of the Fathers of the Church which will enable the Church of today to have a more complete understanding of them. Efforts have been made to do this in the area of Christology but there remains much to be done. Here the Catholic-Orthodox dialogue has much to offer. Certain developments in Western theology concerning the humanity and divinity of Christ have caused preoccupations among Orthodox and Catholics alike. The synthesis achieved in the periods of the great councils of the early Church certainly can be developed further; our understanding of them can be deepened and their meaning for a world entering upon the 21st century must be clarified and expressed in acceptable terms. But the truth achieved in the Spirit through the reflections and debates of our common Fathers cannot be obscured or compromised.

One can understand the perplexity of many Orthodox in the face of some of the developments going on in Catholic theology today. A renewed effort, in which Orthodox must play a more substantial role, is necessary to clarify the picture for both our churches and for the entire Christian dialogue. This clarification does not mean a return to the repetition, by rote, of formulations inherited from the past. It means a renewed expression of the faith these formulations are meant to serve, not to dominate. Father Stylianopolis indicates this when, in his discussion of the *filioque,* he states: ". . . if Catholic and Orthodox theologians can agree on the patristic theology behind the First and Second Ecumenical Synods, it might be possible for them to find a new formula consistent both with the intent of the Creed and with the intent of the *filioque* in the context in which it later prevailed in the Western Church."

Fundamental to this search is the acceptance of the principles of legitimate diversity in unity where diversity is viewed not as a secondary and merely tolerated reality. As Msgr. Charles Moeller has expressed it, diversity is, in a sense, as important as unity.

> "Or better, unity is diversity *in this sense that true union diversifies.* The mystery of the Trinity is a transcendent example of this. Plurality in theology, in canon law, in the liturgy, and in spirituality, is linked not primarily to different cultures and historical situations, even if these play an important role, but to the inexhaustible mystery of Christ."[8]

The Catholic and Orthodox Churches, because of their insistance on a developed trinitarian theology, on the apostolic tradition living in the Church and on the sacramental structure of the Church are particularly able to carry on a dialogue where the issues of profound unity in significant diversity can receive the consideration that must be given them as theological questions and not merely as sociological or cultural ones.

There remains the question of the developments which have taken place in the Roman Catholic and Eastern Orthodox Churches during the centuries of estrangement and division. Catholics and Orthodox have not shared the same problematic. The reforms of the eleventh century, the conciliar movement, the reformation and counter-reformation, the missionary expansion of recent centuries have marked the Roman Catholic Church in a way which the Orthodox have not experienced. Questions of grace, justification, sacraments, primacy have necessitated canonical, theological and even dogmatic developments in which the Eastern Churches have not shared. How are these to be treated in the dialogue?

For the Roman Catholic Church, there is need for a great deal of clarification concerning the roles of the later councils of her history, of the great scholastic theological synthesis, of the dogmatic pronouncements which have been made in the course of the centuries. What does one mean when one speaks of twenty one ecumenical councils? This term is certainly being used in an analogous way, for the medieval councils of the Western Church can hardly be considered on the same level as the four first councils of the *ecumene*. Catholics must research more deeply into the meaning of the definitions of the Council of Trent, for example, as distinct from the post-Tridentine interpretation and application of these statements. How far are they to be considered as necessary and legitimate decisions taken in response to the concrete problems facing the Western Church in particular historical circumstances; how far are they requirements of faith which must be brought directly into the theological dialogue in course.

The Orthodox have not participated in these developments, except sometimes in a peripheral way. The problems behind these developments were not their problems then. If they are problems now, they must be considered in the context of twentieth century needs and not those of the thirteenth, sixteenth or even nineteenth centuries. Here, particular consideration must be given to the statement of the second Vatican Council, brief yet pregnant with meaning: ". . . this sacred Council confirms what previous Councils and Roman Pontiffs have proclaimed: in order to restore communion and unity or preserve them, one must 'impose no burden beyond what is indispensable' (Acts 15:28)."[9] It is not clear how much this principle has entered into the thinking of many Catholics. One of the reasons why there has been such opposition to the formulation of a "Fundamental Law of the Church" is that those responsible for preparing this project did not seem to be guided sufficiently by it. And yet if the Catholic-Orthodox is to make serious progress, it must be seen that Catholic Church authorities and theologians take this principle seriously and are influenced by it in the statements they make and in the actions they take in governing and guiding their Church.

It seems that a common attitude should inspire both Catholics

31

and Orthodox: each Church is accepted as desiring to remain faithful to the Apostolic faith and to have succeeded substantially in doing so. Each will question the other only on what seems clearly against the faith. This point—being guided by what is clearly demanded by the substantials of Christian faith—is essential to allowing for the greatest freedom in expressing and living the Apostolic faith handed on in the Church through succeeding generations under the light of the Holy Spirit, while at the same time not falling into a type of relativism which would allow differences on essentials as alternative interpretations accepted by Roman Catholics but not necessarily by the Orthodox—or vice versa.

The Dialogue and Particular Groups

At the risk of repetition, we must recall the fundamental lesson the history of past relations between the Roman Catholic and Orthodox Churches teaches: unless a broad spectrum of the Church is involved in the dialogue, the results obtained will have limited effect and will not lead to restoring full communion. For that reason both Churches must find ways of keeping the people informed of the work of the official commission and of providing input into, and constructive criticism of this work. The communities of Mount Athos and other groups—Catholic and Orthodox—have expressed strong reserves because of a fear that they will be asked to approve something they do not understand or what they consider to be a compromise of their faith, worked out in secret negotiations. These fears can be dissipated only if there is continuing information about the content and method of the dialogue and of the progress being made.

Towards this end, it is strongly recommended that the major papers being used in the dialogue be communicated to representative Roman Catholic and Orthodox Theological Faculties around the world for their reflection and comment. Where indicated, official dialogue groups on the national and regional level should also be invited to participate in this process. Though the question is delicate and the solution not easy, some way must be found to implicate groups like the communities of Mount Athos and certain Roman Curial offices in the process of dialogue. Even those who consider themselves to be special guardians of the faith and authentic Christian tradition should be able to exercise that function within the dialogue, and not outside, or even opposed to it.

This raises the question of proper representation on the official commission for theological dialogue. On both sides, the geographical distribution could be better. There are large communities of Roman Catholics and Orthodox in the Americas. They have developed a vibrant ecclesial and spiritual life which go beyond the particular theological and pastoral concerns of Europe and the Near East. And yet they have almost no representation on the international commission. Unless this is remedied, there is the risk that an important element will be missing from the dialogue with the concomitant risk of creating further difficulties for the reception of its results. The dialogue is meant to reflect the Roman Catholic and Orthodox Churches in their totalities. Anything else would be a waste of time and effort. It is to be hoped that jurisdictional problems and questions of prestige will cease to present obstacles to a truly representational participation in the work of the international joint commission.

The existence of the Eastern Catholic Churches and their participation in the dialogue has been raised on a number of occasions. It is important that Catholics understand the seriousness of this question for the Orthodox. For many Catholics, these churches are a sign of communion and even bridges between East and West. For Orthodox they are separated portions of their own communities, the results of disloyal proselytism on the part of Latin missionaries, and continual road blocks on the road to communion.

Catholics must recognize that the formation of these churches often took place in circumstances which, instead of leading to reconciliation and communion, resulted in further divisions within the Orthodox Churches and an increase of tension between Catholics and Orthodox. Political and social pressure often accompanied the unions; weaknesses in the Orthodox Churches were exploited; a juridical type of theology which ignored or even denied the ecclesial reality of the Orthodox Churches was used to justify efforts at dividing Orthodox among themselves. Without accepting the exaggerations of polemical literature, which continues to be written even today, Catholics must recognize with sincere regret the actions in the past which are at the roots of the bitterness and suspicion with which many Orthodox still look upon contemporary efforts at reunion between the Churches.

On the other hand, the existence of the Eastern Catholic Churches has permitted certain Christians to express, according to the demands of their conscience, their communion with the Church of Rome. Within the Catholic Church they have given, and continue to give concrete reminders that the Latin tradition is not the only authentic Christian tradition.

Whatever judgement may be made about the political and social factors accompanying these unions or the methods used and the theology originally motivating them, it must be recognized that there were sincere religious and spiritual factors which accompanied the formation and continued existence of the Eastern Catholic churches. Despite political changes and centuries-old pressures, there are significant groups of these Eastern Christians within the communion of the Catholic church who continue today to consider themselves bound to the see of Rome by a communion which they wish to express through appropriate ecclesiastical structures. These Catholics continue to find in their particular churches a fruitful expression of their religious life. The Roman Church considers it her duty to encourage them to remain faithful to their rich spiritual heritage. That is why she could not consider proposals for suppressing their churches and continues to protest when political and social pressures are used, even today, to suppress them in certain parts of Eastern Europe. Involved here are fundamental questions of conscience and human rights which cannot be sacrificed even for the sake of ecumenical dialogue.

At the same time it must be made clear that the Roman Church repudiates all forms of proselytism, "in the sense of acts by which persons seek to disturb each others communities by recruiting new members from each other through methods, or because of attitudes of mind which are opposed to the exigencies of Christian love or to what should characterize the relationships between churches."[10] Pope Paul VI, in his joint declaration with Patriarch Athenagoras I stated: "the dialogue of charity between their churches must bear fruits of a cooperation which would not be self-seeking, in the field of common action at the pastoral, social and intellectual levels, with mutual respect for each one's fidelity to his own church."[11] Furthermore, it is official Roman policy that the partial unions of the past are not to be considered as models of relations with the Orthodox churches today or as a model of any union which may be envisaged for the future.[12]

Ignoring the question of the Eastern Catholic churches would not be a positive contribution to the Roman Catholic-Orthodox dialogue. In fact, just as it was judged useful to find some way for the participation by groups such as the communities of Mount Athos, so it seems indicated that Eastern Catholics take part from the beginning. It is with them—and not without them—that the questions which affect them directly should be resolved. When they see that they are not to be sacrificed on the altar of expediency, they—and all Catholics and Orthodox—can be helped to make a more measured judgement of the past and, more importantly, to open themselves up to more fruitful results in the future. All will also get a clearer understanding of a certain theology of "uniatism" which has led some Orthodox churches to establish "uniate" groups of their own, often basing their actions on arguments quite similar to those used by some Catholic theologians and canonists.

The Papacy in the Dialogue

Catholics and Orthodox alike recognize the truth of Father Stylianopolis' statement that "the place of the pope in a reunited Catholic Christianity is the most difficult of all issues." What is encouraging is that together they have advanced beyond the stage of sterile polemics to one of openness towards facing up to this problem. That is not to say that an easy solution to it will be found. If one continues to look at it primarily from its juridical and canonical aspects, not much progress will be made. That is why the preparatory committee proposed that the theological dialogue begin with a consideration of the Church as the Sacrament of Christ, the visible sign of the mystery of Christ's presence in the world. Within that framework, due attention can be given to the theology of communion and the theology of the local Church. According to Msgr.

Charles Moeller, a prominent Catholic theologian from Louvain and former Secretary of the Vatican Secretariat for promoting Christian Unity:

> "The one Church of Christ is manifested simultaneously *in one single place* where the totality of the means of salvation is present, and *in many places,* geographically speaking. The totality of the means of salvation is present and visible in each case, on condition that the churches are in full communion among themselves; that is, that they recognize the one Church of Jesus Christ, notwithstanding any differences as regards spirituality, the liturgy, canon law and theology. There is no place where the universal Church is made visible other than through local Churches."[13]

Catholics themselves are grappling with this issue of the relations between the local churches and the role of the pope, as the bishop of the local church of Rome, in maintaining and strengthening their communion. The revitalization of the theology of the Spirit in the West will have an important role to play. Through this, it can be seen that authority in the Church cannot be understood primarily in terms of Roman or any other civil law. Authority is derived from the Spirit and must be exercised in the Spirit. There is a real sense in which one can speak about the primacy of the life of the Church, to which even bishops, ecumenical Synods—and popes— are accountable.

It is in the light of these theological developments that research must be made into the whole notion of primacy and the role it plays in the life of the Church. It has juridical aspects but, these should be understood within the wider context of the mystery of the Church as the sacrament of Christ. What has been said above about the historical conditions under which certain theological developments have taken place is particularly important in considering the issue of papal primacy. In the introduction to its constitution "Pastor Aeternus", the first Vatican Council said it was making its definitions "according to the ancient and constant belief of the universal Church".[14] The decree of the second Vatican Council on Ecumenism urges all "to give due consideration to this special feature of the origin and growth of the Churches of the East, and to the character of the relations which obtained between them and the Roman See before the separation and to form for themselves a correct evaluation of these facts."[15] These are not mere rhetoric. They indicate the method by which Catholics and Orthodox should search into Tradition together and discern what may be the exact meaning of the office of service which has come to be known as the Roman primacy. By following this method, it will become clear that there have been different expressions of this office, all of which may throw some light on its meaning but none of which, not even today's, are a necessary model for the Roman primacy of the future, which will be arrived at through a consensus expressing the fullness of Christian truth. Catholics, in particular, must be ready to recognize this and face up to its consequences.

Final Reflection

Father Stylianopolis has indicated that there are some Orthodox theologians who raise doubts about the ecclesial reality of the Roman Catholic Church and of the sacraments celebrated within her. Even if there has been no conciliar declaration, can it not be said that the *consensus fidelium,* the consent of the body of the Church, is in favor of such a recognition? The mutual recognition of each other as Church in the essential sense of the word is at the basis of the tremendous changes which have taken place in our relations in the last two decades. Hierarchs and synods, eminent theologians and the faithful in both churches have recognized this and rejoice in it. To put it in doubt risks reducing the theological dialogue to an academic exercise without roots in reality and with little promise for the future. Exercises like that have been tried in the past and found wanting. It is important, therefore, that the consensus for such a mutual recognition be clear and unequivocal.

There is another reason for such a recognition which can serve as a basis for concluding these remarks.

The Eucharist we celebrate is one; there is not a Catholic Eucharist nor an Orthodox Eucharist. There is the one Eucharist of Christ. The Eucharist is not merely a sign of unity; it is creative of unity, it effects unity. We have been celebrating the Eucharist separately for centuries. Unfortunately, for serious ecclesial reasons we must continue our separate celebration and conscientiously cannot communicate together in the one Eucharistic Body of Christ.

However, over the centuries, perhaps we have not recognized enough the unifying effect the Sacrament should have even through our human weaknesses and divisions. Perhaps it will be precisely through their celebration of the Eucharist, with a renewed consciousness of what that celebration is meant to signify and do, that Catholics and Orthodox will be compelled by the Spirit to seek out and eliminate those obstacles to full canonical communion which have, for too long, prevented them from giving to the world a united witness to the variety and riches of the Spirit in the unity of the one Body of Christ.

NOTES

1. The communique of this meeting will be found in the Documentation section of this issue of *Diakonia*, p. 00.
2. Cf. *Tomos Agapis,* a collection of documents in Greek and French illustrating the communications between the See of Rome and the Ecumenical Patriarchate from 1958 to 1971. Rome-Istanbul, 1971, n. 172, p. 376.
3. Cf. Joseph Gill, S.J. *The Council of Florence.* Cambridge University Press, 1959. p. 105.
4. Brief of Pope Paul VI, *Anno Ineunte,* given to Patriarch Athenagoras on the occasion of the Pope's visit to the Phanar, July 25, 1967. Cf. *Tomos Agapis,* n. 176, pp. 391-393.
5. Cf. Text in *Tomos Agapis,* n. 195, p. 446.
6. Letter to his extraordinary envoy, John Cardinal Willebrands, October 5, 1974. English translation in the Secretariat for Promoting Christian Unity *Information Service,* n. 25, 1974, p. 9.
7. *Vatican Council II, The Conciliar and Post Conciliar Documents,* ed. Austin Flannery, O.P., p. 466.
8. Msgr. Charles Moeller, "Report of the General Secretary to the Plenary Session of the Secretariat for Promoting Christian Unity", *Information Service,* n. 33, 1977, p. 9.
9. Cf. Flannery, *op. cit.,* p. 467.
10. Common Declaration of Pope Paul VI and the Coptic patriarch, Pope Shenouda III, May 10, 1973, (cf. *Osservatore Romano,* 11 May 1981, p. 1).
11. Cf. *Tomos Agapis,* n. 195, p. 446.
12. Letter of Cardinal John Willebrands to Metropolitan Juvenaly, 22 September 1979 (English text in *Diakonia,* vol. XVI, n. 2, 1981, pp. 179-182.) This letter, sent in the name of Pope John Paul II, should be read in its entirety. It is an

authoritative statement on the whole question being considered in these paragraphs.

13. Msgr. Charles Moeller, "Report of the General Secretary . . ." *op. cit.,* n. 33, 1977, p. 6.
14. J. Neuner and J. Dupues, *The Christian Faith in the Doctrinal Documents of the Catholic Church,* Bangalore, 1973, p. 220.
15. Flannery, *op. cit.,* p. 464.

THE HOLY SPIRIT IN THE CHURCH

Metropolitan Damaskinos of Tranoupoleos

Metropolitan Damaskinos is the Director of the Center of the Ecumenical Patriarchate, located in Chambesy, near Geneva, Switzerland. He is general secretary of the preparatory commission for the Great and Holy Council of the Orthodox Church. The following was delivered in the Basilica of St. Peters in the Vatican during the service of first Vespers for the feast of Pentecost, 1981 at ceremonies commemorating the 1600th anniversary of the First Council of Constantinople.

In this atmosphere of evening prayers and meditation, penetrated with love and the vision of spiritual beauty, there ring out in our ears the words of St. Paul addressed to the Romans and to us all, gathered here in the grace of the Holy Spirit.

Words about the Holy Spirit, "the giver of life"; words of the "Spirit of God", "the Spirit of truth, who proceeds from the Father" (*Jn* 15:26), "a new and right spirit", "the spirit that upholds" (*Ps* 51:10, 11, 12), "the source of sanctification, intelligible light . . ."[1]. "Simple in substance", the Spirit "manifests his power through varied miracles, present entirely to each being, present entirely everywhere; 'impassively' he shares himself out, 'indefectibly' he gives himself in participation"[2].

Words about him by whom "hearts are raised, the weak are led by the hand, those who are making progress become perfect. It is he who, illuminating those who have purified themselves of all impurity, makes them 'spiritual through communion with him'"[3].

Words about him from whom everything is derived: "foretelling the future, understanding mysteries, comprehension of things hidden, distribution of charisms, participation in the life of heaven, singing with the angels in chorus, endless joy, permanent dwelling in

40

God, resemblance to God, finally, the supreme good to be desired: 'to become God'"[4].

"For all who are led by the Spirit of God are sons of God. For you did not receive the spirit of slavery to fall back into fear, but you have received the spirit of sonship. When we cry, 'Abba! Father! it is the Spirit himself bearing witness with our spirit that we are children of God, and if children, then heirs, heirs of God and fellow heirs with Christ, provided we suffer with him in order that we may also be glorified with him".

To be adopted sons of God means becoming like Christ himself; not "by nature and in truth", as Athanasius the Great said, but "by disposition and divine grace, by participation in his spirit and by imitation"[5]. That means participating in his glory, being conformed to the image of the Son "in order that he might be the first-born among many brethren" (*Rom* 8:29).

God, becoming incarnate in Christ, becomes humanized, draws close to man, while respecting his own nature: "The Spirit descended on the Son of God, become the Son of man, accustoming himself with him to dwell in mankind, to abide among men, to dwell in the work modelled by God, carrying out the Father's will in these men and renewing their old nature in the newness of Christ"[6].

It is the Holy Spirit that brings about this communion between God and his creature. Since the Son became man, the Spirit of the Father makes us sons of God in Christ. This is a question of a sonship and a brotherhood deified in communion with God. In this communion, "the glory of God is living man, and the life of man is the vision of God"[7]. It is a deep life in God which is realized through the Spirit of the Son; this holy and brotherly life is life in the Church, one, holy, catholic and apostolic. In the Constantinople confession of faith, the article on the Holy Spirit is inseparably linked with faith in the one, holy, catholic and apostolic Church. Because it is the Holy Spirit who gives the Church her existence and keeps her in brotherly communion.

This brotherly communion which does not know fear and slavery is made manifest by the Spirit: "Sons are those whom neither by fear of threats, nor by desire of what they are promised, but out of inclination and habit of the tendency and voluntary disposition of the soul towards good are never separated from God, like the Son who has been told: My child, you are always with me and everything that is mine is yours; they are, by the disposition of grace, what God himself is and is believed to be according to nature and cause. So let us not draw away from the holy Church of God, which contains such great mysteries of our salvation in the holy arrangement of divine symbols which are celebrated in her. Through these mysteries she brings it about that each of us, according to his measure, worthily acquires the way of life according to Christ: she makes manifest as the way of life according to Christ the gift of sonship given by holy baptism in the Holy Spirit"[8].

This way of filial life presupposes a dynamic movement in the Spirit through which man is glorified. "So such is the order", St. Irenaeus says, "such is the rhythm, such is the movement through which created and modelled man becomes in the image and likeness of the uncreated God: the Father decides and commands, the Son carries out and models, the Spirit nourishes and increases, and man progresses gradually and rises towards perfection, that is, draws closer to the uncreated one: for only the uncreated one is perfect, and he is God. As for man, it was necessary that he should first be made, that having been made he should grow, that having grown he should become an adult, that having become an adult he should multiply, that having multiplied he should become strong, that having become strong he should be glorified, and finally, that having been glorified he should see his Lord"[9].

That is the possibility of salvation offered to the whole world by the Father in his Son, in the gift he made of his life for those very people who showed their hatred for him to the extent of delivering him up to death. Christ is always present, through the Holy Spirit, in the Church which is a community of the Son of God glorified, the body of Christ—crucified and risen again—of the first-born of a multitude of brothers, who keep their ontological identity while opening to others.

That means that all men, indiscriminately, if they are guided by the Holy Spirit of God, can be incorporated into the one family of the Son of God, and this in spite of their differences as regards race, language, morals and habits, sex, age, social rank, fortune, way of life, character and behaviour.

Participating in the life of the Church, they are reborn and transfigured by her in the Spirit.

This family, the "body of Christ", is called the Church. This Church, which we ourselves are as members of this body, does not exist for herself or to assert herself, but for the world. Precisely because the Church represents the body of him who "through his humanity becomes identical with us" and who shares in the life of the Church and of history, the Church exists only as an incarnation of the Lord in the world and in history. She has an organic relationship with the world.

This relationship lived in the Eucharist, the accomplishment of the mysteries, is the sacramental event in which renewed communion with God is celebrated and realized in the Holy Spirit. So that there is no renewal in essential historical continuity without the Holy Spirit and, inversely, there is no continuity without faithfulness to origins combined with availability for the Holy Spirit. It is in and by the Eucharist that the Church "sends her sons towards their Father"[10]. Man is placed in a community and created for it. If he should lose this community, his whole relationship is upset. The centre of this communion is the Man-God, the salvation of the world, the divine humanity of Jesus, the sight of the new man, the new society, which is characterized by two movements which are indissolubly interdependent: from the altar towards the world and from the world towards the altar, contemplation and action, the service of man and the service of God, liturgy and diaconia, the spiritual and the temporal.

As ecclesial communion in the Holy Spirit is not juridical, it is characterized by the grace of our Lord Jesus Christ, the love of God the Father and the Spirit of truth. Truth and love form an inseparable whole in the communion of the Holy Spirit. It is in and through love for his neighbour that man, becoming an imitator of God— that is, a servant of the weak, the hungry and prisoners—truly becomes a son of God, led by the Spirit. Heresy consists not only in rejecting such and such a soteriological truth of faith. Since this faith refers to Christ himself—he who is "the way, and the truth, and the life" (*Jn* 14:6), he who identifies himself with his neighbour— every attitude which consists in saying that Christ acts today, but which excludes the neighbour, is only mere ideology and a form of heresy.

Maximus the Confessor, dealing with the central subject of the Ascetic Dialogue on love of one's neighbour, says: "Believe me, my children, nothing else has caused schisms and heresies in the Church but the fact that we do not love God and our neighbour"[11].

These are the conditions for all ecclesial communion in the Holy Spirit, communion of faith and love which overcomes all divisions. This salvific communion is realized within each ecclesial community by the Eucharist, which expresses our unity visibly and our division painfully.

Today the Holy Spirit imposes on us a great task: to re-establish the unity of divided Christendom.

Living today the tragedy of separation and the necessity of putting it right, we are particularly called—in this year of the celebration of the 1600th anniversary of the meeting of the Second Ecumenical Council at Constantinople—to study the creed of faith of this Council, which constitutes the basis of the ecumenical dialogue for the reestablishment of unity.

This year should be for all the Churches and Confessions the year of an urgent invitation to examine in common—through bilateral and multilateral dialogues—to what extent they are obliged, in fidelity to their origins and to their faith, to re-establish unity or not.

This appeal and this invitation apply particularly to those among the Churches which claim to continue exclusively the one, holy, catholic and apostolic Church. They must seek and recognize as the Church, in the full sense of the term "Church", outside their own canonical frontiers, with which they identify the one, holy, catholic and apostolic Church (naturally, if and to the extent to which that is possible) the Churches with which they will be called to eucharistic communion.

My brothers and sisters,

"Let us love one another, in order that, in the same spirit and the same heart, we may all be able to confess together our faith in the

Father, the Son and the Holy Spirit, the consubstantial and indivisible Trinity"[12].

Let us not forget that "in unshakable faithfulness to truth", to quote Gregory Palamas, "God grants us all to be really the image of this supreme and mysterious love which the Holy Spirit is in the life of the Trinity"[13].

And I conclude by quoting a personal confession of Rev. Fr. Yves Congar, expressed a few days ago at the Orthodox Centre of the Ecumenical Patriarchate at Chambésy in the framework of the theological seminar, a confession which I share entirely:

"Brothers, I love you, I love you such as you are and for what you are. I would like, one day, to receive Communion with you at the same cup of Jesus's Blood, full of the fire of the Spirit!"[14].

NOTES

1. Basil the Great, *Treatise on the Holy Spirit* IX; SC 17, p. 146.
2. *Idem*, p. 147.
3. *Idem*, 147-148.
4. Basil the Great, *Treatise on the Holy Spirit* IX; SC 17, p. 148.
5. Athanasius the Great, *Contra Arianos* IXX; PG 25, 361-364.
6. Irenaeus of Lyons, *Adv. Haer.* III, 17, 1; SC 34, p. 303.
7. *Idem*, IV, 20, 7; SC 100, p. 649.
8. Maximus the Confessor, *Mystagogie;* PG 90, 712.
9. Irenaeus of Lyons, *Adv. Haer.* IV, 38, 3; SC 100, p. 955-957.
10. Irenaeus of Lyons, *Adv. Haer.* IV, 32, 1; SC 100, p. 799.
11. Maximus the Confessor, *Prè Spirituel* 74; PG 87, 2925.
12. Invitation to the recitation of the confession of faith in the Liturgy of St. John Chrysostom.
13. Cf. Gregory Palamas, *Capita Physica* 36, 37: PG 150, 1144-1145.
14. Yves Congar, O.P., *Synthese générale de la problématique pneumatologique—Reflexions et perspectives;* lecture given at the Orthodox Centre on 26 May 1981.

COMMENT

MARY AND THE CHRISTIAN
IN THE MYSTICAL POETRY OF ST. EPHREM

by Stephen Bonian, S.J.

Father Bonian, born in Iran, is a Jesuit priest of the Chaldaean Catholic Church. He is presently engaged in theological studies at the Weston School of Theology, Cambridge, MA.

St. Ephrem, Doctor of the Church, and known as "Harp of the Spirit" is the greatest religious poet of the Patristic age.[1] He is the pride of the Syriac churches for his influence on their liturgies and hymns, and even on the Byzantine hymnology. He lived from 306-373 in the two cities of Nisbis and Edessa that fell on the borders of the Persian and Byzantine empire (today near the borders of Iraq and Turkey). As deacon, he taught at the Christian catechetical schools and composed his liturgical poems. Many of these poems were written for different liturgical seasons, and the hymns on Our Lady are among these. Ephrem is also known for his biblical commentaries, homilies and other doctrinal hymns.[2]

My point here is to show that in many of his poems on Mary, Ephrem, in his reflective images on Mary's earthly life, combined with her glorified life in Christ, is continuously bringing Mary and the Christian closer together. I think that Ephrem accomplishes this purpose through his symbolic imagery and parallelism. Ephrem can view Mary in the symbols of the world, such as light, mother earth, Eve; and he can also see her in the sacramental symbols and the Church herself. It is on the latter that I will concentrate our attention.

In Ephrem's words, Mary speaks of her giving birth to Christ as a two-way conception; First Jesus taking on Mary's body, "the 'robe' of his mother", And then Mary taking on Jesus' 'Glory' as a new birth:

"The Son of the Most High
Came to dwell in me
And I became his mother
And as I bore him,
by another birth
he in turn bore me,
by a second birth.
The robe of his mother
which he put on, his body,
I have put on its glory!ʀ

Ephrem explains this new state of Mary's relationship with Christ in a previous stanza:

"How shall I call you
O stranger to us,
Who became one of us?
Shall I call you 'Son'?
Shall I call you 'Brother'?
Shall I call you 'Bridegroom'?
Shall I call you 'Lord'?
Begetter of his mother
By a second birth
from out of the waters!"s

Mary's state here is that of amazement for this new birth in her life, her own rebirth. According to this birth Mary is related to Christ not only as mother but also as sister, bride, and handmaid of the Lord. These new relationships express Mary's depth of relationship with Christ. They could also well be the titles given for the chaste ascetics at Ephrem's time (People of the Covenant) whom Ephrem admired.[5] This poem, along with other similar poems serve as an example of how Ephrem brings Mary close to other Christians as the family and relatives of Christ. The term "from out of the waters" (above) refers to our Baptism.

In another poem, Ephrem draws a parallel between our baptism, symbolized by the river Jordan, and Mary's baptism by Christ who sanctified her from the womb:[6]

"In the pure womb of the river
you should recognize the daughter of man,
who conceived having known no man,

who gave birth without intercourse,
who brought up, through a gift,
the Lord of that gift.[7]

In this poem we see the double role of God as giver and as the gift; Christ, who is given to Mary and to us.

Still in another poem, Ephrem portrays the presence of Christ in Mary as his Light and this 'light of the savior' is Mary's 'glory'. He even compares Mary's light to that of Moses showing that Mary's light is much greater:

"The brightness which Moses put on
was wrapped on him from without,
whereas the river in which Christ was baptized
put on light from within,
and so did Mary's body, in which he resided,
gleam from within."[8]

Ephrem further goes on to say that this light, which is 'the light of Christ', will be fully revealed at our resurrection when we shall also be 'light':

"so too at the resurrection
the righteous are light
for their clothing is splendour,
their garment brightness:
they become their own light,
providing it themselves."[9]

Ephrem calls this light that is in us and in Mary, 'the Light of our Savior'.

St. Ephrem, while showing that we share with Mary our baptism in Christ, also reminds us that it is through Mary that we have received Christ. The symbols of Mary are therefore present in our sacraments; Mary is the font that carries our baptismal waters, the alter-cloth that holds the bread of our communion, the sheaf that gives us the bread of life, and the grape-cluster that gives us the wine from the cup of life:

"'Who has ever'; he asked, 'gathered the waters in a cloth?'
See, a cloth, in the lap of Mary, the Fountain!
Enclosed in a cloth, your handsmaids take
from the Cup of Life, a drop of Life!"[10]

And in another poem:

> "Blessed is your dwelling in which was broken
> That bread from the blessed sheaf.
> In you was pressed
> the grape-cluster from Mary, the cup of Salvation."[11]

In these two stanzas we see that Mary shares with Christ and participates in his work of salvation and in his act of uniting us with God and each other. She is not only the receiver of that gift (Christ) but also the one who fully shares Him with us.

In another one of his hymns, Ephrem shows that the Holy Spirit is present in our sacraments to give us life as He who was present in the womb of Mary:

> "See, Fire and Spirit in the womb that bore you!
> See, Fire and Spirit in the river in which you were baptized!
> Fire and Spirit in our Baptism;
> In the Bread and Cup, Fire and Holy Spirit!"[12]

This stanza draws to our attention that we share with Mary not only Christ but also the Holy Spirit in Christ.

From the above poems we can see that Mary is our example of one who is fully open to God in Christ, and also in communion with us, the Church, For Ephrem Mary and the Church (Symbolized in Mary Magdaline) have always been together proclaiming the Lord and sharing in his life and resurrection:

> "At the beginning of his coming to earth
> a virgin was first to receive him,
> and at his rising-up from the grave
> to a woman he showed his resurrection.
> In his beginning and in his fulfilment
> the name of his mother cries out and is present.
> Mary received him by conception
> and saw an angel before her;
> And Mary received him in life
> and saw angels at his grave."[13]

For Ephrem Mary and the Church are so close together in Christ that they are one:

> "Again, Mary is like the Church,

the Virgin, who has borne the first-fruits by the Gospel
In the place of the Church, Mary saw him;
blessed be he who gladdened the Church and Mary!
Let us call the Church itself 'Mary',
for it befits her to have two names."[14]

In one of his Nativity Hymns, Ephrem expresses in Mary's own words her attitude towards other Christians saying:

"I shall not be jealous, my Son, that Thou art with me, and also with all men. Be Thou God to him that confesses Thee, and be Thou Lord to him that serves Thee, and be Brother to him that loves Thee, that Thou mayest gain all!"[15]

It must have been from such a woman, whom Ephrem described, that Jesus came out to save the world as the Christ; for Mary not only lets him be who he is but also encourages him to go on with his mission of divine love and salvation for all.

It is interesting to notice that Ephrem, in his hymns on Our Lady, does not pray to Mary but rather he prays with her to Christ. Thus we find in these poems that Mary is already in a continuous dialogue with Christ and that Ephrem's attitude in prayerful contemplation is to join Mary in her prayer to Christ. Therefore, Mary is not waiting for us to ask her intercession but she is already praying for us as in the above stanza, and all we have to do is join her in dialogue with Christ.

We can conclude from Ephrem's perspective that Mary, who is the mother, sister, and bride of Christ is one with us Christians (the Church), and that we are one with her in Christ. It is in sharing the same life with Christ through the Spirit and the sacraments that we find ourselves united with Mary. In Ephrem we find the great insight that Mary is not the Mother of the Church only but that she is also *the* Church; one of us and one with us. This is perhaps the reason why we pray with Mary to Christ since she is already with us in Christ. Thus from Ephrem's view, Mary is not a distant (above) intercessor to Christ (who would rank even higher) but they are already here with us; and we are present with them in the life-kingdom of the risen Christ. Therefore our prayer is a prayer of union and closeness with Christ and Mary whose hearts are already close to ours and who are present to us in the sacraments.

In Ephrem's perception all time is present here in kingdom of the risen Lord.[16] Thus Mary's earthly life is part of her present glorified life in Christ, and Ephrem can contemplate the mysteries in the life of Christ and Mary as part of his own present mystery in Christ.

The titles of mother, sister, bride, daughter etc. seem to express the fulness of Mary's relationship with Christ. For the Christian they can express a variety of relationships and mystical levels of union with God. It seems that in Ephrem's time these titles were used by the chaste ascetics known as People of the Covenant whom Ephrem admired. Thus Mary was the model of the ascetic life for Ephrem who saw virginity and Mary's virginal conception as a sign of her holiness.[17]

As Christians, we also participate in the life and family of Christ in a variety of mystical relationships. In Christ Mary is our companion and inspiration and a symbol of our life in Christ. She is present with us as with Christ in his mystical body, the Church. And her presence can always be felt in the people and the things (sacraments) that bring us Christ.

Thus for Ephrem, Mary is present with us as Christ's mother and sister and also as one of us, which in turn also makes us the brothers and sisters of Christ. This again shows the closeness that Ephrem feels in relation to Mary and Christ as a Christian. It is from this closeness that Ephrem writes his hymns and songs. These titles of mother, sister, bride are not far from Jesus' own names for those who are close to him; "For whoever does the will of my Father in heaven is my brother, and sister, and mother." (Mat. 12:50). This is the same closeness that we share with Mary now as she is always present with Christ in glory and with us the Church, his mystical body.

NOTES

1. Robert Murray, 'Ephrem Syrus', in *Catholic Dictionary of Theology,* editor J.H. Crehan, (London, 1967), II, p. 222.
2. Ibid., p. 221.
3. Hymn of Nativity 16, 9-11. Robert Murray, "Mary the second eve in the Early Syriac Fathers," *Eastern Churches Review,* III-4, (1971), p. 376.

4. Ibid.
5. Robert Murray, *Symbols of church and Kingdom,* (Cambridge University Press, 1975), pp. 255-257. About the 'Sons and Daughters of Covenant'.
6. "Ephrem moves on to see the Jordan's womb and Mary's as effectively identical." Sebastian Brock, *"St. Ephrem on Christ as Light in Mary and in the Jordan,"* Vol. 7, n. 2 (1975), p. 140.
7. Brock, "Ephrem on Christ as light in Mary," p. 138.
8. Ibid.
9. Ibid., p. 139.
10. Robert Murray, "A Hymn of St. Ephrem to Christ on the Incarnation, the Holy Spirit and the Sacraments," *Eastern Churches Review,* V.3 (Aut. 1970), p. 144.
11. Hymn Crucif. 3, 9. Murray, "Mary second Eve," p. 381.
12. Ibid.
13. Murray, "Mary second Eve," p. 384.
14. Ibid.
15. Hymn Nat. XI, *Nicene and Post Nicene Fathers,* Phillip Shaff and Henry Wase ed., Second Series, Vol. XIII, (Michigan: Eerdmans Publishing Company, 1964), p. 245.
16. See Brock in "Christ light in Mary" on 'sacred time', p. 141, and Murray in "the theory of Symbolism in St. Ephrem's Theology", *Parole De L'orient,* Vol. VI and VII (1975-6), pp. 7-9.
17. The word for 'Chastity' is 'Holiness' in Ephrem's terminology. Murray, "Mary the second Eve," p. 376.

KHOMIAKOV AND HIS THEORY
OF SOBORNOST

by Mary Grace Ritchey

Mrs. Ritchey graduated from St. Mary-of-the-Woods College through a mission scholarship and is presently studying at John XXIII Institute. She lives with her husband and six children in Birmingham, Ala. where she is Director of Religious Education at St. George Melkite Greek-Catholic Church.

Khomiakov and his Theory of Sobornost

Aleksei Stepanovich Khomiakov was born into a Russian family of landed gentry on May 1st, 1804. He was deeply religious from childhood and deeply concerned for his fellowman while being intellectually gifted. He became a prominent Slavophil with a special devotion to Moscow. He was poet and farmer, philosopher and lay theologian and perhaps even a prophet of sorts. His mother was of strong personal character but not so his father. It was because of his mother that he was a fervent Orthodox. He saw Orthodoxy as intrinsic to the Russian person. He was so compassionate that he was one of the first to free his serfs. His dedication to freedom was later to be painful under imposed censorship and religious constraints. He felt so much affection and concern for his fellowman that he endeavored to learn enough about medicine to treat his peasants during an epidemic when there was a shortage of doctors and medical care. He died of cholera on September 23, 1860.

The concept of *Sobornost,* the reflection of Trinitarian unity in man and his relationship to other men, permeated the faith and living of Aleksei Khomiakov. He believed in the potentiality of the person as intrinsic to the potentiality of society united in fellowship and love with the inspiration of the Holy Spirit as its guide, always in freedom but with a collective moral constraint. He was first

53

impressed by the unity of small farming communities, *obshchina,* that were governed by a parliament, *Mir,* in which rich and poor alike acted together. Personal conduct and wealth were controlled by public opinion expressed in this village gathering in which only unanimous decisions were morally binding.[1] This idea in which all had to agree he saw as the voice of the Holy Spirit and applied this principle to certain problems of church policy which were troubling Orthodox-Catholic relations. He saw the social order manifested in the village group as resulting from "the inner attitude of men to one another."[2] He therefore deduced that "social progress was the fruit of Christian living."[3]

Sources of Church Disunity

The greatest treasure for Khomiakov was his membership in the Church.[4] Its ecclesiological problems, he believed, were not only a concern of the hierarchy but of every member, laity and clergy alike. He felt that infallibility, as conceived by the Western Church, was dividing the Kingdom of God on earth, the Body of Christ, as had been the case for centuries. In 1848 the Eastern Patriarchs signed an Encyclical and sent it to Pope Pius IX. It stated:

> That infallibility resides solely in the ecumenical fellowship of the Church, united together by mutual love, and that the guardianship of dogmas and of the purity of rites is entrusted, not to the hierarchy alone but to all members of the Church, who are the Body of Christ.[5]

In the denial by the West in the infallibility of the membership of the Church, of the totality "transfigured by God . . . in which the Spirit of God manifests Himself,"[6] and the placing of infallibility in an individual were defects of Western individualism and a "defective interpretation of Christianity inherited by the West from Rome."[7] Khomiakov declared: "Modern society in its decay releases every individual to the freedom of his own impotence."[8] The second decline was the Protestant manifestation of individualism, throwing out tradition and community and becoming a law unto itself.[9] The third manifestation was the rationalism of Reformed Christians.

> The Christians of the West were caught in a vicious circle. The reaction at the time of the Reformation against the excessive claims of

the Popes went amiss, for it sprang from the wrong spirit. Protestantism was nothing more than papal individualism brought to its logical conclusion. Rome had imposed upon the Christian West unity without freedom; the Protestants achieved freedom, but at the expense of unity. Yet neither unity without freedom nor freedom without unity was of any use (11, 212). They both meant the isolation of man, and his exclusion from the redeeming influence of true Christian fellowship. The West had rejected the fundamental teaching of love, on which the whole life of the Church was based.[10]

This was completely against the vision of Khomiakov who saw the charisms of the Holy Spirit as incarnate in the community of Christians joined in mutual love and prayer; one life of grace; a sharing experience such as in the Easter night Liturgy which was foremost in his mind. He saw Western civilization as a "deification of political society" rather than the deification of each Christian. The Roman Church's unity was compulsive such as the imposing of Latin universally in their Mass.[11] He longed "to see this burning life of the Spirit pervading the whole life of his country."[12] He saw it resulting in an openness to all brethren "united in love, to the Church."[13]

But this is not what happened in his lifetime or after. Instead the autonomous patriarchate had been abolished by Peter the Great and the priests had become no more than civil servants. Later the seminaries would be closed and many of the Churches also would be closed as the state and law were substituted for communal love and grace. His theory, devoid of the Spirit of God, became atheistic communism. The religious tradition which he saw as inherent in the Russian people was discarded by the state. Khomiakov knew that "a society which had lost its common religious background could be kept together only by fear and compulsion."[14] Although frustrated by the lack of freedom and the censorship of his writing, he continued to write but very little could be published in Russia. Khomiakov believed that the West was dying and that the East would awaken to greatness if only it would reverse its "spiritual backwardness." He wrote in his poem, *The Dream* (1834):

Hark to the call of fate, rise to the new dawn,
Awake, slumbering East![15]

Western thinking in the sciences and in all education of the Russian people perturbed Khomiakov. The West was dying. It did not have the true doctrine of Orthodoxy yet its sciences and education were influencing Russian children. Khomiakov believed that parents should educate their children and only technical training should be given outside the home.[16] He differentiated between the knowledge that comes from God through love and communion and scientific knowledge:

> Many people who, owing to adverse circumstances, lack scientific knowledge, but are penetrated by moral conviction, come nearer to full enlightenment than those who know many things but lack the power of spiritual life. . . .[17]

United In Love

True knowledge comes through love and is beyond the isolated mind but is open to a community of minds: "Truth looks as though it were the achievement of the few, but in reality it is the creation and possession of all."[18] It is the possession of the part of truth of which the Spirit has revealed added to all the other parts, revealed by the Spirit of Truth, who builds up the entire possession of truth for mankind. The isolated, egotistic individual is not sharing his part of the truth. Khomiakov calls such an individual sick.

For Khomiakov the best teacher is the example of those united in love in Christ by the grace of the Holy Spirit whose life exudes morality. He found what was considered to be a God-given right in democratic America was an obligation for the true-believing Russian: "to bring forth a human society founded on laws of the highest morality and Christian truth." He saw America's freedom only in the light of monetary gain.[19] All his life Khomiakov believed that the Russian people would see the folly of discarding their inherent Christian morality based on Orthodoxy and would reverse and awaken to the Spirit of God.

Sobornost

Over a century has passed since the death of Khomiakov. There has been Russian *Sobornost* but its witness has been martyrdom.

(Sobornost comes from the Slavonic word meaning *catholic.* It does not have in the Slavonic the traditional meaning of universality, however, but rather of a fellowship in faith and love.) It has been a *Sobornost* of prison camps and exile. It has been a community of like-minded artists and free thinkers always acknowledging the Creator of their talents, dying and living their witness for the good of all peoples. And the concept of *Sobornost* lives on and has been applied to modern usage.

The first time I came upon the word Sobornost was through a book of the same name by Catherine Dougherty. She used the word to describe the relationship of spiritual sharing of personal experiences and meditations in a situation of material sharing in a common life much as we read about in Acts 2:42-47. This trinitarian overflow of love, which is the basis of Khomiakov's writings, has become the life of many spiritual communities. This trinitarian life spills over into a social apostolate to harbor refugees and fugitives, to feed and clothe the destitute, to evangelize and to teach religious catechesis. But it is especially important today in another community of love, the basic unit of society, the family.

It might seem strange to speak about fellowship of members of the family united together in mutual love where each member is free to achieve his or her potentiality but in the spirit of prayerful consideration and personal constraint. This should be taken for granted. However, today especially, this collegiality is as essential to family life as to the village commune that so intrigued Khomiakov. For it is the Spirit of God working in the family through the marriage charisms given to those who have been joined together in God, that is fashioning a new spirit of society today. It is this concept of family that combats the ills of man's isolation and individualism which Khomiakov labeled as sick. The failure of the love and responsibility of the family is the ultimate failure of Church and all civilization. We can actually apply Khomiakov's idea of society to this basic unit of society:

> Social life (*obschenie*) consists not in mere exchange of ideas, not in the cold and egoistic exchange of services, not in dry respect for an alien law, always reserving its own rights—but in the living inter-

change both of ideas and feelings, in sharing not only grief (sympathy is all too common a feeling) but also the joys of existence.[20]

Unity in the Family

For it is in the context of love and family that mankind learns first to conquer one's *ego* and live for the common good of all. It is in the family that the love of God through other persons is first learned and experienced. It is in the context of family that respect for law and order is first encountered. It is in the protection of the family that is first learned the meaning of truth and right and wrong. It is because of family that the child can learn to have dominion over creation and oneness with the cosmos. It is in the sharing in mutual love of authority, service to one another for the good of the whole family, tolerance and understanding, that prepares the members of the family to become a part of other groups. And, finally, it is because of the family that the person can accept and be accepted into God's family, the Church.

The *New Catholic Encyclopedia* defines *Sobornost* as the Slavonic word for *catholic*. The Creed of Nicaea and Constantinople speaks of the Church as "one, holy, catholic and apostolic." But this word "catholic" has not always taken the meaning of "sobornost" but rather a lesser meaning of universality-merely that the Church is everywhere. But Khomiakov's ideal of catholicity-sobornost is:

> . . . to apply the trinitarian model to the life of the Church; unity in multiplicity, oneness in diversity, togetherness in dispersal, a catholicity realized in quality not in quantity, in depth rather than in breadth, a characteristic communicated by the Holy Spirit which enables individual communities, and even persons, to give full and complete manifestation to the mark of catholicity.[21]

This trinitarian model should also be the real meaning of catholicity for it is distinction yet unity; it is emptying completely but receiving all fullness; it is concentrality in love rather than mere yardage; it is oneness rather than incongruity.

Fellowship in the Spirit

From the word *Sobornost* many Eastern Churches have coined the word Sobor-Synod or Council. Under this context, it becomes a fellowship of the hierarchy who, together with the Holy Spirit and in mutual love and respect, bring order within the Church and unity among the dispersal of local Churches. It has been said that where the Bishop is, there is the Church. He possesses the fullness of the Body of Christ within his fellowship of parishes. The true mentality of infallibility in the Church is that which progresses from the guidance of the Holy Spirit in the local parish leading to the acceptance in love in other parish churches, which, always with the binding together of the charisms of the Holy Spirit, progresses to the Council of Bishops who can, through the initiation of the laity-in-Spirit, bring about unity in the semantics of doctrine and dogma because of the practice of the faith of the people. Stated in perhaps a more clear way:

> The Holy Spirit is leading Christians back into their local Churches and parishes. There they are beginning to experience on a deeper level than ever before a unity that is being evolved as Christians of the same Church group yield to that Spirit. As true conciliarity is found in our families, parishes and local churches, it will become easier to experience true conciliarity on regional and global levels.[22]

But a spirit of renewal and healing must be in the heart of man before man can understand the knowledge of unity in God of all men. Three years ago, I heard an address by a spokesman of one of our divided churches emphatically proclaim in the strongest and most righteous of voices that we shall not intercommunicate until we are in agreement. That would seem to me to be disregarding the healing of union in Christ in communion, among the same family of believers in such healing. Certainly the essence of *Sobornost* is not expressed by such a punishment! The heart of the Body of Christ cries out to be healed of these separations! It cries out to be reconciled of individualism in the civilization of the West by the practice of *Sobornost* in both East and West, sect by sect:

> Sobornost could provide a link between the Catholic and Protestant views of the Church by bringing to fruition true elements of the covenant idea and by assigning to the hierarchy its rightful place as an organizational entity within the living organism of the Church.[23]

Yet ecumenical *Sobornost* can never be so easy among so many years built upon years of distrust, reactionism and hard-hearted misunderstanding, except by the grace of God who makes all things possible and brings order out of our chaos. It will come only after we have realized the difference between the essential Good News of Christ and the non-essentials and cultivate the spirit of growth and progression into the likeness of Christ by the enhancement of His Holy Spirit.

> There will always exist in the Church a fundamental equilibrium, never acquired once for all time, but always in need of renewal, between the principle of tradition, obedience, order and sacramental, liturgical forms on the one hand, and on the other, the principle of liberty, creativity, personal responsibility, the irreducible integrity of the human person of the local community, of the divine grace which interiorizes the forms, places and times which assures a unique vertical relationship between the individual person that the inspiration of the Spirit is always to be renewed and cannot be codified, but incarnates itself; the trust is always pulsating, never content with dogmatic formulas and rules of faith which express and enclose it.[24]

Base Communities

I see the thrust of *Sobornost* today as the search for Truth itself and the mutual comprehension of the truth of each part of the whole practiced in the fellowship of love. This must start at ground roots level: family to family, group to group within the parish community; dialogue between youth groups and catechist groups and ladies' and men's and priests' and bishops' groups and so on and on.

Khomiakov, if he were alive today, would argue (as he did on many occasions before) that the bishops, who are the teachers and protectors of truth, define and proclaim the truth after the fellowship of loving council but these definitions must then be lived. They must be acclaimed by the actual living of the whole totality of the people of God, not just by the hierarchy but also by the laity "because it is the whole people of God that constitutes the guardian of Tradition."[25] Khomiakov would probably insist that church unity, which is the object of ecumenism, may come from ecclesiastical authorities but only after unity has been achieved local Church by local Church—the extension of individual acceptance of unity, concord and harmony, the trinitarian marriage; the love between person and person rather than the distrust caused by labels of Orthodox, Protestant, Catholic.

Therefore, it is the laity who must first take the initiative to achieve a sense of unity before it can progress to the authority or hierarchy of the Churches. Opposed to making a law and enforcing it, we must live in unity and then proclaim it in the name of Jesus Christ, as we remember the prayer of Christ "that they may be one, even as we are one . . . " (John 17:22).

When we understand and live Khomiakov's theory of the potentiality of each person centered in trinitarian unity and attended and renewed by the Spirit of Love, then *Sobornost* will be achieved.

NOTES

1. Nicholas Zernov, *Three Russian Prophets* (London: The Camelot Press Ltd., 1944), p. 72.
2. *Ibid.,* p. 71.
3. *Ibid.,* p. 79.
4. *Ibid.,* p. 51.
5. *Ibid.,* p. 62.
6. Nicholas Arseniev, *Holy Moscow* (London: The MacMillan Company, 1940), p. 6.
7. N. Zernov, *op. cit.,* p. 64.
8. N. Zernov, *op. cit.,* p. 63.
9. N. Zernov, *op. cit.,* p. 67.
10. N. Zernov, *Ibid.,* p. 67.
11. N. Zernov, *op. cit.,* p. 65.
12. N. Arseniev, *op. cit.,* p. 107.
13. N. Arseniev, *op. cit.,* p. 98.
14. N. Zernov, *op. cit.,* p. 76.
15. Richard Hare, *Pioneers of Russian Thought* (London: Oxford University Press, 1951), p. 112.
16. R. Hare, *op. cit.,* p. 126.
17. R. Hare, *op. cit.,* p. 128.
18. N. Zernov, *op. cit.,* p. 58.
19. R. Hare, *op. cit.,* p. 126.
20. R. Hare, *op. cit.,* p. 114.
21. Rev. George A. Maloney, S.J., "A Trinitarian Church of One in Many: A Mysticism of Community," *Diakonia,* 12, No. 3, (New York: John XXIII Ecumenical Center, 1980), p. 215.

Ritchey

22. Rev. George A. Maloney, S.J., "An Emerging New Ecumenism." *Diakonia,* (editorial), 13, No. 1, (New York: John XXIII Ecumenical Center, 1978), p. 2.
23. Rev. George A. Maloney, S.J., "A Trinitarian Church of One in Many: A Mysticism of Community," p. 214.
24. Rev. George A. Maloney, S.J., "Ecumenism and the Holy Spirit." *Diakonia,* (editorial), 13, No. 2, (New York: John XXIII Ecumenical Center, 1978), p. 97.
25. Timothy Ware, *The Orthodox Church,* (New York: Penguin Books, 1963), pp. 256-7.

CHRONICLE OF EVENTS FOR THE YEAR 1981 IN EASTERN CHRISTIAN JURISDICTIONS AND ASSOCIATED ORGANIZATIONS

by *Thomas F. Sable, S.J.*

Father Sable is currently completing a doctoral dissertation entitled "Lay Initiative in Greek Catholic Parishes and Fraternal Organizations (1884-1907)" at the Graduate Theological Union in Berkeley, California.

CHURCHES AND JURISDICTIONS OUTSIDE NORTH AMERICA

Ecumenical Events

On the occasion of the sixteenth centenary of the Council of Constantinople, the Orthodox Center of the Ecumenical Patriarchate at Chambesy, Switzerland held a continuing seminar on the theme: "The Meaning and Reality of the Second Ecumenical Council for the Christian World of Today." An impressive array of scholars and theologians presented talks on five sub-topics: 1. Historical Background by Professors Ritter, Thiraios, Christou, and Metropolitan Chrysostom. 2. The Creed of the Council of Constantinople by Professors Schlink, Stylianopoulos, Schneemelcher, Karmiris, Papadopoulos. 3. The Pneumatological Problematic by Professors Staniloae, Hauschild, Clement, Wiederkehr, Bobrinskoy, Vischer, Garrigues, Aldenhoven, Allchin, Widmer, and Congar. 4. The Canonical Problematic by Professors Pheidas, Meyendorff, and Metropolitan Panteleimon Rodopoulos. 5. The Problematic of Today by Professors Slenczka, Sabev, Metropolitan Damaskinos, Professors Nissiotis, Jevtic, Yannaras, von Schoenborn, Bishop Maximos Agiorgoussis, Metropolitan George Khodr, Father Vitaly Borovoy, Professors Valenziano and Ion Bria. Three formal lectures were held to underline the grand theme. These were given by Cardinal Willebrands of the Secretariat for Promoting

63

Christian Unity, Rome; Phillip Potter, General Secretary of the World Council of Churches, Geneva; and Metropolitan Damaskinos Papandreou of the Ecumenical Patriarchate.

Visits

From May 1 to 5, 1981 His Holiness Vasken I, Supreme Catholikos of the Armenian church (see of Etchmiazin, Armenian S.S.R.), visited West Germany for the first time. He visited various communities of Armenian faithful and established contacts with Catholic and other churches of West Germany. In Munich he visited Cardinal Ratzinger and Johann Hanselmann, Evangelical bishop of Bavaria. The topic ecumenism was discussed at these meetings.

After an Executive Committee session of the World Council of Churches, Patriarch Ilia II of Georgia was the guest of the Federation of Protestant Churches of Switzerland. He was accompanied by Archbishop Nicholosi of Sukhumi, head of the Foreign Relations Department of the Church of Georgia. He met with members of the Georgian Studies Department at the University of Zurich.

Ecumenical Patriarchate

A delegation from the Ecumenical Patriarchate visited Rome to take part in the celebration of the feast of Sts. Peter and Paul. The head of the delegation was Metropolitan Meliton of Chalcedon. The dean of the Holy Synod was accompanied by Bishop Gennadios of Krateas and Archimandrite Spiridon Papageorgiou, director of the Greek Mission in Rome. On June 27, 1981 the delegation paid a visit to the Policlinico Gemelli, where Pope John Paul II was hospitalized.

The sixteenth centenary of the Council of Constantinople was solemnly celebrated at the Ecumenical Patriarchate from June 5 to June 7, 1981 in an inter-Orthodox and inter-denominational context. The celebrations centered on two particular moments of prayer: Vespers on Saturday evening and the Eucharist on Sunday morning. During the Vespers service Metropolitan Chrysostom of Myra gave the anniversary address on the theme: "The Historico-Dogmatic Presuppositions of the Ecumenicity of the Second Ecumenical Council." At the conclusion of the celebration of the Eucharist the Patriarch greeted the delegations with an address in which he stated: "Today, sixteen hundred years later, we Christians are gathered on the soil of the undivided Church in the fellowship of the Holy Spirit; but also—through sins known only to God, but largely because of reasons that derive from non-theological, linguistic and general cultural factors—we return here in division as pilgrims homesick for the ecumenical Christian unity, for the undivided Church, for the One, Holy, Catholic and Apostolic Church of our common Symbol of Faith."

A delegation from Sicily, headed by Cardinal Salvatore Pappalardo, archbishop of Palermo, visited the Ecumenical Patriarchate March 27 to April 3, 1981. The delegation was greeted upon arrival by Metropolitan Chrysostom of Myra. The Patriarch, at an audience for the delegation on March 28, said that he was sure that the visit would help develop a profound relationship between the Church of Constantinople and the local church of Sicily, both of whom have shared such a long and common history.

Dialogues

At the John Knox Reformed Center in Geneva, a bilateral dialogue between a group of theologians from the Ecumenical Patriarchate and a group of theologians from the World Reformed Alliance took place from February 15 to 18, 1981. The participants on the Orthodox side included: Metropolitan Chrysostom of Myra, co-president; Metropolitans Emilianos and Damaskinos; and the theologian Yorgo Lemopoulos. On the Reformed side were: Dr. James MacCord of Princeton, co-president; professors Lochman, Esser, McLelland, Torrance, and Smith. The discussion of the immutability and communicability of God was continued. Two reports introduced the new theme of authority in the Orthodox and Reformed traditions. The next session of the dialogue will take place in the fall of 1982 with the theme of "The Trinitarian base and the Structure of the Faith as Presented to the Church by the Nicean-Constantinople Creed."

The Synod of the Moscow Patriarchate on March 23, 1981

considered the work of the technical commission of the Inter-Orthodox Theological Commission in preparation for dialogue with Lutherans and a letter from Ecumenical Patriarch Dimitrios I to Patriarch Pimen. The Synod decided that the Orthodox-Lutheran dialogue was appropriate, that the Patriarch of Constantinople should be informed of the Moscow position on certain procedural questions, and that the representatives of the Moscow Patriarchate at the dialogues would be Archbishop Vladimir of Dmitrov and Professor Osipov, both of the Moscow Theological Academy.

The Lutheran-Orthodox dialogues were held in Helsinki, Finland from August 27 to September 5, 1981 with three topics on the agenda: 1. Participation in the Mystery of the Church 2. The Creed of Nicea-Constantinople as a Symbol of Ecumenical Faith. 3. Practical Approaches to Continued Dialogue.

In light of these dialogues, the World Lutheran Federation has opened a Documentation Center at the Institute for the History and Theology of the Eastern Church. The center will gather all pertinent documents from the current Orthodox-Lutheran dialogues as well as other Orthodox dialogues for future academic or ecclesial studies. The Center will also help implement the research of the Institute itself. The Institute is located in Erlangen, West Germany.

The projects coordination group of the Dialogue between Anglicans and Orthodox met in London March 27, 1981. The working session of the Dialogue was held at the Orthodox Center in Chambesy, Switzerland from July 20-27, 1981. It studied the following points: the mystery of the Church, Trinitarian dispensations, and Tradition as faith-unifying. This plenary session issued a communique which stated that the Anglicans were pleased with the Orthodox interpretation of the Procession of the Holy Spirit and the new perspectives that this opens for not putting the *Filioque* in the Creed.

The Fourth Series of Theological Conversations between representatives of the Russian Orthodox Church and the Evangelical Church Union of East Germany took place from May 10 to 13, 1981 in Guestrow, East Germany, Metropolitan Filaret of Kiev headed the Russian delegation. Dr. Werner Krusche headed the

East German delegation. The theme of the conference was again "The Following of Christ in the Life of the Christian."

World Council of Churches

The Orthodox Churches continue to examine attentively their relations with the World Council of Churches on the occasion of the preparations for the Sixth World Assembly, scheduled for Vancouver, Canada, in 1983.

At a March 23, 1981 session of the Holy Synod of the patriarchate of Moscow, Metropolitan Juvenaly reported on Moscow participation in the prepatory commissions. The Synod expressed the hope that the work would continue in the best traditions of the W.C.C.

At the invitation of the Orthodox Church of Bulgaria, a top-level delegation of Orthodox church representatives and officials from the W.C.C. met in Sofia from May 23 to 31, 1981. Ostensibly the gathering was to celebrate the 16th Centenary of the Council of Constantinople, but the real discussions centered around relations between the W.C.C. and the Orthodox churches and around preparations for Vancouver.

A communique issued after the meeting made the following points about Orthodox participation in the W.C.C.: 1. The ecclesiological presuppositions of local Orthodox church participation in the W.C.C. should be made clear. The voting procedures at the heart of the W.C.C. allow the customary position of the Orthodox churches to be voted down effortlessly by a majority, composed largely of Reformed churches. 2. The participation of local Orthodox church representatives in all the organizations and staff of the W.C.C. be extended to match the spiritual and historical significance of Orthodoxy. Nominees for positions should not be limited to those suggested by the local Orthodox churches for these organizations. 3. Orthodox representatives should take part in all levels of discussion in the preparation of documents pertaining to questions of Faith and Order and other questions essential to the program of the W.C.C. 4. The representatives of the local Orthodox churches should be more generously allowed to participate in the work of the W.C.C. in the roles of speakers, advisors, experts, presidents, vice-presidents, and facilitators. 5. The local Orthodox churches should be included in the preparation of the Sixth Assembly of the W.C.C. by an active and multi-faceted participation.

Dissatisfaction with the internal workings of the W.C.C. did not disappear after the Sofia meeting, however. At the end of a meeting of the Central Committee held in Dresden three months later some doubts were made public about the Eucharistic celebration planned for the Sixth Assembly at Vancouver. The Orthodox representatives and the Catholic observers agreed that the possibility of a general intercommunion and a general intercelebration was impossible. The Orthodox are also opposed to the conclusions of the Sheffield Consultation on "The Community of Men and Women in the Church." The Orthodox allow for the discussion of the ordination of women, but do not want the conclusions of Sheffield to be imposed contrary to Orthodox convictions.

Orthodox-Catholic Dialogue

The coordinating committee of the Joint Commission for dialogue between the Catholic Church and the Orthodox Church met in Venice from May 25 to 30, 1981. The task of the committee was to examine what work three subcommissions had done on the tasks assigned to them at Rhodes last year. A synthesis of the three themes—1) on the sacramental nature of the church; 2) Trinity, local church, and Eucharist; 3) Trinity, Eucharist, and communion of the local churches—was drafted and sent to all the members of the commission. Along with the reports of the three commissions, these works will serve as the working papers for the next plenary session, which will be held in Munich, Germany, from June 30 to July 4, 1981.

Church of Ethiopia

The largest autochthononous church in Africa, the church of Ethiopia, seems to be experiencing a sort of renaissance. Publishing of religious materials has again been allowed by the government after a period of prohibition from 1977 to 1980. Amharic bibles and bibles in other languages spoken in the country, and small editions of liturgical texts were among the items allowed to be published.

Church of Greece

With the election of the Socialist government of Mr. Andreas Papandreou, the problem of the separation of church and state has again become acute for the Church of Greece. Mr. Papandreou's position on the question became clear in his statement before the fall elections: "The Church will cease to be a sector of the State machinery and will be able to go forward as a free and independent power." In response Athens Archbishop Seraphim declared his agreement with the position of Mr. Papandreou. The Archbishop also agreed with the position of Mr. Papandreou on civil marriage: "We cannot force people to come to the sacrament if they do not believe or do not wish to."

Patriarchate of Moscow

The feast of St. Sergius of Radonezh was marked by a particular solemnity at the Trinity-St. Sergius Lavra at Zagorsk. Metropolitan Theodosius of the Orthodox Church in America took part in the ceremonies. The Greek Orthodox Patriarch of Alexandria, Nicholas VI, was present and presided at a number of the ceremonies on July 18, 1981. Mr. V.G. Furov, vice president of the Council of Religious Affairs, addressed the gathered prelates at a large reception held in the residence of Patriarch Pimen.

In reaction to statements made by Ukrainian Catholics about the reunification of the Ukrainian Greek Catholic Church with the Orthodox church on the occasion of the thirty-fifth anniversary of the event, the Russian Patriarchate celebrated a series of events to mark the anniversary on May 16 and 17, 1981. Present at the celebrations were 15 bishops. Among them were Metropolitans Filaret of Kiev, Sergius of Odessa, Nicholas of Lvov. Also present for the event was N.A. Kolesnik, president of the Council of Religious Affairs of the Ukrainian S.S.R. The participants attended a lecture in which Metropolitan Filaret declared: "Thirty-five years have passed since the Initiative Group for the Reunification of the

Greek Catholic Church with the Orthodox Church held its council in the cathedral of St. George in Lvov. The participants decided to abolish the Union of Brest of 1596 in the Ukraine and to come back to the holy Orthodox faith of their fathers, in the bosom of the Russian Orthodox church. By the grace of God, and thanks to the efforts of enthusiastic promoters of the Orthodox faith and the unity of the church, the dream of the people of God is realized . . ."

The patriarch in his address recalled the role of the military victory and the territorial unification of the Ukraine in this reunion. He also recalled the memory of Father Gabriel Kostelnik, "organizer and president of the Council of Lvov, who gave his life for the holy cause of Orthodoxy" and he mentioned the part taken by Metropolitan Nicholas in this work of "Orthodox unity."

In an exchange of letters between Pope John Paul II and Patriarch Pimen of Moscow, the views of the Roman See on the Ukrainian synod have been expressed. In a letter addressed to Patriarch Pimen on January 24, 1981, the Pope replied: "Somebody, without any preliminary consultation, delivered to the press the projects discussed at the synod. The Holy See, while strongly upholding the positions which it always held in relation to Ukrainian Catholics, regrets this publication, which took place before I myself took cognizance of the documents. At once all the papal nuncios, residing in countries where there are Ukrainian Catholic communities, were informed of the fact that these texts received no approval and are, therefore, deprived of all official character. It was also ordered that the documents be neither published nor distributed. No official publication of the Holy See ever mentioned them."

Patriarchate of Antioch

Patriarch Ignatius IV commented on the necessity of a Pan-Orthodox Synod recently in an interview during his visit to Greece. He said: "I think that a Synod must take place. The bodies designated for this purpose ought to get together as soon as possible. Our faithful expect something to happen. The great majority of topics on the agenda have been resolved by the preparatory committees. There will be no further difficulties because the themes of the Synod are not of a dogmatic nature, but are pastoral questions which can and ought to be resolved quickly. A tentative structure, modeled on the Second Vatican Council, should suffice. All that is difficult to resolve should be put aside. The centuries without a council have created an absense of conciliarity in our Church."

Patriarchate of Serbia

Serbian Orthodox priest Nadjo Jancic, pastor of the parish of Borike, near Sarajevo, was sentenced to six years in prison for "inciting to intolerance and national and religious discord." Three of his parishioners were condemned to prison for the same crimes. The cause of this punishment was that the accused sang a national song at the baptism of the priest's son.

Metropolitan Vladislav of Bosnia, acting in the name of the Serbian Orthodox church, and Dr. Stipe Suvar, representative of the government of the republic of Croatia, signed an agreement to restore control over monuments and other objects of religious art to the Serbian Orthodox Church. The agreement was signed on February 21, 1981.

CHURCHES OF NORTH AND SOUTH AMERICA

Ecumenical Events

A delegation of Orthodox theologians and a delegation of Baptist theologians met in Kentucky from May 25 to 27, 1981. Bishop Maximos of Pittsburgh headed the Orthodox delegation. Dr. Glenn Igletead headed the Baptist delegation. Topics discussed were mission and evangelization, and relations between Church and State. Father Veronis presented a paper on the Orthodox position on mission and evangelization and Professor Stanley Harakas spoke on the topic "Church and State according to the Greek Orthodox tradition."

Dialogues

American Roman Catholic and Eastern Orthodox bishops have set up a joint committee to implement pastoral steps toward unity at the suggestion of their theologians. Archbishop Iakovos, head of the Greek Orthodox church of America, headed the Orthodox group. Also included in this group were Metropolitan

Silas, Bishop Maximos of Pittsburgh, and Bishop Anthimos from the Greek Orthodox Church; Archbishop Michael Shaheen from the Antiochian Archdiocese; Bishop John Martin of the Carpatho-Russian Orthodox Greek Catholic church of Johnstown, Pennsylvania; Bishop Mark of the Albanian Orthodox Church; and Bishop Peter of the Orthodox Church in America. Included in the Catholic delegation was Bishop Michael Dudick of the Byzantine Rite diocese of Passaic, New Jersey. This inclusion was an ecumenical first because many Orthodox prelates continue to object to the very existence of the Eastern Catholic churches [Uniate churches]. Archbishop Iakovos stated about this point: "There's no more discrimination. I think that the Byzantine Rites can help bring about unity. They can provide a better understanding of the Orthodox among Roman Catholics." The Catholic delegation was headed by Archbishop Rembert Weakland of the Milwaukee Archdiocese. Also included in the delegation were Archbishop Francis T. Hurley, Archbishop of Anchorage, Alaska; Archbishop Oscar H. Lipscomb of Mobile, Alabama; Bishop Stanislaus J. Brzana of Ogdensburg, New York; Bishop Arthur J. O'Neill of Rockford, Illinois; and Bishop Ernest L. Unterkoefler of Charleston, South Carolina.

ORTHODOX JURISDICTIONS

Coptic Church in U.S.A. and Canada

In a half-page ad in the New York Times the clergy and the congregations of the Coptic Church in the U.S. and Canada congratulated Hosni Mubarek for accepting the "weighty and momentous responsibility of the Presidency" after the assassination of Anwar Sadat. The ad also congratulated Pope Shenouda III on the tenth anniversary of his enthronement as Pope and Patriarch on November 14.

Orthodox Church in America

A Joint Commission was established by the Antiochian Archdiocese of North America and the authorities of the Orthodox Church in America with the goal of studying together the stages of formation and organization to realize the unity of the Orthodox church of America. The first meeting, held at Englewood, New Jersey on February 24, 1981 issued a statement with four points: 1. The ultimate goal of the commission will be the establishment of one Orthodox church for North America; 2. While recognizing the pluralism and diversity of Orthodoxy in America, steps can be taken now for making the canonical exigency of unity in America a reality; 3. The unity of the episcopacy, a central tenet of Orthodox ecclesiology, has to be seen as a necessity in this day and age of confusion about dogma and moral teaching; 4. While considering the unity of the episcopacy as the corner stone of Orthodox unity in America, the commission underlines other serious needs: cooperation and avoiding of duplication in mission and education.

The commission owes its existence to the initiative of Metropolitan Philip of the Antiochian Archdiocese and reciprocal agreement by Metropolitan Theodosius of the O.C.A. The members of the commission are Fathers Paul Schneirla, John Badeen, and George Corey of the Antiochian Archdiocese; and Fathers Alexander Schmemann, John Meyendorff, and Leonid Kishkovsky of the O.C.A.

On February 22, 1981 the annual meeting of St. Vladimir's Theological Foundation took place at the seminary with some 300 members and guests in attendance. At this time the seminary received the foundation's grant for 1980 for $130,000. Metropolitan Theodosius celebrated the liturgy in the seminary chapel on that day.

On April 1, 1981 Very Reverend Vladimir Sorokin, professor at the Leningrad Theological Academy, and former dean, visited St. Vladimir's Seminary.

Russian Orthodox Church Outside Russia

In a religious ceremony with political overtones, the Russian Orthodox Church outside of Russia canonized as saints of its church Czar Nicholas II, his family, and tens of thousands of others killed during the outbreak of the Russian Revolution in 1917. Metropolitan Philaret, head of the jurisdiction, conducted the two day ceremony at the Cathedral on East 93rd Street in Manhattan.

More than one thousand people and a dozen bishops processed down 93rd Street and carried icons and relics.

CATHOLIC JURISDICTIONS

Melkite Archdiocese

St. John Fisher College, Rochester, New York held a conference December 6, 1981 on the topic "Christians of the Middle East." Speakers included Archbishop Joseph Tawil of Boston, Massachusetts, head of the Melkite Catholics of the United States, and Rev. Marcos A. Marcos, pastor of St. Mark's Coptic Orthodox Church in Toronto. A panel discussion followed the two talks. Members of the panel included: Rev. Jeffrey Kirk of St. Paul's Episcopal Church in Rochester; Atoun Ateya of the Egyptian Coptic community of Rochester; Vahe Zeidtounzian of the Armenian community of Rochester; and Medhi Abhari of the Rochester Presbyterian Iranian Community. A dinner followed.

Ukrainian Catholics

The Ukrainian Catholic Eparchy of Stamford, Connecticut marked its silver anniversary at a Pontifical liturgy on October 11, 1981 in Stamford. Cardinal Wladyslaw Rubin, the Prefect of the Sacred Congregation of Oriental Churches, was present for the luncheon and celebrations. Present also were many Eastern Catholic bishops and Roman Rite prelates from the New England area.

Visits

His Beatitude, Anthony Peter Khoraiche, Maronite Patriarch of Antioch, visited the United States at the invitation of the National Conference of Catholic Bishops and reported on the grave situation in Lebanon and on the need for an immediate solution to the problem. The Patriarch met President Reagan to stress this point with the American government. He celebrated a Pontifical liturgy in Boston, Massachusetts at the Cathedral of the Holy Cross, September 27, 1981. Cardinal Medeiros presided. A banquet was held in the Patriarch's honor at the Sheraton Boston Hotel. The Patriarch also visited a number of Maronite parishes throughout the United States. At the Maronite cathedral in Brooklyn, he celebrated a liturgy, assisted by Bishop Francis Zayek, Ordinary for the Maronites in the U.S.

Appointments and Retirements

On the advice of his doctor, Msgr. Charles Moeller has resigned as the secretary of the Roman Catholic Secretariat for Promoting Christian Unity. He returned to his native Belgium, but will continue on in the role of a consultor of the Secretariat.

Scheduled for March 9, 1982, the installation of the newly-appointed bishop of the newly-created diocese for the Western U.S., the diocese and see of Van Nuys, California will make a total of four Byzantine dioceses in the United States. Currently aiding Bishop Dudick of Passaic, Bishop Thomas Dolinay will be the new bishop of Van Nuys. For his biography, see *Diakonia* 12 (1977): 44.

Most Reverend Nerses Mikail Setian was appointed Armenian Catholic Exarch for the United States on July 17, 1981. His ordination to the titular see of Ancira took place in Philadelphia on December 5, 1981. The sixty-three year old bishop is a native of Sebaste, Turkey, and has been rector of the Armenian College in Rome since 1960. He has also been in charge of the daily Armenian transmissions from Radio Vatican. The new bishop is also a consultor for the pontifical commission for the revision of Eastern Canon Law.

Auxiliary bishop Robert Moskal was ordained to the episcopacy in the Ukrainian Archeparchy of Philadelphia on October 13, 1981. Present at the ordination in the Cathedral of the Immaculate Conception were: Archbishop Steven Sulyk of the Archeparchy of Philadelphia; Wladislaw Cardinal Rubin, prefect of the Sacred Congregation for Oriental Churches; Cardinal Krol, Roman Catholic Archbishop of Philadelphia; and Archbishop Myroslav Lubachivsky, coadjutor to Cardinal Slipyi.

Metropolitan Ireneus has been reelected by the Holy Synod of the Church of Crete to the episcopal see of Kissamos. The metropolitan had already occupied this see for fifteen years until he fell into disfavor with the Greek regime of the colonels and took up the important Greek diocese of Germany. During this last period in Germany, he was noted for his pastoral work among the Greek workers in Germany and for his many ecumenical contacts. His successor in Germany, Bishop Augustinos, was named to fill the post in October, 1980. The popular sentiment to bring back Ireneus was so strong that the faithful of Kissamos refused to accept the decision of the Cretan Holy Synod to appoint Metropolitan Nektarios as their ordinary the previous year.

At a general assembly of the diocese of Western Europe, gathered together at the cathedral of St. Alexander in Paris, France, Bishop George Wagner, a German national, was elected as a successor to Archbishop George, who passed away in March. [Cf. Deaths] Born in Berlin Bishop George did his theology at the Institut Saint-Serge in Paris before being ordained to the diaconate and priesthood in 1955 in the diocese of the Moscow Patriarchate. His thesis was on the origins of the liturgy of St. John Chrysostom. He became titular bishop of Eudokias in the Orthodox Archbishopric of France in 1971 and taught canon law and liturgy at the Institut in Paris. He became first auxiliary of France and Western Europe in 1979. The election has to be confirmed by the Holy Synod of the Ecumenical Patriarchate.

Metropolitan Angelarij of Debar-Kicevo was elected to the archepiscopal see of Ohrid and Macedonia by an ecclesiastical and popular assembly. The election took place on August 18, 1981 in the church of Santa Sophia in Ohrid. His installation took place in the church of St. Clement in the presence of the religious authorities of the country, the Catholic bishop of Prizren, and the civil authorities of the Serbian, Macedonian, Croatian, and Bosnian republics.

Archbishop Diodoros was elected Greek Orthodox Patriarch of Jerusalem on February 16, 1981. After long debates the names of three candidates were selected: Metropolitan Basil of Caesarea, Bishop Diodoros, and Father Amphilochios, abbot of Mar Kosiba. In the subsequent election Archbishop Diodoros received nine votes, Metropolitan Basil five, and one ballot was blank. Patriarch Diodoros I was born in Chios in 1923 and arrived in Jerusalem in 1938. He made his theological studies at the University of Athens and was made a monk and deacon in 1944. He was ordained to the priesthood in 1947 and made archimandrite in 1948. He subsequently worked in the translation service of the Patriarchate. He taught in the seminary and served on the church tribunal. He was named the archbishop of Hierapolis in 1962 and lived in Amman, Jordan since 1963.

The Metropolitan of Attica has ordered Bishop Dorotheos to proceed with the installation of the new hegumen of the Paraclitou monastery, Archmandrite Timotheos Sakka, who received his theological training both in Russia and in Greece, and will serve as the pastor for the Russian Orthodox parish in Athens.

On April 9, 1981 Patriarch Pimen of Moscow accepted the resignation of Metropolitan Juvenaly of Kruticy and Kolomna from the presidency of the Department of External Affairs of the Russian Orthodox Church. The metropolitan cited reasons of health as the cause of his resignation. He took the office over in 1972 from his predecessor, Metropolitan Nikodim. Metropolitan Philaret of Minsk was elected President of the Department of External Affairs over three other candidates. Archbishop Platon of Sverdlovsk replaced Archbishop Chryostom of Kursk as one of the vice-presidents of the department.

Deaths

The first primate of the Orthodox Church in America, Metropolitan Ireney, passed away on March 18, 1981. Shortly after his death, the Office of the Dead, presided over by the actual head of the O.C.A., Metropolitan Theodosius, was recited in the Pokrov Cathedral in New York. The Divine Liturgy and the funeral rites were conducted at the monastery of St. Tikhon in South Canaan, Pennsylvania. His remains were interred on the monastery grounds.

Born Ivan Bekish on October 20, 1892 in the south of Russia, Metropolitan Ireney finished his studies at the Chelm seminary in 1914. After he was ordained a priest in 1916 he was named assistant at the Cathedral of Lublin, Poland and a member of the consistory of the Pinsk diocese. In 1944 he emigrated to Germany as a displaced person. He became pastor of the Russian Orthodox church in Charleroi, Belgium in 1947. He came to America in 1952 with his wife, Xenia. After her death in 1953, Father John took monastic vows as Ireney, was consecrated bishop, and sent to Japan as bishop of Tokyo. The Orthodox Church in Japan came to life under his direction. He was named Archbishop of Boston and New England in 1960 and served as assistant to Metropolitan Leonty. After Metropolitan Leonty's death in 1965, he was named temporary administrator until September 23 when he was elected Archbishop of New York and Metropolitan of America and Canada. After the Moscow patriarchate issued the Tomos of Autocephaly in 1970, he was given the title of Beatitude and became the first primate of that church. He retired in 1977 from active administration and lived at the Home of St. Cosmas and Damian until his death.

Bishop Ceslau Sipovich, the Apostolic Visitator for the Byelorussians in exile, died in London, October 1981 while celebrating the tenth anniversary of the Francis Skaryna Byelorussian Library and Museum, which he founded. Born in Dziedzinka, Byelorussia, on December 8, 1914, Bishop Sipovich began his service as a local pastor. Shortly before World War II he went to Rome to study church history and liturgy. As the war worked to its close, he was sent to London to work with Byelorussian refugees there. He founded a center for these refugees and began organizing parishes and missions as well. A member of the Marian Fathers, he was consecrated a bishop during the Eucharistic Congress in Munich in 1960. He was the author of four books on church history and liturgy. A funeral service was held October 13 at St. Albans church in North Finchley, England. He was buried later in London.

Archbishop George [Tarassov] died in Paris, France on March 22, 1981 following a long illness. Born in Tambov, Russia, in 1893, he was received into the jurisdiction of the Ecumenical Patriarchate in 1931. He directed the Russian diocese of Western Europe since 1960 and became the Orthodox Archbishop of France and Western Europe in 1965.

Archbishop Dositej of Ohrid and Macedonia died May 20, 1981 at Skopje. He was 75 years old. In 1958 he was elected as head of the Orthodox church of Macedonia at the second Assembly of Church and People. He convoked the third such assembly in 1967 to proclaim the autocephaly of the Church of Macedonia. The Church of Macedonia to this date is recognized as autocephalous by no other Orthodox church.

Archbishop Gabriel Bukatko, ordinary of the eparchy of Krizhevsi for Croatian Greek Catholics, died October 19, 1981 in a hospital in Verbas, Yugoslavia. Born January 1, 1913, he was ordained a priest in 1939 by Bishop Dionysius Naryadi at St. Josaphat's Seminary in Rome and was a classmate of Archbishop Stephen J. Kocisko, current Archbishop of the Byzantine Metropolitan See of Pittsburgh [formerly Munhall]. Pope Pius XII named Father Gabriel titular bishop of Severoiu in 1952 and was consecrated in Zagreb on April 27, 1952. On July 20, 1960 he was appointed ordinary of the diocese of Krizhevsi, and was appointed Archbishop and ordinary of the Roman Catholics of Belgrade in 1964. Funeral services were conducted October 22, 1981 in Russkij Kerestura by Bishop Miroslav Marusin, Rev. Sofronius Mudry, O.S.B.M., and other clergy in attendance.

Bishop Giuseppe Perniciaro, first resident bishop of Pianadegli-Albanesi in the province of Palermo, Sicily died June 5, 1981 at the age of 74. Ordained a priest in 1929, he was made auxiliary bishop in 1937 and titular bishop in 1967. He was noted for his ecumenical contacts in Greece, Constantinople, and Romania. His ecumenical initiatives helped promote the growth of ecumenism in Sicily.

DOCUMENTATION

JOINT COMMUNIQUÉ

RUSSIAN ORTHODOX ROMAN CATHOLIC
CONVERSÁTIONS AT ODESSA
March 1980

At the theological seminary of Odessa in the Soviet Union from March 13-17 there was held the fifth series of theological conversations between representatives of the Catholic Church and the Russian Orthodox Church. Preceding conversations took place at Leningrad (USSR) in 1967, Bari (Italy) in 1970, Zagorsk (USSR) in 1973, and finally in Trent (Italy) in 1975.

Those who took part in the Odessa conversations were:

For the Catholic Church:
— Cardinal Jan Willebrands, Archbishop of Utrecht, president of the Secretariat for Promoting Christian Unity;
— Archbishop Antoine Hacault of St. Boniface, president of the ecumenical commission of the Canadian bishops' conference and member of the Secretariat for Christian Unity;
— Archbishop Lucas Moreira Neves, secretary of the Congregation for Bishops;
— Canon Jacques Desseaux, secretary of the ecumenical commission of the French bishops' conference and consultor of the Secretariat for Christian Unity;
— Father Pierre Duprey, undersecretary of the Secretariat for Christian Unity;
— Father Emmanuel Lanne, OSB, of the Benedictine monastery of Chevetogne (Belgium), consultor of the Secretariat for Christian Unity;
— Father Stjepan Schmidt, SJ, official of the Secretariat for Christian Unity;
— Father John Long, SJ, official of the Secretariat for Christian Unity.

For the Russian Orthodox Church:
— Metropolitan Filaret of Kiev and Halych, patriarchal exarch of the Ukraine;
— Archbishop Vladimir of Dmitrov, rector of the theological academy and the seminary of Moscow;
— Bishop Ilian of Solnetchnogorsk;
— Archpriest Livery Voronov, professor of the theological academy and the seminary of Leningrad;
— Archpriest Vassily Stoikov, professor of the theological academy of Leningrad;
— Archimandrite Augustin (Nikitine), professor of the theological academy of Leningrad;
— Archpriest Vladimir Mustafin, professor of the theological academy of Leningrad;
— Mr. A.S. Buevsky, secretary of the Department of Foreign Church Affairs of the Patriarchate of Moscow;
— Mr. A.I. Ossipov, professor of the theological academy of Moscow;
— Mr. K.E. Skourat, professor of the theological academy of Moscow;
— Mr. V.V. Ivanov, professor of the theological academy of Moscow;
— Metropolitan Sergei of Odessa and Kherson attended the conversations as guest of honor.

Metropolitan Filaret and Cardinal Willebrands presided over the work. Before beginning the colloquy, the participants took part in a liturgical prayer service in the Church of the Virgin's Assumption at the monastery of Odessa.

The conversations were opened by Metropolitan Filaret, who placed them in the context of the development of relations between the two churches. He highlighted the interrelationship between these conversations and the preparation of the pan-Orthodox dialogue with the Catholic Church. Finally, Metropolitan Filaret read a report by Metropolitan Juvenaly of Krititsy and Colomna, president of the Department for Foreign Church Affairs, on the main events of the Russian Orthodox Church's life since the last conversations, held at Trent in 1975, and the development of relations between the Russian Orthodox Church and the Roman Catholic Church during that period. Metropolitan Sergei of Odessa and Kherson greeted the participants in the name of the Odessa diocese, the monastery and the seminary.

For his part, Cardinal Willebrands reviewed recent events in the life of the Catholic Church, citing in particular the 1977 Synod of Bishops on catechesis, the "year of three popes" in 1978, and the broad outlines of Pope John Paul II's pontificate. Referring to the four previous series of conversations, he emphasized the natural and logical development of their themes.

The speakers also commemorated the deceased metropolitan of Leningrad, Nikodim, who worked so hard to begin the conversations and continue their progress.

The main theme of the conversations was "the local church and the universal church." The issue had already been raised at Trent. On that occasion it was decided to take it into consideration again and deepen it. In the course of its work the group studied reports on issues of the nature of the church (Archpriests Vassily Stoikov and Vladimir Mustafin); the bishop's authority in the church (Archpriest Vassily Stoikov); the theology of the local church (Father Raniero Cantalamessa, director of the department of religious sciences of the Catholic University of the Sacred Heart in Milan, whose report was read by Father Duprey in the author's absence, with additional comments by Father Duprey); and finally, various theological and practical aspects of the relations among local churches and between them and the universal church (Canon Jacques Desseaux).

The authors of the reports tried to deepen the theme, basing themselves on the teachings of the fathers of the primitive, undivided church. Also taken into consideration were subsequent theological and canonical developments, verified in the course of centuries, in our two traditions, taking particular account of the decisions of the Second Vatican Council of the Roman Catholic Church, and the various reflections of contemporary theologians of the two churches as well. The Catholic theologians informed their Orthodox brothers of some recent developments in the Catholic Church, citing specific examples of reinforcement of the principle of collegiality within their church.

The discussion on this theme was developed in a spirit of brotherhood and good will. It allowed participants to understand better each other's positions, the meeting points, and the divergences which, at the present moment, are hard to overcome.

The two parties found themselves in broad agreement on the following points:

1. The local church, in the ambit of the diocese, represents the people of God united around the bishop, legitimately ordained in an uninterrupted apostolic succession. The bishop, with whom the other members of the clergy collaborate and to whom they are subordinate, is the teacher of the faith, the minister of the sacraments, first of all of the eucharist, and the one in charge of the Christian life of his flock.

2. The concept of catholicity, understood as organic wholeness of the church, as the fullness of the possession of the truth revealed by God and of the means of grace given for man's salvation, was discussed. The presence of the episcopate in the local churches guarantees the fullness of their eucharistic life in grace. Particular attention was given to this aspect of catholicity, which implies the necessity of communion among the local churches.

Despite their state of separation, the Catholic and Orthodox churches recognize one another as sister churches. In the East, the local church is seen above all as an example of different dioceses which, in the course of history, were brought together to respond to certain pastoral needs, in conformity with a set canonical tradition. For this, in the East the local churches, quite early on, overwhelmingly took on the form of autocephalous patriarchates with their own canonical structure, preserving among themselves communion in faith, sacramental life and brotherly relations.

In the West, dioceses were grouped together in ecclesiastical provinces or in the framework of geographical regions. Most recently these groupings have taken on, in the Catholic Church, the form of bishops' conferences. This development was favored by the role played by the principle of conciliarity.

Both parties recognized the importance of the 34th Canon of the Apostles, which serves as the norm in relationships between the bishops of the local churches and the first among them, even if there is not agreement about the levels at which the canon applies or the reasons why one bishop comes to be considered first among his equals.

There arose the issue of the role of the church of Rome and its bishop in the service of communion among the churches. In this regard the Catholic participants explained in detail their convictions. This allowed better clarification of the problems that still remain to be resolved between our churches, as was recognized by both parties. Among these problems are the dogmatic formulations of the First Vatican Council concerning the primacy and infallibility of the bishop of Rome. Despite these divergences, both parties agree on the fact that the authority or spiritual power of the church differs from any other power as regards its origin, the purposes for which it was constituted and the means by which these goals are pursued.

In the course of the conversations, the following themes were presented and discussed: the role of women in the church, and the bilateral and multilateral dialogues in which the Roman Catholic and Russian Orthodox churches are participating. Reporters for the first theme were Archbishop Lucas Moreira Neves and Archimandrite Augustin (Nikitine), and for the second theme Father Emmanuel Lanne, OSB, and Professor V.V. Ivanov.

The Christian faith has contributed to a deep renewal of the view of women: Men and women are equally creatures redeemed by the blood of Christ, called to become members of his body and to share in its glory. Still, much remains to be done so that the dignity of women will be fully recognized and expressed in actual life without any discrimination. There are, in fact, in many parts of the world, numerous situations that are the cause or result of discrimination against women at the cultural, social and political level.

In today's world in rapid and profound transformation, the role of women is growing in all areas of life. The church cannot remain indifferent to or outside of this important phenomenon of our times. It is concerned with giving its own contribution with openness and discernment. It does so to the degree that it stimulates the participation of women, in conditions of full equality and collaboration with men, to the pursuit of their proper social functions and, their tasks within the ecclesial community.

Above all this is a matter of revaluing in society the woman's function as wife, mother and educator, which are her primary and irreplaceable roles. But the church does not forget the other functions of women, whether in the world or in consecrated life, in prayer and contemplation or in discerning service to the most needy. Within the ecclesial community, in both the Russian Orthodox and the Catholic churches, there are more and more women who are taking up ever more varied tasks, such as education of new generations in the Christian faith, promotion of mutual aid in communities, etc.

Still, the two churches today consider as one of their main tasks that of facilitating, wherever possible, the access of women to posts of responsibility in the life of the church and inviting them to participate in the construction of peace and more just relations in society.

Nevertheless the two churches do not see how it is possible to change a universal and uninterrupted tradition, continued from the Lord and the apostles, of not allowing the ordination of women to the ministerial priesthood.

As regards the theme of bilateral and multilateral dialogues, both parties have recognized their usefulness in the search for Christian unity, and for this they deserve considerable efforts by each of our churches. Professor V.V. Ivanov provided a detailed perspective of the various dialogues conducted by the Russian Orthodox Church. These dialogues are very similar to those being carried on by the Roman Catholic Church, whose approach was analyzed by Father Emmanuel Lanne. From the discussion there emerged the need to clarify the precise role of the church's magisterium in validating results of these dialogues and the significance and importance of their acceptance by the people of God.

In the course of the conversations, in several reports and interventions, the problems were addressed concerning the service that the two churches fulfil in promoting peace in today's world, seeking to reinforce the principles of peace and justice in the relationships among peoples, contributing to the progress of human society along the path of detente, encouraging the effort for disarmament by every means. The need to continue and intensify this important action of both churches was also emphasized.

The conversations were carried out in a candid atmosphere of brotherly love. In the course of their work the participants received strength from praying together. The Catholic participants learned about the religious life of Odessa and its environs. They met with the local clergy, monks and members of the local parishes. They prayed during the divine liturgy, celebrated on Sunday, March 16, with the assembly of bishops and members of the Orthodox clergy in Odessa's Assumption Cathedral. They celebrated holy Mass in the Catholic church of St. Peter in Odessa, with the members of the orthodox delegation in attendance.

Professors and students showed their interest, assisting the participants in the conversations.

Metropolitan Sergei gave a reception in honor of the participants at his residence in the Assumption Monastery of Odessa, with representatives of the city's clergy and professors of the local theological seminary attending.

The participants in the conversations express their deep gratitude to His Eminence Metropolitan Sergei and to all those who gave them their affectionate and generous hospitality. It accompanied them throughout their unforgettable visit to Odessa.

VISIT TO ROME OF HIS HOLINESS, ILIA II
Catholicos-Patriarch of all Georgia
June 5-8, 1980

On this, the first visit to Rome of a Georgian Patriarch in the long history of the Patriarchate, His Holiness, Patriarch Ilia was accompanied by Archbishop Nikolosi of Sukhimi, Bishop David of Batum, an Archdeacon, and his private secretary. On Friday, June 6 the Patriarch was received by the Holy Father and addressed him as follows:

83

Documentation

Your Holiness,
Blessed and Beloved Brother in Christ,
First Bishop of the most ancient Church of Rome.

How marvellous and incomprehensible to human understanding is Divine Providence, by whose will we have come to the Holy City in which once suffered the great Apostles Peter and Paul, as well as many other luminaries of the Universal Christian Church.

We attach great importance to our visit, for this is the very first occasion on which the Chief Pastors of the Roman and Georgian Churches have met.

We have come here from the land in which is preserved the Tunic of Our Lord Jesus Christ; the land in which St. Andrew, the first-called, and St. Simon the Canaanean preached; the land in which St. Nina carried out her work, she who bears the title "Equal to the Apostles"; the land in which the bishop and universal doctor St. John Chrysostom died.

We have come to the city in which there is the Chair of St. Peter, to reestablish those ancient and brotherly relations which traditionally existed between our two ancient Churches.

Sadly the complexities of history have brought about the division of our Holy Church. Nevertheless we believe that the Lord, with his almighty power, will grant us once again the unity which we have lost and which we desire.

Despite this sad fact, there have always been good mutual relations between our two Churches, and these have found expression in political, spiritual and scientific collaboration.

The Georgian Church and the people of Georgia form the great bridge that links the two great cultures of Europe and Asia.

Today the Christian Churches face many common problems; to resolve these we must draw closer together.

We value greatly the great contribution the Roman Catholic Church is making to mutual understanding between peoples and to the maintenance of peace in the world.

As we raise our prayers for the well being of the Roman Catholic Church, we wish Your Holiness and long pontificate, full of grace and rich in abundant fruit.

Christ is in our midst; may he always be so!

In reply, Pope John Paul II spoke as follows:

Your Holiness and Beatitude,
Dear Brothers in the Lord,

Today is indeed a joyful day in the long history of our Churches, for it is the first time that a Catholicos Patriarch of the Ancient Apostolic Church of Georgia has visited this Apostolic See of Rome to exchange the kiss of peace with its Bishop. In recent years there has been a steady growth in the good relations between our Churches as each has shared in the sorrows and the joys of the other, in accord with the words of the Apostle: "Rejoice with those who rejoice, weep with those who weep. Live in harmony with one another" (*Rom* 12:15-16). Bishop Nikolosi of Sukhumi and Abkhasia, whom I am glad to greet once again, represented Your Holiness at the funeral of my predecessor John Paul I and also at the Mass which inaugurated my own pontificate; it was indeed a joy for me to be assured of your Church's solidarity in prayer for God's blessing as I began my ministry. Three years ago Paul VI was represented at the funeral of your own predecessor, Catholicos Patriarch David V; and last year Cardinal Willebrands, President of the Secretariat for Promoting Christian Unity, led a delegation to bring you my own brotherly greetings. We have, then, greeted each other, but

84

from afar. Now God has enabled us to meet and to speak "face to face, so that our joy may be complete" (*2 Jn* 12).

We meet as brothers. The Church of Georgia treasures the preaching of St. Andrew; the Church of Rome is founded on the preaching of St. Peter. Andrew and Peter were brothers by blood, but they became brothers in spirit through their response to the call of Jesus Christ, true Son of God and "the first-born among many brethren" (*Rom* 8:29), who, in taking to himself the nature of all men, "was not ashamed to call them brethren" (*Heb* 2:11).

As heirs of Andrew and of Peter we meet today as brothers in Christ.

It is with brotherly love and concern that the Church of Rome has taken a keen interest in the joys and sorrows of the Church of Georgia. In time of peace and in times of persecution alike your Church has born a faithful and exemplary witness to the Christian faith and the Christian sacraments, a witness borne by many holy men and martyrs from the days of St. Nina onwards.

Your Holiness's concern for the renewal of the Church, a renewal firmly rooted in the apostolic tradition and in the particular traditions of the Church of Georgia, is a cause of special joy. You are well aware that the renewal of the Christian life is likewise the concern of the Church of Rome. It is this concern for renewal that has made us so keenly aware of the need and obligation to restore full communion between our Churches. The long course of our history has led to sad, and sometimes bitter, divisions which have led us to lose sight of our brotherhood in Christ; and our concern for renewal is one of the factors that has led us to see more clearly the need there is for unity among all who believe in Christ. The Second Vatican Council said: "Every renewal of the Church essentially consists in an increase of fidelity to her own calling. Undoubtedly this explains the dynamism of the movement towards unity" (*Unitatis Redintegratio*, 6). It went on to remind all the faithful that "the closer their union with the Father, the Word and the Spirit, the more deeply and easily will they be able to grow in mutual brotherly love" (*ibid.*, 7).

Today this task of restoring full communion between divided Christians is a priority for all who believe in Christ. It is our duty to Christ, whose seamless robe is rent by division. It is our duty to our fellowmen, for only with one voice can we effectively proclaim one faith in the Good News of salvation and thus obey our Lord's command to bring his Gospel to all mankind. And it is our duty to each other, for we are brothers and must express our brotherhood.

For this reason the Catholic Church has been praying earnestly in these last weeks for God's blessing on the first meeting of the Joint Commission for theological dialogue between the Catholic Church and all the Orthodox Churches. How fitting it was that the Commission first gathered on the Island of Patmos, where John was privileged to receive the revelation which enabled him to bid us "hear what the Spirit says to the Churches" (*Apoc.* 2:7). I am glad to learn that two members of your delegation, Bishop Nikolosi and Bishop David, took part in that meeting as representatives of the Church of Georgia, and I look forward to talking with you about it.

We join together in prayer that this dialogue will indeed bring us to that full unity of faith which we both so ardently desire. But our progress towards unity in faith must be matched by constant growth in knowledge and understanding of each other and by an everdeepening love. When I returned from my own visit to the Ecumenical Patriarch last year, I said: "Union can be only the fruit of the knowledge of the truth in love. They must both operate together, one apart from the other is still not enough, because truth without love is not yet the full truth, just as love does not exist without truth" (*General Audience*, 5 December 1979).

85

Documentation

Your Holiness, it is indeed timely that your welcome visit to Rome should occur so soon after this beginning of our theological dialogue, for it enables us to witness to the need for this to be rooted in a dialogue of brotherly love which must characterize relationships between the Churches of which we are the Pastors. As I renew my cordial greeting to you, I recall the words of Saint Peter, the brother of Saint Andrew: "All of you, have unity of spirit, sympathy, love of the brethren, a tender heart and a humble mind" (*1 Pt* 3:8). may the Three Divine Persons, whose unity is the highest exemplar and source of the mystery of the unity of the Church (cf. *Unitatis Redintegratio,* 2) grant us this grace, and so bless our meeting today that it will contribute to the attainment of that goal for which Christ prayed and for which we so ardently long.

BOOKS RECEIVED

GLEANINGS, The Monks & Nuns of New Skete (Cambridge, N.Y., 1982) pp. 94, $4.50.

L'ICONE, Image de l'invisible, Egon Sendler (Desclee De Brouwer, Paris, France, 1982) pp. 251.

CRY OF THE PEOPLE, Penny Lernoux (Penguin Books, N.Y., 1982) pp. 535, $6.95.

TOUS SCHISMATIQUES?, Elias Zoghby (Heidelberg Press, Lebanon, 1982) pp. 156.

MOLCHANIE, The Silence of God, Catherine De Hueck Doherty (Crossroad Publ. Co., N.Y., 1982) pp. 79, $8.95.

INTRODUCING THE ORTHODOX CHURCH, Anthony M. Coniaris (Light & Life Publishing Co., Minn., Minnesota, 1982) pp. 214.

MEISTER ECKHART, Edmund Colledge, O.S.A. & Bernard McGinn (Paulist Press, N.Y., 1982) pp. 366.

FRANCISCO de OSUNA, Mary E. Giles (Paulist Press, N.Y., 1982) pp. 624.

BYZANTINE-RUTHENIAN ANTIMENSIA IN THE EPISCOPAL AND HERITAGE INSTITUTE LIBRARIES OF THE BYZANTINE CATHOLIC DIOCESE OF PASSAIC, Edward Kasinec and Bohdan A. Struminsky (EHI Libraries, Passaic, 1981).

John XXIII
INSTITUTE FOR
EASTERN CHRISTIAN STUDIES

June 24-July 31, 1982

The John XXIII Institute for Eastern Christian Studies was inaugurated in 1971 as a four-summer program leading to the Master of Arts degree in the theology of the Eastern tradition of Christianity. Inquiring Christians—Catholics, Protestants and Orthodox—have been turning with increasing interest in recent times to the Eastern origins of their faith: particularly to the Fathers of the Church, the first interpreters of Christianity, but also to the Medieval Byzantine theologians who have developed the doctrine of the Fathers in a much less philosophic and systematic manner than it was developed in the West. Every Christian today, who is interested in promoting a greater understanding and, hence, a greater ability among all Christians will realize the ecumenical possibilities of an institute that seeks to study the rich and authentic theology and spirituality of the Christian East.

It would be difficult to find a more appropriate location for the John XXIII Institute than New York City. Not only are there university theological departments and seminaries of all the principal religious denominations with their excellent libraries, but there are also many Orthodox and Eastern-rite Catholic Churches. New York is certainly unique in liturgical, academic and cultural resources.

The courses of the John XXIII Institute are given academic credit through Maryknoll School of Theology. These courses will be applied to the requirements of an accredited master's degree upon completion of the full program, or they can be transferred to other academic institutions as fully accredited courses.

1982 Summer Courses

1. Church and State in Byzantium
2. Centering on the Lord Jesus
3. Growth into Personhood in the Byzantine Tradition
4. Icons and Their Meaning
5. Liturgical Offices and Feasts of the Byzantine Church
6. Eastern Orthodox Ethics: Theoria and Praxis
7. The Holy Trinity
8. Catholics and Orthodox in Dialogue
9. Methods and Materials of the "God with Us" Series
10. Pavel A. Florensky: An Introductory Exposition of his Thought

1982 Faculty

Archbishop Joseph Raya; Rev. George A. Maloney, S.J.; Rev. John F. Long, S.J.; Rev. Stanley Harakas; Rev. Philip O'Shea, OFM; Rev. Thomas Hopko; Mrs. Fran Colie; Rev. Robert Slesinski; Richard Novak; Rev. Basil W. Kraynyak.

For further information write:

Rev. George A. Maloney, S.J., Director
John XXIII Institute
2502 Belmont Avenue
Bronx, New York 10458
(Telephone: 212-298-8752)

THE FIRST DAY OF ETERNITY
Living the Mystery of the Resurrection

by George A. Maloney, S.J.

There are various degrees of "knowing" about resurrection. But the highest level of knowing the resurrection is to be led into the mystery that is at the heart of all reality—love. Whether it be your love for God or for another human person, you know in that awesome experience that you have attained a knowledge beyond your own rational knowledge.

The experience of resurrection is at the source of all reality. It is love moving out of self-controlled reason to trustful abandonment as one takes the risk to "believe" that in losing one's life, one finds it in greater abundance in loving union with another through a dying process.

This latest book by George A. Maloney, S.J. seeks to present the message of resurrection of Jesus and our own participation as a mystery. It is an attempt on the part of the author to de-objectivize the habitual understanding of the resurrection of Jesus and our own personal resurrection in order to enter into a daily experience of death-resurrection.

The author draws upon the latest biblical scholarship as well as the writings of the Eastern Fathers and Eastern liturgical texts to present the resurrection as an experience of sharing, even *now* in Christ's victory as we die to our selfishness and rise by the Spirit of love to live by loving service to others.

CONTENTS

1. God Calls His People
2. New Time and New Space
3. A Light That Shines in the Dark
4. Death Is Resurrection
5. The Risen Lord and the Eucharist
6. The Spirit of the Risen Jesus
7. Resurrection and Ascension
8. Today Is the Last Day

Published by Crossroad Publishers

ORDER FROM: Icon and Book Service
2502 Belmont Ave.
BRONX, N.Y. 10458

DIAKONIA

INDEX

VOLUME XVI

1981

Editorials   No.   Page

LONG, Rev. John F., S.J.: New Hopes 3   185

MALONEY, Rev. George A., S.J.: From Frog to Prince 1   1

_____, Ecumenism "In Trouble" 2   89

Articles

BOURDEAUX, Rev. Michael: Religion and Human
Rights: The Case of Soviet Ukraine 3   262

CHRYSOSTOMOS, Archimandrite: Additional Comments on the True Orthodox Christians of Greece 2   138

_____, Hieromonk Auxentios: Some Summary Re-
marks on the Development of Byzantine Liturgical Ves-
ture: Its Social and Mystical Significance 1   55

_____, A Comparative Treatment of Scripture and Tra-
dition in the Orthodox East and the Catholic and Protestant West 3   212

CLAPSIS, Rev. Emmanuel: Prolegomena to Orthodox
Dogmatics: Bible and Tradition 1   16

COREY, Rev. George, S.: That They May Be One ... 1   2

FIAND, Sr. Barbara: The Prayer of Listening: A Form of Contemplation 2 168

HOGAN, Joseph: Our Bodily Union with Christ 1 10

KIRK, Rev. David: Hospitality: The Essence of Eastern Christian Lifestyle 2 104

KLIMENKO, Dr. Michael: The East-West Dialogue: Thoughts of An Orthodox 2 192

MALONEY, Rev. George A., S.J.: Jesus, The Lover of Mankind 3 204

MATTHEWS, R.J.H.: Jottings on the Holy Mountain 2 158

MOROZIUK, Dr. Russel, P.: Byzantine Slavic Frescos in Poland 1 63

PATHIKULANGARA, Rev. Varghese, CMI: Liturgical Reforms in the Chaldeo-Indian Church 2 147

PETRAS, Rev. David M.: The Liturgical Theology of Marriage 3 225

RAYA, Archbishop Joseph: The Crowning: Sacrament of Union 3 188

REXINE, Dr. John E.: The Teachings of the Orthodox Church 3 272

SABLE, Rev. Thomas F., S.J.: Chronicle of Events Concerning Eastern Christianity: 1980 .... 1 29

SAINT-LAURENT, Dr. George E.: Pre Baptismal Rites in the Baptismal Catecheses of Theodore of Mopsuestia 2 108

91

TEASDALE, Wayne: Contemplation as the Heart of the
World 3   247

TSICHLIS, Rev. Deacon Steven Peter: The Nature of
Theology in the Theological Orations of St. Gregor
Nazianzus 3   238

WALKER, Rev. Anselm: Sophiology 1   40

WOOTTON, Raymond, J.: Depth Psychology and
Desert Spirituality 2   127

Documentation

The Announcement of the Extraordinary Joint Conference of the Monks of Mount Athos Concerning the Dialogue Between the Orthodox and Roman Catholics ...· 1   80

An Exchange of Correspondence: Cardinal Willebrands
and Metropolitan Juvenaly 2   178

DIAKONIA

Devoted to promoting Eastern Christianity in the West.

edited by REV. JOHN F. LONG S.J.

MANAGING EDITOR
Rev. Richard d. Lee

ORTHODOX ASSOCIATE EDITORS
Dr. John E. Rexine
Bohdan Demczuk

CIRCULATION MANAGER
Mrs. Rita Ruggiero

  Editorial and Business Correspondence: Manuscripts should be typed double-spaced, with footnotes separate. Authors should retain a carbon copy and enclose return stamps. All manuscripts, subscriptions and correspondence should be sent to the following address: DIAKONIA, John XXIII Center, Fordham University, Bronx, N.Y. 10458.

Published by the John XXIII Center
2502 Belmont Avenue
Bronx, New York 10458

Copyright 1982 by the John XXIII Center for Eastern Christian Studies

Fordham University

Subscription price:

USA and Canada:	$7.00
FOREIGN:	$8.00
Single numbers:	$2.00

DIAKONIA
Published by the John XXIII Center
2502 Belmont Avenue
Bronx, New York 10458

Non-Profit Org.
U.S. POSTAGE
PAID
BRONX, N.Y.
Permit No. 4445

diakonia

DEVOTED TO PROMOTING A KNOWLEDGE AND
UNDERSTANDING OF EASTERN CHRISTIANITY

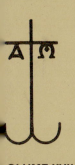

OLUME XVII
NUMBER 2
1982

DIAKONIA   Volume XVII   Issue 2
                       1982

EDITORIAL
   EASTERN AND CATHOLIC
      Rev. John F. Long, S.J. 93

ARTICLES
   THE ACTIVE ROLE OF CHRIST
   AND THE SPIRIT IN THE DIVINE LITURGY
      Edward J. Kilmartin, S.J. 95

   LIFE GIVING
   AN INTERPERSONAL ACTION
      Metropolitan Emilianos Timiades of Silibria 109

   FRUITS OF THE EUCHARIST:
   HENOSIS AND THEOSIS
      Rev. Mr. Jonathan Morse 127

   THE THEOLOGICAL ANTHROPOLOGY OF THE
   BYZANTINE RITES OF CHRISTIAN INITIATION
      Rev. Myron Tataryn 143

COMMENT
   CONTEMPORARY ESSAYS IN ORTHODOX
   TRADITION AND LIFE
      Rev. Robert Slesinski 151

   PURPOSE, SCOPE AND METHOD OF THE DIALOGUE
   BETWEEN THE ORIENTAL ORTHODOX AND ROMAN
   CATHOLIC CHURCHES 168

DOCUMENTATION
   PRESS RELEASE 176

   THE MYSTERY OF THE CHURCH AND OF THE
   EUCHARIST IN THE LIGHT OF THE MYSTERY
   OF THE HOLY TRINITY
      Joint International Commission for the Theological
      Dialogue between the Roman Catholic Church and the
      Orthodox Church 178

BOOKS RECEIVED 188

EASTERN AND CATHOLIC

One of the effects of the Second Vatican Council has been the efforts to put into practice its insistence that the Eastern Churches in full communion with the See of Rome have a particular role to play in the life of the entire Church. In order to carry out this role, they are asked to dig deeply into their own traditions, rediscover their own roots and search out ways whereby this new understanding of who and what they are may serve the pastoral needs of their own people and contribute to the general movement of renewal and reform going on in the Church as a result of this Council.

This question is a very complex one. It cannot be treated adequately within the framework of these few pages. Perhaps a few general observations may provide a modest contribution to the discussion surrounding this subject.

It is clear that one of the essential foundations of the movement of renewal is a deep and wide knowledge of the authentic traditions of the Eastern Christian Churches. These traditions include much more than just a few liturgical rites. Accompanying and supporting rites are theological expressions of the divine revelation, as well as forms of spiritual life which are rooted in the practice and experiences of humble, yet gifted servants of God and of their brothers and sisters. There is a whole area of pastoral experience and devotional life which have accompanied the development of the Eastern Christian Churches and communities within them. Knowledge and understanding of this rich heritage is absolutely essential before anyone starts presenting himself as a champion of "our traditions."

An archeological approach to this question can be positively harmful. It easily forgets that Churches are living communities, imbued with the Holy Spirit, who have tried to remain faithful to this Spirit in the course of centuries. They may not always have succeeded, but it must be recognized there is no "golden age" from the past which can be recaptured and imposed on the present in the name of renewal. The present situation and future possibilities of these living communities must be in the forefront of the thinking of those who seek a genuine renewal based on the authentic tradition of their own church.

At the same time, another important principle is that of legitimate diversity within the unity of the one Church, where diversity is viewed not as a secondary and merely tolerated reality. True unity diversifies; plurality in the Church finds its theological foundations in the mystery of the Holy Trinity and in the inexhaustible mystery of Christ Himself.

The validity of these principles makes it particularly unfortunate that some members of the Eastern Catholic Churches, in their efforts to react to the excesses that have sometimes been committed by enthusiasts of renewal, seek to withdraw into an attitude of defense, and even of intransegeance, in the face of the many legitimate efforts which are being made in the area of reform and renewal. Liturgical and devotional practices, theological formulations, forms of external discipline—many of them of relatively recent origin, and strongly influenced by the practices of the dominant Latin communities—are extolled as being more "Catholic". In defense of this attitude one sometimes hears the statement that one must be a Catholic first and Eastern only second. At a time when the communities of the Latin tradition are painstakingly making changes in order to renew and reform themselves on the basis of what is most authentic in that tradition, it is ironic that some Eastern Catholics will continue to judge their own catholicity by how closely they resemble their Latin brothers and sisters.

Communion with Rome does not mean that one must start making distinctions of more or less, of first and second. For one who really understands what the unity and catholicity of the Church mean, Catholic and Eastern are perfectly synonomous.

Rev. John F. Long, S.J.

ARTICLES

THE ACTIVE ROLE OF CHRIST
AND THE SPIRIT IN THE DIVINE LITURGY

by Edward J. Kilmartin, S.J.

*Father Edward Kilmartin, S.J., Professor
of Theology at Notre Dame University,
has been active for many years in the
dialogue between the Roman Catholic
Church and the Eastern and Oriental
Orthodox Churches. His book* Toward
Reunion *(Paulist Press) and this article are
part of his extensive contributions to these
dialogues.*

The last forty years of scholarly research have yielded a more accurate account than was previously possible of the evolving theologies and liturgies of the Eucharist of the first four centuries. The results have special significance for the ecumenical dialogue between the Oriental and Roman Catholic Churches. The formulations of theologies of the Eucharist and their impact on the liturgy, occurring at the end of this period, have greatly influenced the subsequent traditions of both Churches. Through a better grasp of the various factors which contributed to these developments, these Churches are in a better position to address the task of arriving at a common understanding of the Eucharistic mystery.

One of the most interesting and important aspects of the history of the theology of the Eucharist is the changing perspectives on the role of Christ and the Holy Spirit which came to the foreground during the first four centuries. This essay is confined mainly to a review of Eastern theological reflection on this subject and the contrasting ecclesiological approach of St. Augustine to the Eucharistic celebration. It concludes with some brief observations on the relevance of this history of theology for an ecumenical age.

I. Theologies of the East before the Council of Ephesus (431)

The documentary evidence of the period under consideration shows that our theme was discussed under the following headings: Christ, dispenser of the Eucharistic food; Logos, consecrator of the bread and wine; Logos and/or Holy Spirit, consecrator(s) of the bread and wine; Christ, High Priest of the Eucharist sacrifice of the Church. This data determines the structure of the first part of this study.

Christ, Dispenser, High Priest and Consecrator

Dispenser: The active presence of Christ as the dispenser of the Eucharistic food is a common theme of the 3rd and 4th centuries. It reflects the experience of believers that just as Christ gave himself to the disciples at the Last Supper under forms of bread and wine, so also he gives himself in the same way in the Divine Liturgy. In writings of this period Christ is viewed not only as the content of the Eucharistic food but also as the host of the holy meal. As yet the popular religious experience, which does not differentiate between the person who symbolizes Christ and the Christ who is symbolized in the act of distribution of Holy Communion, does not come into conflict with reflex theology's attempt to deepen the understanding of the mode of Christ's active presence as dispenser of the gifts of his Body and Blood.

The description of Christ as active dispenser of his own Body and Blood is a theme favored by Church Fathers of Egypt, Asia Minor and Syria. One can name, as examples, the *Apocryphal Acts of Thomas* (200-250), Aphraates (c.300), Ephraem of Syria (306-373), Cyril of Jerusalem (c.313-386). This traditional teaching was popular in the school of Antioch, mediated by Lucian the Martyr (d.312) and Diadorus of Tarsus (c.275-337). John Chrysostom (344-407), a faithful recorder of the theology he received, is a good witness to this teaching.[1] On the other hand, Theodore of Mopsuestia (c.350-428) does not repeat it during his creative period. He holds to the notion that Christ "nourishes us still with the grace of the Holy Spirit in the Eucharistic food".[2] But the accent falls on the content: the grace of the Holy Spirit contained in the Eucharistic species.[3] This neglect of a traditional mode of speech about Christ as dispenser is linked to his theological reflection on the implications of the ascension of Christ, the symbolic function of the earthly priest and the ritual actions of the Divine Liturgy.

High Priest: The active presence of Christ as high priest of the Eucharistic sacrifice is a favorite subject of the early Alexandrian theology, as exemplified in the writings of Clement of Alexandria and Origen. However it is explained in terms of the *archiereus-logos* theology and so focuses on the role of the Logos. As is well known, the role of the humanity of Christ in the Eucharistic celebration is not developed in the theology of the earlier Alexandrians. The stress falls on the mediatorship of the Logos with respect to the worship of the earthly Church.[4]

However, even in Alexandria an Eastern Church liturgical formula keeps alive the notion of the mediation of the humanity of Christ in the Divine Liturgy. The phrase "to him through Jesus Christ his Son in the Holy Spirit" conveys the idea that the prayer of the Church comes before God through the mediation of the humanity of the exalted Lord who is actively present in the worship of the Church. "In the Holy Spirit" expresses the belief that the prayer of the Church is sent forth in the power of the Spirit, bestowed on the Church at the first Pentecost.[5]

Consecrator: The role of Christ in the consecration of the bread and wine is taken for granted during most of the 3rd and 4th centuries. Typically the early Fathers view the transformation of the elements as analogous to the Incarnation. Just as the Logos took flesh in the Incarnation, so now Christ makes the bread and wine his Body and Blood. An early witness to this thinking is Justin Martyr (c. 100-167). He attests that the *pneuma* (= energetic principle) of the Logos both effected the Incarnation and now transforms the bread and wine.[6] Eventually the notion that the 2nd Person of the Trinity consecrates led to liturgical invocations directed to Christ himself.[7]

However at the end of the 4th century the controversies over the equality of the Logos with the Father (Arian) and the divinity of the Holy Spirit (Pneumatomachi) led orthodox theologians to a new interpretation of Christ's role in the consecration of the elements as well as of his high priestly function in the Eucharistic sacrifice.

Holy Spirit as Consecrator

At the end of the 4th century the Logos epiclesis of the Divine Liturgy practically disappeared in the East. Its place was taken by the epiclesis of the Holy Spirit. The historical occasion for this change was the intensive theological reflection on the divinity of the Holy Spirit, prompted by the Pneumatomachi who explicitly rejected the equality of the Spirit with Father and Son.

In their reaction to this heresy, Church Fathers were led to a consideration of the role of the Holy Spirit in the Eucharistic celebration. As a result they unanimously attributed a consecratory role to the Spirit. John Chrysostom, Theophilus of Alexandria[8] (d. after 413) and Theodore of Mopsuestia can be mentioned in this regard. Some Fathers, as Isidore of Pelusium (d.c.440), point to this activity of the Holy Spirit as proof of his divinity.[9]

It is noteworthy, however, that Chrysostom offers ambiguous testimony to his understanding of the principal subject of the consecration of the Eucharistic gifts. In several texts he mentions only Christ as consecrator.[10] More often he simply attributes the consecration to the descent of the Holy Spirit.[11] However one cannot conclude from this that Chrysostom changed his mind from exclusive attribution of the consecration to Christ to the exclusive attribution of the consecration to the Holy Spirit.

Chrysostom understands that there exists a correspondence between the Incarnation and the Eucharistic consecration.[12] It is, therefore, reasonable to suppose that he would ascribe the transformation of the elements both to an act of Christ himself who, as Logos, took flesh and to the Holy Spirit who exercised an active role in the Incarnation. No such ambiguity is found in the extant writings of Theodore of Mopsuestia. These sources indicate that Theodore exclusively attributes the consecration of the elements to the Holy Spirit—a viewpoint which corresponds to his theology of Christ's high priesthood.

Christ, High Priest of the Eucharist Sacrifice

By the end of the 4th century the traditional understanding of the mediatorship of the exalted Lord in the Divine Liturgy underwent some revision in the speculation of the more outstanding theologians of the East. Among these were John Chrysostom and

Theodore of Mopsuestia. At the same time a change in liturgical
formulas took place which had the effect of obscuring the notion of
the high priestly activity of the humanity of Christ in the Liturgical
celebration.

The historical occasion of these developments was the teaching
of the Arians. Arius (256-336) himself appealed to a passage of the
Epistle to the Hebrews, which speaks of Jesus as faithful high priest,
for his Logos theology. Hebr. 3:1-3 describes Jesus as the one sent
and high priest who was faithful "to him who appointed him." Arius
interpreted this to mean that the Logos ("the one sent") was made
("appointed") by the Father. Therefore he concluded that the Logos
was created. Athanasius (295-373) refuted this argument by con-
tending that Hebr. 3:2 refers to the descent of the Logos and his
being made high priest in the Incarnation, a process which involves
Christ's suffering and death. But in keeping with the tradition of
Alexandria, he teaches that the Logos is the person who bears the
high priesthood on the grounds of his humanity. As such the Logos
draws the faithful to the Father, offers them and obtains reconciliation for all.[13]

In the subsequent reaction to Arianism, orthodox theologians
had two possibilities. They could affirm the liturgical texts which
speak of the subordination of the mediator Jesus to the Father and
at the same time restrict this high priestly activity to the humanity of
the exalted Lord. In this way the divinity of the Logos would be
secured. It was also possible to follow the direct route and simply
confess the equality of the Logos with the Father.

The second way was taken by many influential theologians.
However the Arians used the orthodox Eucharistic prayers to refute
this claim of the divinity of the Logos. They argued that the formula
"to him through Jesus Christ his Son in the Holy Spirit" refers to the
inner-Trinitarian relations and not to the economy of salvation!
Consequently they could assert that the official prayer of the
Church of their opponents contradicts their reflex theology. The *lex
orandi* proves that the Logos is inferior to the Father.[14]

The anti-Arian liturgical reform shows the way in which some
influential orthodox theologians met this objection. They met the
Arian objection by substituting other formulas which affirm the
equality of Father, Son and Spirit. Under their influence corres-

ponding changes were made in the liturgy. Such formulas as: 1. "Glory to the Father and to the Son and to the Holy Spirit" (Antioch); 2. "Glory to God the Father with the Son with the Holy Spirit" (Caesarea), placed Jesus clearly on the side of God. They replaced formulas which contained "through him," expressive of Jesus' mediatorship and his belonging to the human race. Thereby Jesus was no longer viewed precisely as mediator of the prayer of the Church but as the recipient of human adoration.[15] The effect which this anti-Arian liturgical reform had on Eucharistic piety and frequency of the reception of Holy Communion is well known. Fear (*phoberos*) was understood as the proper attitude for reception of the Body and Blood. Basil the Great (330-379) provides the first written evidence of this new attitude toward Holy Communion.[16] By the end of the 4th century it is commonplace, as the writings of Chrysostom and Theodore attest.

Chiefly, however, theologians countered the Arian position on the nature of the Logos by affirming that the high priestly position and function of Jesus corresponds to his humanity. Ps-Athanasius, Epiphanius of Salamis, Gregory of Nazianzus, Gregory of Nyssa and Eunomius of Cyzicus can be mentioned.[17] Correspondingly, in their writings the concept of the Eucharist as representation of the past saving acts of Jesus came to the foreground. In this connection John Chrysostom and Theodore of Mopsuestia deserve special attention.

John Chrysostom's Theology of Christ's High Priesthood

Chrysostom links the high priesthood of Jesus to his humanity and understands that the offering of himself on the cross is the goal of the Incarnation. But peculiar to this Church Father is the interpretation of the Scriptural texts which speak about Christ's sitting at the right hand of the Father (e.g., Rom 8:34; Acts 2:33-35). According to him this concept expresses Jesus' equality with the Father, his claim to equal honor. Only insofar as Jesus can be said to stand before the Father can one speak of active adoration on his part.

This point of view determines Chrysostom's interpretation of Hebr. 7:25: "Therefore he is always able to save those who approach God through him, since he forever lives to make intercession for them." In his commentary on Hebrews, Chrysostom places the accent on the fact that Jesus "forever lives." He states explicitly that it would be nonsense to say that Christ continually intercedes for us.[18] The rest of the text is explained away as a manner of speaking adapted to our feeble human intellect.

Chrysostom restricts the priestly activity of Jesus to his earthly life and views the exalted Lord almost exclusively from the divine side. Still he cannot avoid the conclusion that the glorified Lord is always priest, even though sitting at the right hand of the Father. Hence he does not explicitly reject the notion of any activity of Jesus in the Eucharistic worship of the Church.

In his earlier writings, Chrysostom describes Christ as host, consecrator and distributor of the Eucharistic gifts. The human priest provides only the outward appearances. In his *Homilies on the Epistle to the Hebrews* (c.402), the presence of Christ and his activity is viewed in a more nuanced way. He admits the active presence of Christ the high priest in the Eucharistic celebration up to a certain level, corresponding to the anti-Arian narrow view.

Since the high priestly activity of Christ is relevant to the present realization of the work of redemption, it is present in the Eucharist. But the mode of this presence is described in a much more precise way than in *The Homily on the Betrayal of Judas* I.6. The High Priest seems to be present, not in himself, but only in the priest. Elsewhere Chrysostom refers to the priest as "*symbolon* through whom God works."[19] This statement was made in the period when he was preacher at Antioch (386-397). By the time Chrysostom wrote the *Homilies on Hebrews,* he is in the position to clarify the meaning of this expression more precisely.

From the standpoint of the *Homilies on Hebrews,* a direct intervention of Christ in the Eucharistic liturgy, insofar as sacrifice of the Church, is not possible. This would entail a repetition of the once for all saving acts and so contradict the explicit teaching of Hebr. 9:11: "But when Christ came as high priest . . . he entered once for all into the sanctuary." Consequently the grounds for the presence of the high priestly activity of Christ in the Divine Liturgy is no longer described with the vague reference to the power of God. This was done in In 2 Tim hom. 2,4: "All comes from the grace of God. His task (= earthly priest) is to open his mouth, but God effects all."[20] In *Homily on Hebrews* 17.3 the relative presence of the High Priest Christ is grounded on the anamnesis character of the Eucharist of the Church.[21] But because the Eucharist is the anamnesis of the once for all sacrifice of Christ, it is identical with it.[22]

Theodore of Mopsuestia's Theology of Christ's High Priesthood

Theodore's understanding of Christ's high priesthood is based on the principle: "He (Jesus) exercises his priestly activity in heaven and not on earth. For he died, rose and ascended into heaven in order to open the way for us all to rise and ascend into heaven."[23] The task of the high priest is conditioned by his approach and nearness to God. It consists in drawing the others into this nearness. Hence Theodore typically stresses the results of Jesus' death which ground his heavenly position. Because of the historical priestly sacrificial act of Jesus, he is raised from the dead and placed at the right hand of the Father. Through this process the mortal body of Jesus obtains complete unification with the divine nature. It becomes immortal and cause of immortality for others: "Through the resurrection from the dead the unification with the divine nature (is attained), it becomes cause of immortality also for others."[24]

It is also characteristic of Theodore to ascribe the high priestly status of Jesus to the work of the Holy Spirit and not, in any way, to the Logos. The Spirit equips the human nature of Jesus and makes it capable of mediating life and immortality to others. The high priest makes the grace of divinization, which he receives from the Holy Spirit, efficacious among the others by drawing them to God after himself.

But how does Jesus work as high priest? Theodore responds that he does this insofar as guarantee of the destiny of the others.[25] As first fruits among human beings to rise and become immortal, he is the exemplary cause of our destiny. Primarily Jesus is high priest through his being. Theodore cites Rom 8:34: "Christ Jesus, who died or rather was raised up, who is at the right hand of God and also intercedes for us." But he does not interpret this to mean that Jesus intercedes for us with words. The intercession consists in the acts of resurrection and ascension, constitutive of the heavenly high priestly activity of Jesus: "His ascension into heaven is itself a kind of prayer which he makes for us."[26] The intercession of the exalted Lord does not consist in a repeated intercession of Jesus for us. It is anchored in the once for all act of ascension. The concept of Jesus

functioning as mediator of our prayers has, as in the case of Chrysostom, faded into the background in the wake of the anti-Arian
liturgical reform. Consequently he holds that the glorified Jesus is
the receiver, not the mediator of human worship of God.

Theodore does not deny any present intercession of Jesus for
others. The ascension is past but its efficacy remains. Through his
being as exalted Lord, Christ intercedes for us now. Consequently
the high priestly activity of Jeus consists in his exalted being which is
the ultimate fulfillment and validation of the sacrifice of the cross.
As glorified Lord, Christ is the guarantee and proof of the coming
glorification of the others. Still Theodore can also speak of a high
priestly activity of Jesus whereby he draws others to heaven and he
conceives this as liturgy: "There (= in heaven) he exercises the
priestly service . . . He exercises a real high priesthood and offers to
God no other sacrifice than himself, as he had also delivered himself
to death for all."[27] This activity is linked to the earthly liturgy: "We
are ordered to perform in this world the symbols and signs of the
future things so that, through the service of the mysteries, we may be
like men who enjoy symbolically the happiness of the heavenly
goods."[28] The earthly mysteries are symbols of the reality: the
situation of the ascended Christ. As such they excel the Old Testament types which pointed to the existence but not to the essence of
the reality. The New Testament symbols reveal the being of the
coming reality.

Accordingly, the Eucharist is symbol of the heavenly reality.
The earthly priest is *eikon* of the heavenly high priest. He mediates
the presence of the exalted Lord. Christ, therefore, acts in the
Eucharist by means of the visible priest: "He (= earthly priest) does
not offer his own sacrifice . . . rather he accomplishes in a kind of
image the liturgy of the unspeakable sacrifice."[29] Christ really acts in
the Eucharist, but he acts by means of the visible priest.

Moreover, according to Theodore, the external liturgy as a
whole is the representation of the succession of historical events of
Christ's life by which he accomplished his saving work. Through
these ceremonies Christ himself lives through the stages of his once
for all historical life and so exercises his proper priestly activity. It is
not because Christ intercedes before the Father in the mediation of

human prayers and sacrifice—therefore in a completely present activity—that he can be said to act in conjunction with the earthly liturgy. This was an earlier concept of Christian Fathers. Theodore, on the contrary, restricts the proper high priestly activity of Christ to his earthly life. Accordingly he holds that the past high priestly activity of Christ is re-presented through the liturgical ceremonies. Through the power of the liturgical acts the once for all historical saving activity of Christ obtains a relative presence. In short, just as the presence of the person of the high priest is mediated through the earthly priest, so the presence of the historical saving acts is mediated through the ceremonies. Christ is not even directly present and active as "co-consecrator" of the Eucharistic gifts: "Those who have been chosen as priests of the New Covenant are believed to perform mystically, by the descent of the Holy Spirit . . . those things which we believe Christ our Lord performed . . ."[30]

II. Relevance of Pre-Ephesus Eucharistic Theology for Today

The late 4th century Eastern theological reflection on the meaning of the Divine Liturgy was both prompted and determined by Christological and pneumatological controversies. As a result several important theological conclusions were reached by orthodox Church Fathers which remain valid today. The rejection of any repetitious intercession of Christ before the Father on the occasion of the Divine Liturgy was, at the same time, a statement about the once for all historical saving activity of Christ. The teaching about the presence of the historical saving acts of Christ in the Divine Liturgy, "somehow re-presented," highlighted their efficacy for every generation of the Church. The confession of faith in the consecratory role of the Holy Spirit is a necessary consequence of the dogma of the Trinity. However the theology of the Eucharist, which resulted from these new reflections, was impoverished because it left little room for the development of the more original insight of the early Church that the Risen Lord is actively present as subject of the Eucharistic celebration in a corporeal, albeit invisible, way.

If the Eastern Church Fathers had to contend with a heresy which involved the ecclesiological dimension of the Eucharist, a different development might have occurred. If, for example, they were faced with the explicit rejection of the notion that the whole community is active participant of the Eucharistic sacrifice along with the priest, they would have been forced to reflect more profoundly on the "we" aspect of the prayer of the Divine Liturgy and its implications for the active presence of Christ.

In North Africa the situation was different. Augustine (354-430) had to deal with the Donatist heresy. The Donatists held that the sacraments belong to the Donatist Church, the true communion of saints, and that they do not exist outside its confines. As a consequence only the holy priest who belongs to the holy Church can be dispenser of a true sacrament. Augustine, on the other hand, held the view that the Church is an *ecclesia permixta*: made up of sinners and saints.[31] He could, without difficulty, affirm that a sinful member of the Church can act as dispenser of a sacrament. Moreover he also held that the holy members of the Church act in the administration of a sacrament. Therefore he could grant that a heretic acts as instrument of the Church.

In Augustine's view it is the living organism of the people of God, enlivened by the Holy Spirit, which acts in the dispensation of the sacrament of baptism. The *communio sanctorum* is the properly active factor in the sanctifying activity of the Church. This does not preclude the idea that the Church must employ ordained ministers. But the minister is understood to represent the authority of the whole Church.[32]

In the Eucharist, it is the whole Church which offers acceptable sacrifice to God in union with Christ in the power of the Spirit under the leadership of the priest. It is the whole Church which also dispenses Holy Communion through its representative. In short, it is the whole of the holy Church which offers acceptable sacrifice to God in union with Christ, begets new children in baptism and nourishes them in Holy Communion. It does this insofar as living in the Spirit in union with Christ.

The holy Church is the *Totus Christus*: Head and Body. Therefore when the holy Church acts, it is Christ who acts. The *res* ultimately signified in all the sacramental activity of the Church is Christ and his redemptive work. But since it is the holy Church and its activity through which Christ works, the *res* of the sacraments includes the holy Church itself. Hence when the Church baptizes "Christ baptizes . . . by hidden power in the Holy Spirit . . . Where the ministers are seen to work corporeally, he (= Christ) washes, he cleans . . ."[33] When the Church offers acceptable sacrifice, the offering is that of the *Totus Christus*: Head and Body: '*Hoc est sacrificium Christianorum: multi unum corpus in Christo.*"[34] The sacrifice is the offering of the *caritas* which is ultimately that of Christ flowing through the whole Body. Correspondingly, Augustine can say: "Since you are the Body of Christ and his members, it is your mystery which is placed on the altar."[35]

This view of Augustine corresponds to the more original description of the Lord's Supper as the *Eucharist of the Church*. This ancient notion reflects the Church's understanding of itself as the community of Christ united in the one Spirit. Accordingly the Divine Liturgy is interpreted as the means by which the new people of God manifests and realizes itself. Here the symbolic action and the reality coincide. The problem of the relation between symbol and reality does not arise.

Within this frame of reference one does not interpret the liturgical acts in such a way that certain activities are exclusively identified with the priest and others with the community. Much less does one interpret the liturgy as a sacred drama which represents stages in the life of Christ. Rather the liturgy is viewed, first and foremost, as representing what the community does, or rather as the activity of the community realizing itself as the true people of God.

The Western approach to the theology of the Eucharist is determined by the Pauline theology of the Body of Christ; the Eastern approach by the implications of the glorification of Christ and the theology of the Holy Spirit. Both theologies have their advantages. Neither offers the possibility of an adequate Eucharistic theology by themselves. It is time for the formulation of a new systematic theology of the Divine Liturgy which takes into account the contributions of the Fathers of the Church, of the undivided Church before the Council of Ephesus. However this will not be achieved unless modern theologians exercise the same kind of reflection on all aspects of the mystery of the Eucharist which is exemplified by John Chrysostom, Theodore of Mopsuestia and Augustine of Hippo.

NOTES

This essay contains the substance of a lecture given at a meeting of the Oriental-Roman Catholic Dialogue, New York, December 4, 1981. This dialogue is sponsored by the Oriental Churches in the U.S.A. and the National Conference of Catholic Bishops' Committee for Ecumenical Affairs.

1. *De proditione Judae hom.*, 1.6 (MPG 49. 380-381).
2. *Homily* 15.2 (R. Tonneau & R. Devreesse, *Les homélies catéchétiques de Theodore de Mopsuestia.* Studi e Testi 145 (Vatican City, 1949), 465).
3. *Homily* 15.3 (Tonneau—Devreesse, 467).
4. Clement of Alexandria speaks of honoring "God through the high priest Logos" (*Stromata* II. 45,7 (O. Stählin, GCS II (2nd ed. 1939) 137, 11-12). This holds for the Eucharist in which praise is rendered to God "through the all righteous Logos (*Stromata* VII. 31,7 (GCS III (1909) 23,26). In *Dialogue with Heraclides,* Origen clearly states that the *prosphera* (= Eucharistic prayer) "is made always to the all powerful God by the intermediary of Jesus Christ, insofar as he communicates with the Father through his divinity" (*Entretien d'Origene avec Heraclides* IV. 24-27 (J. Scherer, ed. Sources Chrétiennes 67 (Paris: Cerf, 1960) 63).
5. J.A. Jungmann, *The Place of Christ in Liturgical Prayer* (Staten Island, N.Y.: Alba, 2nd rev. ed. 1965) 150. Origen expressly recommends that a prayer end "by praising the Father of all through Jesus Christ in the Holy Spirit" (*De Oratione* 33 (P. Koetschau, GCS II (1899) 401, 15,25). However he has the high priest Logos in mind (Jungmann, *ibid.,* 160-161).
6. *I Apology* 66.2 (J.C. de Otto, *Corpus Apologetarum Christianorum saeculi secondi* I (Jena, 1847) 180-182). In *I Apology* 1.13 (Otto, CAC I.102) Justin equates the Spirit of Lk 1:33 with the Logos, following a common tradition (Cf. E.J. Kilmartin, "The Eucharistic Prayer: Content and Function of Some Early Eucharistic Prayers," in R.J Clifford & G. MacRae, eds., *The Word in the World* (Cambridge: Weston College, 1973) 122).
7. The anaphora in the *Euchologion* of Serapion (4th century) petitions: "God of truth, let your holy Word come over the bread, in order that the bread may become the body of the Word . . ." (A. Hänggi & I. Pahl, *Prex Eucharistica.* Spicilegium Friburgense 12 (Fribourg, Switzerland: Éditions Universitaires, 1968) 130). For other examples, cf. J. Betz, *Die Eucharistie in der Zeit der griechischen Väter* I/1 (Freiburg im Br.: Herder, 1955) 335-336.
8. It is significant that Theophilus, around 400, states that "The subsisting Wisdom of God . . . shares his body as bread . . ." (Ps.Cyril of Alexandria, *Hom. 10 in coenam myst.* (MPG 77.1017C). However in his Easter letter of 402 he attributes the consecration of the elements to the Holy Spirit: "The Lord's bread . . . and the holy cup . . . are sanctified by the invocation and descent of the Holy Spirit" (Jerome, Ep. 98.13 (CSEL 55, 196, 29 to 197,12).

9. Ep.1.109 (MPG 78. 256C)

10. *In 2 Tim hom* 2.4 (MPG 62.612): "Christ is also present and works." *In Mt hom* 82.5)MPG 58.744): "The work before us is not of human power. He who did it then at that meal (= Last Supper), this one accomplishes it now." *De proditione Judae hom* 1.6 (MPG 49.380): "For it is not man who makes the oblations become the body and blood of Christ but this one, the Christ crucified for us."

11. *De sacerdotio* 3.4 (MPG 48.642); *ibid.* 6.11 (MPG 48.681); *De sancta pentecosta* (MPG 50.459); etc.

12. *In beato Philogono hom* 6 (MPG 48.753).

13. J. Betz, *Die Eucharistie . . .* 1/1, 121-122.

14. *Ibid.* 123

15. *Ibid.* 124-126.

16. *Reg. brevius tract.* 172 (MPG 31.1196A).

17. J. Betz, *Die Eucharistie . . .* 1/1, 126-127.

18. *In Hebr hom* 13.3 (MPG 63.107).

19. *In 2 Tim hom* 2.4 (MPG 62.612).

20. MPG 62.612.

21. *In Hebr hom* 17.3 (MPG 63.131).

22. J. Betz, *Die Eucharistie . . .* 1/1, 190-192.

23. *Hom* 15.15 (Tonneau-Devreesse, 487).

24. *Hom 15.10* (*Ibid.* 475).

25. *Hom 12.4* (*Ibid.* 329).

26. *Hom 15.16* (*Ibid.* 491).

27. *Hom 15.16* (*Ibid.* 487).

28. *Hom 15.18* (*Ibid.* 492).

29. *Hom 15.21* (*Ibid.* 497).

30. *Hom 15.19* (*Ibid.* 495).

31. Augustine relates "The field is the world" (Mt 13:38) to the Church. In the Church weeds and wheat are found together. It is not the task of the saints to reject sinners but seek their conversion (*Contra ep. Parmeniani* 3.2,6 (CSEL 51.107)).

32. Hence Augustine can call the Church *columba,* because the power of the Holy Spirit works in it (F. Hofmann, *Der Kirchenbegriff de hl. Augustinus in seinen Grundlagen und in seiner Entwicklung* (Munich, 1933) 266). It is the whole mother Church, composed of the saints, which acts as instrument of the Spirit: *Tota hoc ergo mater Ecclesia, quae in sanctis est, facit, quia tota omnes, tota singulis parit* (Ep. 98.5 (CSEL 51.74, 5-6).

33. *Contra litteras Petiliani* 3.54,66 (CSEL 52.220).

34. *De civitate Dei* 10.6 (CSEL 40.1, 456).

35. *Sermo* 272 (MPL 38.1247). Cf. E.J. Kilmartin, "Eucharist: Nourishment for Communion," G. D'Ercole, ed., *Populus Dei*: Ecclesia. Communio 11 (Rome: Christen, 1969) 1069-1070.

LIFE GIVING
AN INTERPERSONAL ACTION

by Metropolitan Emilianos Timiades of Silibria.

*The Metropolitan Emilianos of Silibria, is
the representative of the Ecumenical Patriarchate of Constantinople to the World
Council of Churches in Geneva. The following was a contribution to an Orthodox
Theological Symposium discussing the
theme of the forth-coming General Assembly of the WCC: Jesus Christ—the Life
of the World.*

Person to Person

The belief that the Triune God is the true giver of life raises the question of the particular function of the actions of the Spirit in the divine economy. The Nicene Creed names the Spirit as 'Lord and Giver of Life'. As such, the Spirit must be considered as Person with His own hypostasis. This pneumatological subject becomes so important that many have spoken of a 'rediscovery of the Holy Spirit' ('Wiederentdeckyng des Heiligen Geistes) in recent theological discussions.

Being equal (isotimia) to the Father and the Son, the Spirit cannot be regarded in any sense as merely an impersonal celestial force or as the 'link' between the Father and the Son, but as truly God. This is the standpoint of Hebrews 9:14 when it attributes divine properties to the Spirit ('eternal'); of 1 Corinthians 2:10 (omniscient); of Luke 1:35 (creative force). To say 'person' is also to say 'will' and 'action'. Thus the Spirit is described in the New Testament as actively communicating God's blessings to humanity. He speaks, sends out, distributes, and so on (Acts 2:4; 10:19; 13:4; 1 Cor.12:11). When in a few passages (e.g. Lk. 4:14; Acts 1:8; Rom.15:13,19; Eph.3:16), He is linked with the concept of power (*dynamis*), this cannot be used as an argument for reducing the Spirit to an inferior divinity and an impersonal force. The best way to interpret these passages is to take them as declaring that the Spirit empowers or is the very source of creative force (cf.Lk.1:35; Rom.15:19).

Implicit in the divine personhood of the Spirit is His transcendence in respect of creation and the history of humanity. He descends to us and even to non-Christians, illuminating their intelligence, as the early Apologists maintained (Justin, Origen, Clement of Alexandria, etc.), on the basis of the doctrine of the *logos spermatikos.* Since the Spirit is God, the concept of His existence cannot be used to bridge the gap between God and humanity. He is not an 'intermediate being', nor is He equivalent to any power already existing in humanity. God's Holy Spirit is clearly separate from humanity and the human spirit (Rom.8:16; 1 Cor.2:4).

As far as the history of salvation is concerned, the outpouring of the Holy Spirit in the Old Testament was limited in scope, anticipating the charismata which would characterise the messianic period. Now, under the new covenant, the coming of the Spirit is final and accomplishes the fulfilment of the promises of the old covenant. The Paraclete witnesses that God is Emmanuel, remaining with us for ever. He continues to operate since Christ's incarnation and now through the Church (*Christus praesens*).

For the Fathers, the Holy Spirit means a synergistic soteriology to the exclusion of all semi-Pelagian concepts of the appropriation of salvation. The proffered divine grace is not an infused gift (*gratia infusa*), as if it were transmitted through sacramental channels. It is a *koinonia* of persons. This is the relationship between the Holy Spirit and humanity (anthropological). The Church is a fruit of the Spirit's activity and this explains why, in the Nicene Creed, the article on the 'One, Holy, Catholic and Apostolic Church' follows immediately on the confession of the Holy Spirit.

The work of sanctification, illumination and giving new life, therefore, is performed in unison by the Father, the Son and the Holy Spirit. There is no claim that the Spirit alone has the power to sanctify. Basil of Caesarea declares that all the other powers are equally granted, to such as deserve them, only by the Three Persons.[1] The Spirit never acts alone but always together with the other two Persons of the Blessed Trinity, so that the Church as a whole and in each of its members always remains within the unbroken and undivided energy and sovereignty of the whole Trinity. As St. John Chrysostom teaches, the actions of the Trinity are inseparable. Where there is communion of the Spirit, there will also be communion of the Son. And where the action of the Son, Jesus Christ, is operative, there also is the action of the Father and the Holy Spirit.[2]

While the Spirit is given so that its blessings may permeate all liturgical acts, it is also obtained personally by Christians who struggle constantly for this end. It is worth recalling that in the 4th century, when the Massalians launched an anti-ecclesiastical and anti-liturgical spirituality, there was a real danger of an anthropocentric and moralistic ethic. This error originated with the early 4th century Massalians or Euchetes, who denied any assistance from sacramental life and relied on personal individual prayer (*'merias-kesis'*). Another unhealthy spirituality was equally dangerous, a moral *'imitatio'* of Christ and the saints, a kind of mimetism or 'habitus'. What the Fathers affirmed was not an improvement of human nature but a radical regeneration, a 'rheosis' and 'newness of life', a 'christification' of all our being. The prayer of the Festival of Pentecost (3rd prayer) is addressed to the Fount of all gifts:

> 'O God, who, on this redeeming day of the Pentecostal Feast, didst reveal unto us the mystery of the Holy Trinity as one in essence, co-eternal, undivided and unmingled, and didst pour out the holy and life-giving Spirit in the form of tongues of fire upon Thy holy apostles and didst appoint the same to be heralds of the glad tidings of our holy faith, and didst make them confessors, . . . hear us . . .'

Yet the Spirit could not perform this service unless it derived the power to do so from the Father and manifest it through the Son, or if the Son did not manifest it through the Spirit. Each operation fulfils its end because the perfect communion in God, which exists not only in the common essence but also in each divine operation, is manifested and accomplished in the Third Person. It is clear to us, therefore, that the Spirit plays an extremely important role in the relationship which God the Father has established with His creation in accomplishing its salvation.

In practical daily life, the love of God and a sense of responsibility for this life are the work of the Spirit. Where this life is pure, these take the form of adoration, or when we realise our sinfulness and disobedience to the supreme will, in the form of trembling fear and tremendous awe. Only the Spirit can awaken in us an appropriate response to the loving invitation of the Father which is conveyed to us by the same Spirit. Only the Spirit can give to this response its fervour and joy. Only the Spirit can make us share the Son's sensitivity and sense of responsibility to the Father.

The indwelling and operation of the Spirit in the human soul is the essential mission and role of the Spirit. By its nature, the soul is prepared for this visit and unique communion. As an expression of the human hypostasis, the soul is the image of the Logos and, by the Spirit's natural attraction towards the personal Father, it has this tendency in itself from the very beginning. Our soul expects to be visited by the Spirit, to be loved, to be completed. Sin, by weakening this desire to relate to the supreme Person and to other (human) persons, has placed the soul in an embarrassing situation, in a state contrary to its nature. The indwelling of the Spirit thus reestablishes and strengthens the soul in its capacity to relate to God and fellow human beings. In other words, the Spirit restores the soul to its nature and original beauty when this has become disfigured (*pro to ek physeos kallos*), in the profound remark of Basil of Caesarea.[3]

God's Intervention in Our Life

God was not interested in creating slaves and misfits. Humanity is divine because of its noble origin. Humanity is given perfection in creation: the perfection of humanity aimed at and subordinated to the impossible possibility of having God as the content of human life. This human life was damaged by Adam's own perfection and not by any personal defects. He believed the suggestion of the Devil that he could be like God and have 'life in himself'. His fault was in rejecting God as the true content of his life. In doing so, however, he separated himself from the only possible source of life. Because of sin, because humanity desired life apart from God, humanity became the slave of sin and life turned into death. For all these reasons, humanity was in desperate need of salvation. Communion with God needed to be restored, a new relationship established, thereby giving back to human life its meaning and content, or, rather, giving back life to humanity's non-life. In the Orthodox experience, we find our entry into the joy of salvation in the Church.

In the Eucharist, Christ gave us once and for all the means whereby we may be totally united to Him, may have Him totally in us and be ourselves totally in Him. In every Eucharist we proclaim the presence of God in us. The Church is the presence in this world of the Christ who is in us and we in him. Here we see the cosmic dimension of our communion as *'totus Christus corpus et caput'*. This concept, a great favourite with the Greek Fathers, was prominent in the teaching of St. Augustine, and nowhere more so than in his great commentaries on the Psalms:

> 'Christ prays for us as our priest; He prays for us as our Head; He is prayed to by us as our God. Let us then recognize our words in Him and His words in us.'

Perfect life should therefore seek its oneness. Clement of Alexandria uses a significant term for this movement: *monadikos*. In practising the *apatheia*, humanity becomes *monadikos* (*Sir.* IV, 152,1). Believing in Christ the Unique One, we also become 'unique', like Him, united to Him, with no inner division or dissimilarity (*Sir.* IV, 157). Once human life is distanced from Christ, it becomes fragmented and deformed. Origen and Evagrius (the church historian of the 6th century) would describe the life of the monks as *monadikos* in contrast to the life of those living in the secular world.

Yet to embrace spirituality in this way is only possible through *askesis*, a certain aloofness from earthly life, rising above it, constantly striving for self-liberation. This is the reason for the saint's choice of inner or external exile. Concern with actuality is not his only motive here. His search is for freedom from the present in order to recover the *true* reality—i.e. to contemplate God. Today, the obsession with the present and temporal has encouraged the refusal to remember. People become more and more afflicted with *amnesia*. Certainly the illiterates of past centuries knew little of history. For modern people, history is present but blurred, strangely confused. Essential events and facts become hazy and are presented in an anachronistic and irrelevant way.

The question remains: how are we to be above earthly realities and yet at the same time to see the earth? 'Seeing' means not only having eyes. It also means keeping in remembrance, reconstructing and actualising past events. The distance is achieved thanks to the faith. Every event, every date, then becomes eloquent and persists as an eternal reminder of human depravity as well as of human greatness.

St. Macarius the Egyptian was preoccupied with the problem of maintaining the true life. How was a Christian wrestling against evil passions to achieve victory over the enemies of the spiritual life? Is it only by asking God to send sufficient grace, or does He come directly to our personal succour in such critical moments? Macarius' answer is as follows:

'The infinite and inaccessible God made Himself accessible in a bodily form, in His immeasurable and unfathomable love. God diminished Himself from His inaccessible glory so that He might be united with His visible creatures, namely, with the souls of His saints and angels, so that they might partake of the life of the divinity . . . Because of His *philanthropia,* therefore, God is transfigured, mingles with us, becomes accessible to us in bodily form. He takes with Him these saintly, faithful and God-pleasing souls and thus becomes one with us in Spirit. Hypostasis meeting another hypostasis, so that the soul might live its very youth and feel tangibly the immortal life, becoming partaker of the incorruptible glory . . .'

So the whole life given by God derives its existence from God at every point, because it lives with the life which comes from Him, a gradual revelation of the being and nature of God. What we call spiritual powers are all an effluence from God who abides and works in the universe of His making. We recognize that all this vast display of infinite skill and wisdom is but the reflection of the infinite, perfect wisdom, beauty and glory of God.

God, then, is the source of all life and as such does not leave it to its own devices but abides in it. God is the Creator and indwelling Sustainer of all life. In Him we live and move and have our being, as St. Paul reminded the Athenians (Acts 17:27). Yet God is not confined within this life which reflects Him. He is eternally complete in Himself. In other words, He did not need this creation in order to express Himself. He made this lower world because of the pure love which animates His being and because of the simple desire that there might be beings knowing the joy of existence and delighting to praise, serve and enjoy Him. In other words, His life does not depend on the creature. He lives in Himself a life of perfect completeness, perfect movement, perfect beatitude and Trinitarian communion.

In a sense, God only began to create in time; but He was productive, active, long before He was a Creator. God is eternally active, living and manifesting His love through His divine energies. In God there was an eternal love, a love which never failed of its object, a love of the Father and the Son in the embrace of the Holy Spirit. One simple lesson may be derived from this: is we are to serve the living God, our own lives must display a good deal of vitality.

We belong to a continuously acting, sustaining and living God. 'I am come that they may have life and have it more abundantly'. God estimates us not so much by the attainment of this or that virtue but simply by the degree of real spiritual vitality (*zoe*) in our lives, by how much we are really alive. The Pharisee in the parable was condemned because he had ceased to go higher, to grow, to move. This is why he is condemned by the 'living God' who looked at the publican and there saw vitality, a movement towards *metanoia,* life. God is a source of life and if He is at work in us we can trace this operation in us by an increased vitality in us. Faith is transformed into deeds, an energetic instrument which does not merely repeat the words of a Creed but makes them the life-giving motives for an *'orthopraxia'* which justifies the *'orthodoxia'.*

In this context, the meaning of church membership needs to be clarified. It is not just the sum total of the many liturgical forms and proclamations of faith but, more specifically, the personal response to God's invitation and offer, the unique saving redeeming relationship of the human person to the divine Person, a relationship which is itself a way of life—life as God meant it to be. The interrelationship of salvation and faith does not permit us to deal first with one and then with the other. The moment we speak about God we must also speak about the human being and the human response to Him. The impression was often given in the West that faith is concerned exclusively with certain parts of our soul; this encouraged the growth of piety. For the Church Fathers, salvation has an immeasurably wider effect; it embraces not only the soul or what is called the 'spiritual' or 'inner' life but the whole of our being, with all this implies in the world in which we live, including the whole cosmic dimension of creation. Religious life is not a narrow sectarianism, something taking place in an inner sanctuary isolated from the wider secular world and its unredeemed life. To understand what salvation is about we must try to get beyond our ordinary and often decadent religious grasp, which seeks many things which are not beneficial for our human life.

If we fail to take the incarnation seriously, we shall simply be reasserting the selfsufficiency of humanity rather than the need of salvation. This Pelagian attitude has its complete antithesis in another distinctive theology which reduces humanity to utter passivity, allowing it to do no more than listen and hope. Here even faith itself is regarded as totally God's gift, thus leading to the inescapable conclusion that there is nothing to prevent the salvation of all. Christ's incarnation is an event, the historical Event in the Person of the Son of God. The Church is the historical form of this event, where each member becomes a person, appropriating the personal outpouring of the charismata. United with God, humanity defines the new way of life, the new ethos, which is not simply a more complete system of moral imperatives but rather an actual transfiguration of human nature.

For the Fathers, sin is not simply a transgression, a violation. It is above all a broken relationship, an unbridgeable gulf between humanity and God, one which could not be crossed by the personal will condemned by sin to remain an isolated individual will. It is in the Church that this restoration of fellowship in the realm of human nature is carried out, making possible a natural communion in the new Divine-human nature of Logos. The wall of separation having been destroyed, humanity can now renounce its self-sufficiency and rise to the new catholicity, the new wholeness of union with God. This is the new way of life. In fact it is a hard struggle, an asceticism, a familiar process for saints and disciples of Christ. Piety may surely be defined as a yearning for holiness, a yearning for segregation from everything which stands in the way of our integration into the life of Christ. In this respect, the historical experience of the Church, the stories of martyrdom, the *Acta Sanctorum,* the commemoration of the saints and confessors, is extremely important for personal piety. It provides us with models, faithful prototypes, so that we can become imitators of them, living in harmony and symphony with their way of life. Their experience becomes a spur to us, a living lesson. More important still, they are praying for us, encouraging us in our struggle, in the context of the solidarity of the *communio sanctorum.* Thus we acquire the same experience and at a personal level attain what the church has already achieved collectively: salvation. Christian salvation is not an individual matter to be achieved in personal isolation: 'Unus christianus nullus christianus' applies here. A true Christian cannot be a solitary and isolated being.

Life—A Subject of Improvement

From childhood on we are so familiarised with all that life has to offer us that it is hard for us to realise that it does not belong to us. Life is not our exclusive property. It is a gift, given by God, but a gift we are completely free to use or misuse by our own personal decision. The whole question of human freedom and human responsibility is here involved. The words of St. Paul are relevant here: 'What hast thou that thou didst not receive? But if thou didst receive it, why does thou glory as if thou hadst not received it?' (1 Cor.4:7).

With the passage of time, we realize that we are not self-made. One day, sooner or later, we have to return this life we have been given. We become aware that even our life has relative value. And in some moments we are thankful for this exceptional gift. We are still in the first phase of the full communion with God. Such acknowledgement is not enough. More is expected—a full relationship between the Life-Giver and the life-receiver, between the Other-Thou and me. This personal and intimate communion, once established, transforms the whole meaning, content and direction of our existence. Such communion is a constant reminder that we cannot fall away without grave consequences. Here we touch the summit of Christian life: holiness.

Holiness is nothing other than the absolute communion of life with God's life as lived by the Holy Trinity. Just as there we find full communion of interpersonal relationships, sealed in perfect love, so also is it in our case. The Trinitarian communion is the model for human communion. Human life is created to be everything that God is by nature. Men and women are called to be persons, united in perfect love. This being so, the Fathers are opposed to all forms of individualism as well as of collectivism. The Church is not an impersonal group, nor a collective mass of anonymous beings. It is a communion patterned on the perfect hierarchical and interpersonal life of the Trinity who is Love. The Church is a covenant of those who live the fullness of life. If they do not live such a life and are dead, they exclude themselves from such an organism. Their vitality is also shown by the distribution of 'spiritual life' or 'living sacrifice' to others. Sharing in God's life, they offer it to others, warming their hearts instead of making them cold. They keep their inner fire constantly glowing by prayer and love, careful lest the emotions dissipate this glow.

Every one may have moments of anxiety for his spiritual insufficiency. Few even feel a certain deep sorrow, for the distance existing between what remains their final object, and what they actually are. Others, in time, become accustomed to these gaps and open empty places in their life. This emptiness becomes a dangerous habit, and even slowly, an integral part of their thinking and living. Subsequently, they forget to fight, they lose all appetite for improving their situation, for finding ways and means to fill the existing gaps. With such a manner of living communion with God does not exist. Religion then flees taking with it faith, hope and trust. Thus there enters an awful vacuum, the absence of fulness, the small concern for noble gains.

And yet, God, the Life-giver, offers so many chances for a person to renew and to complete this gift of life. Knowing our weaknesses, He takes the initiative to propose a new birth, a re-creation which is a real adventure, but which promises a new sunrise; the real life has to be re-made many times, in spite of our shortcomings. And here enters the role of God's love, whose concern is that our life not be wasted, nor lost, but repaired, re-built.

Broadening one's life, allowing others to share its blessings, constitute another basic problem needing further study. Natural law is restrictive, imposing limits. "Life is mine", with all consequent possessive arguments. But love ignores limits; it abolishes existing distances and rights of one's "self". From this moment we are able to distribute, to offer. Love even sacrifices its own legitimate right. It accepts injustice, self-emptiness for the sake of the "other". Sacrifice, kenosis then become the natural element of one's life transformed by love.

What practical conclusions emerge from an abstract spirituality which makes no reference to personal relations with a personal God?

Often we trace a liberal conception of ethics deviating from the old established order without any reference to an Incarnate Christ, the second Person of the Holy Trinity or to the Holy Spirit as Person. Religious life then becomes a subjective, elastic moralism, a humanitarian "orthopraxia", determined by circumstances, shaped and reshaped according to each one's view and a degree of good will. And yet it is a constant belief that subjectiveness and human fragility hinder the perfect realisation of virtues and personal communion with God; doing takes precedence over "being". A Christian belongs to a God who has lived as true man and true God, who has left us an example to be followed.

For Christianity cannot be reduced to a simple humanitarian spontaneity, however generous it might be. Living as a Christian the "very life" given to us implies always a "perpetual reference" which is connected with the sayings and the pattern of the life and teaching of Jesus of Nazareth as a concrete historical person. This piece of sacred history, coherent and challenging, marks the limits of any dangerous deviating initiative. Creative plans, often animating contemporary renewal movements within and outside of the Church, have to be seen in the light of the living example of Christ. Such a confrontation determines the quality of the authenticity of our faith. Such a judgement saves us a lot of abuses, although good intention and merits are not absent from an autonomous "dis-incarnated" spirituality.

Yet such an approach poses a serious problem. It defines neither the origin of piety in general, nor its source animating any activity. One clearly sees an ambiguity, masking a theological error. Spiritual life should be a consecration to God, through Christ, not to an abstract absolute supreme Being, or as a commitment to vague moral principles.

The Patristic anthropoligy that man is created in the "image of God" is taken very seriously. This means that he can never lose his link with God, even though he falls. Retaining this link, he can cooperate with God. Although this cooperation might often be inconsistent and inadequate, step by step it can proceed in trans-forming fallen nature and life. The beautiful sentence of John Chrysostom on synergism: "Let us transform together the earth into heaven" (Homily on St. Matthew 43,5: PG 57, 463) sees man as a partner of God in transforming a world darkened by sin and man's fall, but one which, because of God's philanthropia, awaits trans-formation into a new Jerusalem. This is biblical, and expressed eloquently in the last chapters of the Apocalypse.

God's Partners

This faith in God as a person bears anthropological conse-quences. God wants free will partners. God treats man as a son, not a slave. Patristics reject any doctrine of redemption and salutary intervention which might seem to infringe upon man's freedom. Man, having before him a God who is Father, full of love and compassion, motivated in all his dealings with humanity by divine philanthropia and not tyranny, has to cooperate, that is either to accept God's offer or to reject it. He is even free to refuse any dialogue with God. Without man's consent and "synergia", salva-tion remains inoperative; in Paul's words: "We are fellow workers with God" (1 Cor. 3,9). If man is to achieve full fellowship with God, he must play his own part. The incorporation into Christ requires the cooperation of two unequal, but equally necessary persons and forces. God respects human attitude and reaction. He does not break it down.

God invites all but compels none, as John Chrysostom develops it:

"God never draws anyone to Himself by force and violence. He wishes all men to be saved, but forces no one"[5]

Life is the field of many conflicts, oppositions and hardships. But their very nature does not lie in external phenomenological elements like structures of society, laws, etc., although even such things influence to a certain degree, human life in a society. What constitutes above all the root of tension and struggle is the attachment to this life or the faith in another kind of life. Even history is not just a move for the better, for the progress, but a struggle for finding real liberty, and even better, a fight between two opposing liberties, as Saint Augustin said: "a conflict, permanent and painful, between love of God, arriving and resulting in the neglect of one's self; or love for ones' self, arriving at the despisal and neglect of God.[6]

Humanists of all times have claimed that man could live by moral principles alone, without the help of a grace-giving God. The answer to life, as an existence and as spiritual being, lay in man's own hands, and his purpose was to try by his own efforts to change the world. If Christianity is true, we have to get out beyond values or abstract moral standards and our own experience however high and noble. It is to God as person, acting, intervening, saving and speaking that we must listen and hear when we address our supplications. Because of his reliance on human experience, man has too often been deceived. We have had enough bad copies of masterpieces in art, reproductions of Greek sculpture, to put us on our guard. If this is so of man's work, how much more careful should we be to ascertain with objective certainty where the divine message is to be found.

The ultimate love which makes human love meaningful and stimulating for the fulfilment of high tasks in every generation, is the idea and reality of God, One who as Alpha presides at the beginning, and as Omega closes the book of life at the end. God is the same in the Old Testament as in the New, not only because He is in possession of necessary, immutable essence, but because the whole of salvation history is a progressive revelation of the way in which the Divine Logos enters into relationship with the world.

God is the loving Creator of a world independent of Himself, a world of things and of free persons. These free persons will find their final bliss in union with this same living God, a union in which human personality will still persist. We commit ourselves and become optimists relying on the promises of a living God. Unnecessary mortification need not be imposed, because the crosses of daily life which we meet will make us Christ-like. It is in the life of the Church that the Spirit shapes and forms our gradual sanctification, in time and in history. In the history of Salvation, the Spirit's activity is the people of God (I Sam.16,13; Ps.50,13;I Cor.3,16). This is the kernel of truth in the attitude of Cyprian of Carthage that "extra ecclesiam nulla salus".

It is clear that from the moment life ceases to be related to a partner who is God, rather than to a dubious being or idea, the duration of the link itself is at stake. The commitment of the Christian is based on the fidelity and the unshaken stability of God, who is beyond time, space and finitude, all characteristics of human fragility. There is no question of change or modification in accordance with the different ages and historical conditions, when one is dealing with the Eternal and Absolute One, who is God of all ages for ever. One understands then that the absence of a divine "partner" disintegrates the relationship and injures its irreversible character.

Any silence about concrete commitment is the logical consequence of God's absence, a personal absence. Such a problematic empties any religious life of its Christian density, its evangelical specificity. If one, for example, looks at Buddhism, lacking a relationship with a personal God, it is evident that Christianity, continuing the monotheistic background from the Old Testament, is centered round, and grounded on a personal God. It would be interesting to develop the contrast in terms of spiritual results. A Christian believes he is responsible to God as a person, as love, and not to a law or moral rule. He tries to shape his life according to the degree of faithfulness to God's love or to its violation. He obeys or disobeys God, a living person. Between this God and the believer an encounter takes place in full conscience, in liberty to agree or disagree. We can characterize this as an ontological encounter since it determines the believer's existence. Between these two personal poles is created an existential relationship which binds together in some way the freedom of the one and the fidelity of the other. Because God is a person, he is bound to his creation, sustaining and taking care for it.

This personal God is recognised by His unique name and His action in the history of mankind, particularly in that of His chosen people who depend on Him. Thus Yahweh becomes the privileged partner of Israel:

> "The Lord, the God of your fathers, the God of Abraham, the God of Israel, and the God of Jacob, has sent me unto you: this is my name for ever, and this is my memorial unto all generations" (Exod. 3,15).

Jesus of Nazareth further defines this name:

> "Go ye therefore, and make disciples of all the nations, baptising them into the name of the Father and of the Son and of the Holy Ghost" (Matt. 28,19).

Christian life is incorporated in this personal relationship, human-divine and intimately personal, which is distinctive of Christianity. Against any view of a pure "ideology" which develops a coherent system of values, Christian life inaugurates a bilateral communication. Christianity delineates the space where a word is pronounced placing God and man in dialogue. Jesus inaugurates the basic discourse which channels the divine-human communication. In all human life communication is multiform, variously diversified. It is done with many partners according to intimacies great or small, and at different depths. The Christian is one who lives out a relationship of dialogue with God. A Christian is precisely one for whom God becomes the privileged living "partner", "heteros" and not the "heteron". Communication with God inspires all other dialogue and is established in a priority relationship to all other dialogues. It defines the history of a life in faith to such a degree that it becomes the major preoccupation: "Do you not know that I must be in my Father's house?" (Lk 2,49)

Precisely this communication with God gives value to and orders all other dialogue and activity. Because Christ has a unique relation with God, being His Son, He influences the mode of dialogue. Hence any Christian act is a "sequela Christi", a sequel to Christ, and its scope will reach beyond the individual Christian's own achievements, reaching unimaginable targets, what Gregory of Nyssa describes as *Epektasis.*

In short, Christian spirituality is fundamentally "referential" and not ideological, self-merited. It is "reference" to a permanent standard, that is the Gospel and Christ, consecration to God, in the biblical sense of the term. "For thou art a holy people unto the Lord thy God: the Lord thy God has chosen thee to be a special people unto himself, above all peoples that are upon the face of the earth" (Deut. 7,6). Our life is not a relying upon values, abstract ideas, principles and theological truths but on a God who has sent His Son to be with us for ever. This life is shaped, linked and nourished by God. All virtues spring from this personal love and intimate relationship. From the moment God enters as a constituent of human history, its space of action excludes any limitation, since the initiative lies with God: "another shall gird thee, and carry thee whither thou wouldest not" (John 21,18). This Other Thou remains our permanent companion and protector.

Furthermore, this dialogue offers a promise for eternal life. The personal God lives in an eternal existence. Faith in Him produces a hope of sharing this everlasting life. Christianity, in its religious essence, offers a liberation from the most rebellious alienation of man: that of death. If death works its rupture bringing all to nought, then a superior or force is needed to halt and to overcome its dominion. Christianity bases and secures its credibility on this capital problem. St. Paul saw clearly the danger of this possibility: "But if there is no resurrection of the dead, neither has Christ been raised; and if Christ has not been raised, then is our preaching vain, your faith also is vain, and we are found false witnesses of God" (I Cor.15,13-14).

The fundamental role of Christianity is to liberate man from his biological limitations and earthly destiny: death, bodily dissolution and return to earth. This liberation is achieved in communication with God, the promise of immortality. The more we take God as our privileged partner, the more we proceed to the ground of our liberation and detachment from earthly bonds and slavery to ourselves and to fragile pleasures. The whole of Patristic teaching about God's essence and energies presupposes a personal God. And because God is a living Person, He is eternally in redeeming liberating action—"en ergo"—for the benefit of mankind, manifesting His "energies" towards man and the world.

Refuting any impersonal metaphysical view, leading finally to an unknown or anonymous God, Gregory Palamas had developed a thorough analysis on this point[7]. God's energy is manifest and perceptive, since the relationship and the dealing is between two personal beings. All divine properties known to us: creativity, providence, Lordship . . . flow from a common origin: that of a personal action of will. God shows His being hypostatically; all His energies proceed from His ousia. God exists, and consequently, is acting! God is seen, ontologically felt through His "energies".

It is through the Spirit that God rules and maintains the whole world, intervening through the mystery of the Church and leading it to its "telos", its final accomplishment, i.e. its divinisation. The Spirit waters the roots of the Church, dispensing to its members wisdom, strength, faith, hope, spiritual growth and joy in facing the tribulations and sufferings on earth. Thus, as in the Trinity the Spirit shows that the Father and the Son are two distinct persons but One in essence, united by love, likewise the Spirit consecrates us as distinctive persons while incorporating us into the Church, uniting all in the joy of a unique communion: "Ubi Spiritus Sanctus, ibi Ecclesia", Irenaeus said. Thus we see that the whole mystery of the Church lies in its pneumatological structure.

One might conclude by saying that the experience of full personal communion is made possible and real because of Christ's Incarnation. No total communion is possible except with a perfect person, who can incorporate us in his infinity—and He alone can achieve this, through His obedience to the Father, and the grace of the Spirit. In giving us the Spirit, Christ offers us the perfect "life-giving" trinitarian communion. Man is in agony when deprived of communion with others. But the communion with human beings leads to another agony, deception, if it is not associated with its source in God, infinite Person.

NOTES

1. *Letter* 109 PG 32, 693.
2. *Comm. 2 Cor. Homily* 30, 2 PG 61, 608.
3. *De Spiritu Sancto,* PG 30, 109.
4. *Homily* 4, 9-10. PG 34, 480.
5. *Sermon on the words "Saul, Saul . . ."* 6, p. 51, 144.
6. *De Civitate Dei,* 14, 28: CSEL 40, II, 56-57.
7. *Chapters on Nat. Theol.* 136: PG 150, 1220.

FRUITS OF THE EUCHARIST:
HENOSIS AND THEOSIS

by Rev. Mr. Jonathan Morse, M.R.E., M.A.

The Rev. Mr. Morse is a deacon of the Ukrainian Archeparchy of Philadelphia and teaches in the Religious Studies Departments of Manor Junior College and Holy Family College, Philadelphia, PA.

The goal of every Christian's life is Henosis, which is union with Christ, and Theosis, which is sharing in the divine nature.

The root of the theology of the relationship of the eucharist and Henosis and Theosis is in the Hebrew Scripture's thought on the concept of "meal."

Genesis

The Lord appeared to Abraham by the terebinth of Mamre. As Abraham was sitting at the opening of his tent in the heat of the day, he looked up and saw three men standing in front of him. When he saw them, he ran from the opening of his tent to meet them and bowed low to the ground. "Sir," he said, "if I have deserved your favour, do not pass by my humble self without a visit. Let me send for some water so that you may wash your feet and rest under a tree; and let me fetch a little food so that you may refresh yourselves. . . . So Abraham hurried into the tent to Sarah and said, "Take three measures of flour quickly, knead it and make some cakes." Then Abraham ran to the cattle, chose a fine tender calf. . . . He took curds and milk and the calf he prepared, set it before them. . . . (Gn 18:1-9, N.E.B.)

This meal story shows the intimacy that Abraham had with the Lord God, as well as the tradition of hospitality. It is at this meal that a covenant is reached and ratified. Abraham's wife is to give birth in a year's time to a son.

In Genesis there are many other accounts of meals used as the sealing of a covenant: 26:26-31; 31:53f.[1]

Hebrew Scriptures

These are not just to be found in Genesis. They are found in I

Sm. 9:22, Lv. 24:6-9, Ex. 12:13, Dt. 26 and most importantly in Ex. 24:11 and Dt. 27:7. These last two are important because it is between God and Israel.

Meals were to take the place of animal sacrifices.[2] For in the meal fellowship you have two points of view, first it is man's response to the word which God has already addressed to him and it also is man's entry into familiarity with God, who now communicates His life to the people.[3]

The reason for God's usage of meals is because God's word, like a meal becomes the food and drink of His people. This idea is especially brought out in the prophet Isaiah.[4]

> It is an ancient oriental idea that a common meal binds the table companions into a table fellowship. This table fellowship is religious and therein rest its obligations: its violation is a particularily heinous crime (Ps. 41.10), and hence the deep grief felt by Jesus, Mark 14.20 par. Above all, the passover table fellowship is religious; this is seen most clearly in the fact that membership of every *haburah* had to be determined before the lamb was killed and its blood sprinkled on the altar of burnt-offerings. . . . When at the daily meal the *paterfamilias* recites the blessing over the bread—which the members of the household make their own by the "Amen"—and breaks it and hands a piece to each member to eat, the meaning of the action is that each of the members is made a recipient of the blessing by this eating; the common "Amen" and the common eating of benediction unite the members into a table fellowship. . . . The same is true of the cup of blessing . . . drinking from it mediates a share in the blessing.[5]

Christian Scriptures

This was the perspective that Jesus and his apostles brought with themselves at the Last Supper and to all their meals together. This is important because for those who believe that the Eucharist was instituted at the Last Supper, a fellowship is important in the Eucharist. For those that hold that the Eucharist's origin is not in the Last Supper, but in the meals that Jesus had with his followers, the meal fellowship is still there.[6]

As part of the meal fellowship there is joy because Jesus is present. While the Bridegroom is present there is rejoicing. This is just one of the characteristics of the messianic age. In the age to come there is going also to be a superabundance, which can be seen when Jesus multiplied the loaves and fishes and there were twelve baskets left over. There will also be salvation (Lk. 19:9) and pardon (Lk 7:47), where the repentant woman shows the reconciliation that Jesus was to bring. "In accepting this initimate community with sinners, Jesus showed that He had come to destroy the barrier between sinful men and God. . . . It is an act with a religious significance which sheds light on what is most essential in the mission of Christ."[7]

The table fellowship with sinners is to point out that God and man are to be reconciled here on earth as a foretaste of what is to come in the Kingdom. This reconciliation is to be seen in the present by the reconciliation of members of the community.

It is for this reason that St. Paul demands that there must be charity toward others (cf. I Cor. 11: 17-33) before there can be a Eucharist. In Corinth people were dividing themselves into groups destroying the symbolic table fellowship. They had turned the Eucharist into a personal picnic. They had become removed from the ideal, which was, "In celebrating this meal the early Christians had the experience of being a Church—an eschatological community on the basis of their personal relationship with Jesus, whom they had come to know explicitly as the Christ in the resurrection."[8]

In the post-Resurrection appearances, there is usually some form of eating together. In every sense of the word then this would be the Eucharist in this authors opinion. Because these meals happen with a kind of frequency. Something that happens often develops a history, but then again it usually comes out of some history. "The Eucharist comes about, not by a creation out of nothing, but by what we call today a "transignification," when Our Lord gives to the simple table rituals of the Jews an altogether new meaning. This new meaning points these rituals away from the Exodus of Moses (if the Last Supper was a Passover meal) towards its fulfillment in the "exodus" of the new Moses."[9]

Moses led his people to a new life with God, Jesus led his people to a new life in God, as St. Paul says "in Christ."

The term "in" shows a very close connection and a union that has a totally new character. "Paul has the most varied expressions for this new life principle, union with Christ. It is life in Christ: the Christian must consider himself dead to sin but alive for God in Christ. (Rm 6:11). It is love in Christ: no created thing can ever come between the Christian and the love God made visible in Christ Jesus, our Lord (Rm 8:39). It is the grace which is given in Christ (I Cor. 1:4) freedom in Christ (Gal. 2:4), blessings in Christ (Gal 3:14), unity in Christ (Gal 3:28), incorporation into Christ's body through the one Spirit (I Cor 12:13)"[10]

To summarize the meals in the Christian scriptures, they are a table fellowship binding all the community together in charity so that they may become one in Christ and Christ in them.

The Fathers

The Fathers continued the thought of the eucharistic as a meal of unity. In the *Didache,* the eucharist can be seen in chapters 9 and 10 as a common meal. The one line that is of special interest here is: "As this broken bread was scattered upon the mountains and being gathered together as one, so may Thy Church be gathered together from the ends of the earth into Thy Kingdom."[11] This passage on the surface deals with the unity of the Church one with another, but on a deeper level it points to the multiplication of the loaves and fishes, meaning therefore union with Christ.

The multiplication, as pointed out earlier, deals with the Messianic Banquet, of which we all shall partake after our resurrection. By receiving the Eucharist we are taking into ourselves the seed of our resurrection which is joined to Christ's. St. Ireneaus makes this point very clearly:

> Therefore when the chalice has been mixed and the bread has been made, receive the word of God and become the Eucharist of the blood and the body of Christ, from which the substance of our flesh is increased and supported. How do they (the heretics) deny that the flesh is capable of the gift of God which is life eternal, which is nourished by the blood and body of Christ and is his very member? . . . So also our bodies nourished by them and placed in the earth . . . shall rise in their own time when the Word of God grants them resurrection unto the glory of God the Father.[12]

Following upon this theme of the eucharist as the communicator of everlasting life many of the Fathers pick up on the comparison of the manna from the Hebrew Scriptures. For St. Ambrose, a western father highly respected in the east, states:

> The manna was a great marvel, the manna that God rained down on the Fathers. . . . But this nourishment that you receive, the Bread descended from heaven, communicates to you the substance of eternal life. It is the Body of Christ. As the light is greater than the shadow, the truth than the figure, so the Body of the Creator is greater than the manna from heaven.[13]

The manna in the desert was able to give the Fathers nourishment for their bodies, the Eucharist gives more than physical nourshment. As St. Cyril of Alexandria says:

> . . . He who has taken part in Christ by the communion of His whole Body and Blood, should also have His spirit and live to enter into his interior dispositions in having the understanding of what is in him . . .[14]

A person receiving the Eucharist receives the spirit of God. This spirit lives in him and when God enters matter things do not remain the same. As St. Gregory of Nyssa observes:

> Those who have been tricked into taking poison counteract its destructive influence with another drug, but the antidote must, like the poison, enter right into a man's entrails for the effect of the remedy to spread through the whole body; so also we who had tasted of that which rots our nature needed that which would undo decomposition, an antidote that would enter into us and remove by counteraction that harmful effects of the poison that our body had taken in. What is then this antidote? Nothing other than that body which was shown to be stronger than death and became a source of life for us. Just as a little leaven, as the apostle says, assimilates the whole lump to itself, so also the body which was immortalized by God, once it has entered into our body, changes and translates it totally into itself. Just as the addition of a destructive agent to a healthy body reduces it to uselessness, so also the immortal body, once it has entered the man who receives it, changes him totally into its own nature.[15]

To summarize the thought of the Fathers in a paraphrase of a

131

current expression, "We become what we eat." It is necessary then to examine what is "in" the Eucharist.

The Real Presence

This term is being used in the eucharistic context and so therefore cannot be looked upon in isolation. When Jesus gave the command "Take and eat, this is my body," it was the meal that was the sacrament, not just the bread and wine. At that supper Jesus was present. Likewise Jesus, the dead and risen Jesus is today. Therefore the eucharist is also an anamnesis.[16] It is a rememberance, which he told us to do, a rememberance of him and what he stood for. It is a rememberance that brings him to us. What and who are we remembering? What did He say that is important to remember especially on the subject of the eucharist?

"Whoever eats my flesh and drinks my blood dwells continuously in me and I dwell in him." (Jn 6:56)

"I live because of the Father, so he who eats me shall live because of me." (Jn 6:57)

In these two lines taken literally, Jesus is giving us himself to eat and drink and by doing so we are given the life of the Father. The second part is verified in Jn 14:20 where He says, "because I live, you too will live; then you will know that I am in my Father, and you in me and I in you." It is Christ who lives within us upon receiving the Eucharist. As the contemporary author Father Dubay summarizes:

> The Word made flesh dwells among us under the appearances of bread and wine with his flesh and blood, soul and divinity, but without external quantity. . . . Needless to say, the eucharistic presence shares in the uniqueness of the incarnational.[17]

The belief that it is Christ is verified in the writings of the Fathers, for example, St. Justin,

> For not as common bread and common drink do we receive these; but in like manner as Jesus Christ our Saviour, having been made flesh and blood for our salvation, so likewise have we been taught that the food which is blessed by the prayer of His word, and from which our blood and flesh by transmutation are nourished is the flesh and blood of that Jesus who was made flesh.[18]

132

This is verified in *Against Heresies* Book 4, chapter 18, by St. Ireneaus and by St. John of Damascus in *On Orthodox Faith* 4,13.[19]

This Christ we receive as spiritual nourishment cannot be separated from the Christ who was crucified. In the Eucharist we participate in this sacrifice. "And communion is precisely the manner in which these effects are applied to the soul. By this, the theology of Communion is seen not to differ from that of the Consecration in being a participation in the mystery of Christ dead and risen again. It is important, in fact, to note that, for our catecheses, Communion is seen to be as much a participation in the Death of Christ as in His Resurrection."[20]

The how of the consecration in the west is usually referred to as transubstantion, even though this is only the most common conception as opposed to being mandatory.

> This reduction (of transubstantiation) to time and logic seeks to reduce the Eucharist to one moment of time, to a special action of human causality. It forces the Eucharistic mystery into the same framework within which we live. The Eucharist is a certain change of time, but it cannot be reduced to any one human act of causality. We must put on a completely different understanding of natural, supernatural, visible and invisible. The Eucharist cannot be reduced to these categories, not even to the substance-accident theory.[21]

In all reality we cannot fully understand what we are partaking because of our finite minds. We are partaking of divinity, which is infinite, as St. Cyril of Jerusalem encourages us:

> So let us partake with the fullest confidence that it is the body and blood of Christ. For his body has been bestowed on you in the form of bread, and his blood in the form of wine, so that by partaking Christ's body and blood you may share with him the same body and blood. This is how we become bearers of Christ, since his body and blood spreads throughout our limbs; this is how in the blessed Peter's words, "we become partakers of the divine nature."[22]

This passage of Cyril and the earlier sections on the eucharistic meal show us the two fruits of the eucharist: Henosis (union with God) and Theosis (deification.)[23]

Henosis

As Jeremias states in eating and drinking we are connected with the atoning death of Jesus. So much so as Lussier notes:

> In St. Paul our mystical union with Christ originates at the high moment of redemption, the time of the Passion, and from that moment on it is continuous and the *communicatio idiomatum* between Christians and Christ is henceforth complete.[24]

Since the Fathers were concerned that this teaching be based upon Scripture, they looked at the sections dealing with eating or incorporating wisdom into a person, and then took it into the Christian context as can be seen in this passage of St. Ambrose:

> You wish to eat, you wish to drink. Come to the feast of Wisdom which invites all men by a great proclamation, saying "Come, eat my bread and drink my wine that I have mingled." Do not fear that in the Feast of the Church you will lack either pleasant perfumes, or agreeable food, or varied drink, or fitting servants. There you will gather myrrh, that is to say, the burial of Christ, in such a way that, buried with Him by Baptism, you also will arise from the dead as He Himself is risen. There you will eat the bread that strengthens the heart of man, you will drink the wine so that you may grow to the full stature of Christ.[25]

In the heart of man according to the prophet Jeremiah the new covenant was going to be written. Also, the above passage is dealing with the sacrifice of Cain and Abel. As noted earlier, sacrifices were replaced by meals, but we have the sacrifice of Christ and it is the flesh and blood of this sacrifice that we partake in. The Fathers at time expressed this in very crude almost cannibalistic language.[26] But, the sacrifice of the New Covenant (Testament) had to be written in our hearts and this could only be done by partaking of the sacrifice.

Jesus sacrifice was done in the flesh. Jesus worked his miracles through the flesh.[27] Now Jesus joins us through his new flesh, the Eucharist, in order to give us the "Bread of Life," the bread that will make us grow.

Bread nourishes our whole self. The Eucharistic bread nourishes our bodies and our souls. It nourishes our souls by giving us the virtues, dispositions, and the soul itself of Christ. Since we are whole persons, our bodies which carry these virtues are nourished. When we are fed it effects the whole of us, just as after a meal, our physical bodies are nourished and we feel good. Christ is not lifeless, but life itself. He was active in love in becoming the eucharist. He acted again in love by joining himself to us, freely. Christ is "active love" in our lives. The Eucharist gives us the very act of love *(dilectio)*, it makes the soul rebound anew in a living flame of love, a flame like the Burning Bush which burns but does not consume.[28]

But this unity does not last forever, like that of Baptism. We can look at the Hebrew Scriptures for many examples of when the Spirit of God came upon a person and then left, for example, Saul and the Judges.[29] Most of the work of the Spirit is transitory in nature. The union with Christ in the Eucharist is the work of the Holy Spirit, which Theodore of Mopsuestia points out:

> When you have undergone the real birth of the resurrection, you will eat another kind of food which is wonderful beyond description; you will feed upon the grace of the Spirit, which will make your bodies immortal and your souls unchanging. . . . It enables those who have been born by the resurrection to remain firm, so that their bodies do not decay, and their souls experience no change inclining them to evil.[30]

It may appear that he is separating a person into parts. Theodore is keeping man whole, but just as I can talk about my arm, I can talk about my body. But, I must always remember that I am a whole and never think of my body as something other than myself. What then effects any part of me, effects the whole of me.

Our bodies following the resurrection will be made by the Eucharist into the same "glorified" body that Jesus had following His resurrection. As St. John of Damascus says:

> Thou has vouchsafed me, O Lord, that this corruptible temple—my human flesh—should be united to Thy holy flesh, that my blood should be mingled with Thine; and henceforth I am Thy transplant

and translucent member . . . I am transported out of myself, I see
myself—O marvel—such as I become.[31]

Union with Christ changes the person we are because it changes
our bodies, it transforms us into what we can be. Hensois ends in the
second fruit, Theosis.[32]

Theosis

As Dionysius defines this term:

> Theosis is assimilation to and union with God to the extent that is
> permitted. It is the common end of all hierarchy that a continual love
> *(prosekes agapesis)* of God and of divine things, carried out in a holy
> way in God and in unity, and, previously, the total and irreversible
> flight from what opposes it, the gnosis of what is as being, the vision
> and the science *(episteme)* of the holy truth, participation in God
> *(entheos)* in uniform perfection and in the One Himself so far as this is
> permitted, the satisfying intuition that nourishes intellectually whom-
> ever tends toward it.[33]

Theosis began at the creation of Man as found in the book of
Genesis. When God created man out of the slime of the earth, He
breathed into him and gave him a share in His divine and immortal
life. Man's breath is from God. Breath is part of the nature of man so
by nature he is filled with the spirit of God in an embryonic form.[34]

This makes up part of the image and likeness of God that man
was created with (Gn 1:26-27). The image denotes the powers that
man is endowed with and the likeness is his goal. Therefore, man
cannot lose image but his likeness depends upon his moral choice.
Man then at creation was perfect in a potential sense.[35] His perfection comes in theosis.

The scriptural basis of theosis and its understanding starts
usually with John 10:34: "Jesus answered: 'Is it not written in your
Law:' I said, you are gods? So the Law uses the word gods of those to
whom the word of God was addressed and Scripture cannot be
rejected." It was God, the God of the Hebrew Scriptures and Jesus,
who creates a God by grace, not by his very nature.

I John 3:2 states, "We are already the children of God but what we are to be in the future has not yet been revealed; all we know is that when it is revealed we shall be like Him. The idea of deification must always be understood in the light of the distinction between God's essence and His energies. Union with God means union with the divine energies not the divine essence."[36] We do not become the Father or the Son or the Holy Spirit, rather we share so intimately with their life-creating energies that we are joined to them, and that even in this union we still remain ourselves. We chose to be joined with the whole Trinity, Father, Son and Holy Spirit. This in the east is in the Holy Spirit, which differs from some in the west, who believe it is in the Son. The Eastern principle is "To the Father, through the Son and in the Holy Spirit."

> When Saint Maximus wrote "God and those who are worthy of God have one and the same energy," (*Amibgua.* P.G. 91, 1076) he did not mean that the saints lose their free will, but that when deified they voluntarily and in love conform their will to the will of God. Nor does man, when he "becomes god" cease to be human.[37]

"We remain creatures while becoming god by grace, as Christ remained God when becoming man by the Incarnation."[38]

The most theologically developed quote is from 2 Pt 1:4, ". . . you will be partakers of the divine nature."

The teachings of the Fathers use this passage as the starting point for statements like that of St. Ireneaus, "God became man in order that man might become God."[39] or in St. Athanasius, "The Logos in the Spirit gives to men glory and by deification and adoption leads them to the Father."[40]

Theosis comes out of the hypostatic union of the two natures of Christ.[41] It comes from the power of the Incarnation, when Christ joined our humanity (reverse henosis—divinity becoming united to humanity as opposed to Henosis where humanity joins divinity). Christ in his humanity joins with our humanity, especially through the Eucharist, when we are joined to the still human Jesus. (For if he can lose humanity, by dieing he was never truly human. The Church teaches that He is in the Nicean-Constantinoplian creed.)

When talking about humanity, we are not just talking about the soul, but the body as well. Deification involves the body, because man is a union of body and soul. Since Jesus the Christ redeemed man, he redeemed the total man, his body and his soul. The body has its own special place in salvation, as St. Paul points out. "Your body is the temple of the Holy Spirit."[42]

Since the Trinity cannot be divided, where the Spirit is the whole Trinity is present. God then is present within us. We then have two natures, human and divine. This is how we are in the image of God, because we are in the image of Christ. We have the potential of being transfigured. At the end of time man, his body, and all of creation will be transfigured, not all at once but in degrees. As it says in Revelation (21:1) "The I saw a new heaven and a new earth; for the first heaven and the first earth had passed away."

The creation of the new earth, which is created through Christ and His Body, is called anakephalaiosis *(recapitulation)*.

> Irenaeus is the first to introduce the principle of anakephalaiosis in Christ as an integrating structure by which he could explain to the Gnostic heretics and his own flock at Lyons the immanence of Christ in the material world. God became man that man might become God. Jesus Christ is God's Logos, and in Him God is gathering up His entire work, fulfilling it according to His original plan. Christ's work and the whole real progress in the universe are measured in terms of the restoration of the first creation through Christ's activities in the cosmos.[43]

It was a sense of nostalgia for the original state of affairs when the cosmos, man, and the world submitted to the divine element in man. It is the completion of creation the way God planned it before Adam interrupted it.[44]

Man cannot do this alone. It can only be done in a mirror image of the Trinity. First, God and man must work together. This is the reason for the Eucharist. It places the Christ in a person's heart motivating in love back to the Father, back to the original plan of creation. Man then freely out of love is motivated to put his will in accordance with the divine will, so they work together. The term for this is synergy. The third leg of our image is that of the community, the Body of Christ to which we are joined in the Eucharist.

Love of God and love of man are inseparable. (I Jn 4:20) As St. Antony of Egypt points out: "From our neighbor is life and from our neighbor is death. If we win our neighbor, we win God, but if we cause our neighbor to stumble we sin against Christ."[45] We must be joined with our neighbor and with God. The three must become one, a divine *imago*. The Eucharist, as it is seen in the Divine Liturgy, joins us to our neighbor, the eucharist joins us to our neighbor and to Christ. When we are joined with Christ we become divine, and we can make our neighbor divine as well.

This potency to act comes from a three-fold origin, 1) The source of all, the Father, 2) the eucharist which puts the act of love in our heart; 3) the image of God within us.[46]

Man then finds his fulfillment in being what he was created to be and this should fill his life with joy.[47] Christ in his heart in the eucharist leads him in synergy towards the paradise dreamed of at creation, recapitulation.

I would like to note that this theology is obvious in the east, but it is not absent from the west. Hippolytus of Rome wrote:

> You, who, living on this earth, have known the heavenly King, you will be the familiar friend of God and co-heir with Christ, being no more subject to the desires of the passions nor to maladies. For you have become God *(gegonas gar theoi)*. All the trials you have endured being man, God has sent to you because you are man: in return, all the goods that are natural to God, God has promised to give you, when engendered to immortality, you will be deified *(hotan theopoiethes athanatos gennetheis)*. By obeying His holy precepts, by rendering yourself good by the imitation of His goodness, you will be like Him, honoured by Him. For God is not poor, He who has made you God also in view of His glory.[48]

In an attempt to synthesize henosis, theosis and eucharist, it is convenient to look at the Council of Florence which said, "The effect of this sacrament which it works in the soul of a worthy recipient is the union of man to Christ. . . . Every effect which material food and drink produce regarding bodily life—sustaining, increasing, repairing, delighting—this sacrament produces regarding our spiritual life."[49] "Union of man to Christ" is henosis, and "repairing" is recapitulation, while increasing can be considered to be Theosis, since it is the increasing of divine life and grace within us.

Morse

For in the Eucharist as in any sacrament, we encounter Christ. When we encounter Christ we encounter God. When God joins himself with us we have the potential for theosis and grace, uncreated energies. The East differs from the west on how it looks upon the graces involved. Sacramental grace is then a personal communion with God, while sanctifying grace is the relationship between us and God.[50] The relationship between God and man is that they share the same nature. (2 Pt 1:4) This is different from the west where these two graces are seen as the same.

After the "Body" of Christ in the Eucharist is no more, the person of Christ still remains.[51] Yes, it is Christ who remains. St. Paul does not hesitate to say that we are Christ's members and spiritually incorporated into him. Every increase of grace in us is an increase in this "incorporation." "It is not you who change me into yourself, it is I who change you into myself." Through eucharistic communion, Christ constantly assimilates us more and more to himself, makes it actual. We might almost say that he grows in us, perfects and completes himself in us. Christ is present in us so that we can and should become "two-natured," our created nature is joined to the uncreated grace, divinity, adapted to each member.[53] We can become in reality what we were only in potential by our image.

NOTES

1. Schanz, John. *The Sacraments of Life and Worship.* (Bruce: Milwaukee: 1966). p. 200.

2. Gn 31:54; Ex. 12:5; 14:23; 25:20; 18:12.
3. Grelot, Pierre. "God's Presence and Man's Communion with Him in the Old Testament." *The Breaking of the Bread.* Concilium 40. (Paulist: NY: 1969). p. 13.
4. Isaiah 55:1-3. Cf. Grelot. p. 21.
5. Jeremias, Joachim. *The Eucharistic Words of Jesus.* (S.C.M.: London: 1966). p. 232.
6. Cf. Jungmann, Josef. *The Early Liturgy: To the Time of Gregory the Great.* (Univ. of Notre Dame: 1959). p. 33. and Lietzmann, H. *Messe und Herrenmahl.* (Bonn: 1926).
7. de Montcheuil. *La signification exhatologigue du repas eucharistique.* (R.S.R.: 1936). p. 5f.

140

8. Schmemann, Alexander. *For the Life of the World: Sacraments and Ortho-doxy.* (St. Vladimir: Tuckahoe: 1973). p. 123.

9. Moloney, Raymond. "The Early Eucharist: An Hypothesis of Development." *Irish Theological Quarterly.* 45/78/3. p. 170f.

10. Lussier, Ernest. *LIving the Eucharistic Mystery.* (Alba House: NY: 1975). p. 182-3.

11. *Didache.* 9.

12. *Adv. Haer.* 5:2-3.

13. *On the Mysteries.* 46.

14. *On Adoration.* 68.

15. *Cat. Or.* 37 (P.G. 45, 93)

16. Schillebeeckx, E. *The Eucharist.* (Sheed & Ward: NY: 68) p. 127.

17. Dubay, Thomas. *God Dwells Within Us.* (Dimension: Denville: 1971). p. 122.

18. *1st Apology.* 66.

19. Cf. Wainwright, Geoffrey. *Eucharist and Eschatology.* (Oxford: NY: 1981). p. 49f.

20. Danielou, Jean. *The Bible and the Liturgy.* (Notre Dame: 1966). p. 139.

21. Schmemann, Alexander. "Liturgical Spirituality of the Sacraments." *John XXIII Lectures.* vol. 2. (1969), p. 25.

22. As found in Yarnold, Edward. *The Awe-Inspiring Rites of Initiation.* (St. Paul: Slough 1971). p. 85.

23. Monk of the Eastern Church. *Orthodox Spirituality.* (S.P.C.L.: London: 1974). p. 22.

24. Lussier. p. 182.

26. *Orthodox Spirituality.* p. 83.

27. Dubay. p. 125.

25. *Of Cain and Abel.* 1.5.

28. Cf. Nicholas, Marie-Joseph. *What is the Eucharist?.* (Hawthorn: NY: 1960). p. 82-3.

29. Monk of Marmion Abbey. *Becoming Christ.* (Dimension: Denville: 1980) p. 30-1.

30. As found in Yarnold. p. 212.

31 As found in Lossky, Vladimir. *The Mystical Theology of the Eastern Church.* (St. Vladimir: Tuckahoe: 1976). p. 181.

32. Bouyer, Louis. *The Spirituality of the New Testament and the Fathers.* (Des-clee: Pais: 1960). p. 416.

33. *Hier. Eccl.* 1.4.

34. Gleason, R. W. *Grace.* (Sheed & Ward: NY: 1962). p. 225f.

35. Ware, Timothy. *The Orthodox Church.* (Penguin: NY: 1969). p. 224-225.

36. Ibid. p. 237.

37. Ibid.

38. Lossky. p. 87.

39. *Ad. Haer.* V. Praef.

40. *Ad Adelphium.*
41. Cf. Ryk, Marta. "The Holy Spirit's Role in the Deification of Man According to Contemporary Orthodox Theology." *Diakonia.* 10/75/2. p. 109-130.
42. I Cor. 6:19
43. Maloney, George. *The Breath of the Mystic.* (Dimension: Denville: 1974). p. 117.
44. Gleason. p. 226.
45. *Apophthegmata.* 9.
46. Cf. Burghardt, Walter. *The Image of God in Man according to Cyril of Alexandria.* (CUA: Washington: 1957). p. 3f.
47. Schmemann. p. 24.
48. *Philosophoumena.* 10:34.
49. As found in Dubay.
50. *Orthodox Spirituality.* p. 180.
51. Nicolas. p. 84.
52. Ibid. p. 85.
53. Lossky. p. 182.

THE THEOLOGICAL ANTHROPOLOGY OF THE BYZANTINE RITES OF CHRISTIAN INITIATION

by Rev. Myron Tataryn

Rev. Myron Tataryn is a priest of the Ukrainian Catholic eparchy of Toronto, Canada.

The Eastern Church's rites of Christian initiation make a powerful but often misunderstood statement about the human person. All too often, the maintenance of the exorcisms, the triple immersions and the churching are seen as magical ceremonies and signs of the acceptance by the East of a myth-filled, dualistic world. The contention of this paper will be that in fact the anthropology which subsumes these rites is wholistic and entirely congruent with a contemporary anthropology. In fact, a further contention will be that the rites of baptism, chrismation and first eucharist express a deep sensitivity to the sanctification of humanity wrought in the world and not beyond it or outside it. The resultant theology is one within which the natural and supernatural are inextricably complementary and not separate.

The method by which we hope to test our contention is twofold. Firstly, we will proceed with a study of the initiation rites themselves. We will study these rites under three categories: the first will be the image and likeness theology recognized by the person and presented in the prayers; secondly, the communitarian aspect involved in the "new" person and thirdly, the capacity for the person to participate in a synergic relationship with the divinity. The second part of our study will involve testing our insights for their compatibility with historical tradition. In order to maintain brevity we will refer to a single theologian from the period of the Fathers, the 14th century and the contemporary period. All in all, we hope that our thesis will be justified and serve to enhance our understanding of the Eastern rites of Christian initiation.

Eastern theological anthropology is well-known for being

rooted in an image and likeness theology first mentioned in Genesis 1:26 but developed primarily in Irenaeus (*Adversus Haereses,* IV, ch. 38). This theology is clearly referred to in the first priestly prayer after the triple exorcisms. We hear:

> O Lord and Master, who created man in thine own likeness, and bestowed upon him the power of life eternal.[1]

Herein we hear a reminder of the Eastern Church's teaching of what it means to be human: it means to be created in some way as to resemble the divinity and to strive to increase that resemblance during our life. In other words, to be human is to be God-like and to be able to increase that likeness. This concept helps us understand more fully a number of the other prayers. Specifically, let us look at the initial prayer of the priest during the reception into the catechumenate. Here we see reference to the person caught in-between two realities and deciding for God:

> I lay my hand upon thy servant, (name), who has been found worthy to flee unto thy Holy Name, and to take refuge under the shelter of thy wings. Remove . . . delusion, and fill him/her with the faith, hope and love . . . that he/she may know that thou art the only true God . . .[2]

Therefore, the person already (prior to baptism) has a consciousness of the true, the good and the divine and it is this consciousness which brings the person to seek "refuge" and to "know" God. We can easily say that this consciousness is the image of the divine because it is that which enables the person to grow in their understanding and knowledge of God. It is the achievement and deepening of this understanding and knowledge which constitutes growth in the likeness of God.

Let us return to the first prayer which we mentioned. In this prayer we can see what constitutes the likeness talked about. Firstly, it involves freedom from "the enemy"; an enemy who from the prayers of exorcism we recognize as bringing death, fear, deceit, impurity and alienation. But then it also involves accepting salvation, a salvation made historic (and thus part of the world) in the incarnation of Christ. The prayer goes on to explain how this is all done. In symbolic language, the prayer speaks of three necessary elements: understanding, discernment and reason. It is by the proper use of these human faculties that the human person is enabled to accept salvation (fulfillment), and is freed from the negative conditions brought by the "enemy" (which we equally recognize as a part of our human condition). All in all, we recognize that to grow in likeness is to grow as a person, for who among us does not recognize the value of understanding, good judgment and reason. Further, which of these qualities are extrinsic to our experience as intelligent and conscious human beings?

Now let us go on to a further how: how is all this attained in this ceremony? We go on therefore, to the prayers of the blessing of the water. In the latter part of this prayer the water (proclaimed as water of redemption and salvation) is the agent by which the person is "renewed after the image of him who created him/her."[3] This very worldly element, this universal symbol of life and death is now made an agent of transformation, an agent of regeneration. In this water, many elements coalesce: first we recognize water as a symbol for life and death, secondly, we recognize it as an agent of cleansing and renewal and thirdly, we recognize it in its function as a symbol of life and death as a reminder of the historic event of the death and resurrection of Christ. It seems then that we can learn in this that growth in this likeness is somehow bound to all three of these elements: it is a recognition of the need to participate fully in life (and so pen-ultimately die), it is a recognition of the need for cleansing and renewal (something very analogous to the self-correcting process of learning) and finally, it is to recognize a value in human history and specifically in the history of the person of Jesus Christ.

Flowing out of this third element is our second category and that is human community. Although a very significant element in growth in the likeness it will be treated separately here. Throughout the rites of initiation the communitarian aspects of the human person are constantly underscored. The very setting of the rites is communal: the Church with the faith community gathered in prayer. The first words of the priest are a call for communal prayer: "Let us pray to the Lord." The initiate is brought to the service by sponsors and this in itself creates community. But even more clearly, the prayers throughout the ceremony emphasize community. The very first prayer in the rite clearly states that one of the goals of this ceremony is to unite this person to a community: "unite him/her to the flock of thine inheritance."[4] As we continue we recognize that this person is coming to participate in a community which is not only here and now, but is historic: it has its origin in the past and membership in the past, present and future. In other words, the human person finds a bond not just with the here and now but is able to transcend the immediate in order to find commonality across time and space. This is strongly reinforced by the readings of the ceremony of chrismation (Romans 6:3-11 and Matthew 26:16-20). In these readings we can recognize the foundation of the community: it lies in a real historic event (Christ's death and resurrection), it recognizes a common experience (life and death, salvation and sin) and it establishes a common mission (proclamation of the teachings of Christ). It is in this community, now established, that we gain sanctification; after the illumination granted in baptism. Clearly, the lesson in this section is that to be a human person and to grow in personhood involves recognition of and membership in a human community. We have then progressed in our view of the person, for, to our original point of the need for reason, understanding and good judgment, we now add the need to be in a community. This involves shared history, shared experience and shared mission. All these elements are made most explicit in the ceremony of Chrismation.

Finally, we turn to the third element: a synergic relationship with the divinity. Although we recognize examples of this in the ceremonies of baptism and chrismation it is expressed most clearly in the third ceremony: the communal celebration of the eucharist. Initially in the prayers of baptism we see this synergic relationship expressed in the human action allowing God to act. In the opening prayer the person's action of fleeing to God allows God to now save him/her. The triple prayers of exorcism are fulfilled with the human action of renunciating Satan. In the chrismation prayer the sanctification is truly a gift of God but still it awaits the human action: "that he/she may please thee in every deed and word, and may be a child and heir of thy heavenly kingdom."[5] But clearly the apex of the synergic relationship is expressed in the Divine Liturgy. It is here that the human and divine intertwine, the historic and the eschaton meet and ultimately the human person is transfigured and divinized. The eucharist fulfills the rites of initiation because in it we have the fullest expression of humanity: unity with the divinity through synergic action.

Let us now turn to the teaching of tradition and see whether the three elements of an anthropology are in fact recognized in this tradition. In the mystagogical catecheses of St. Cyril of Jerusalem we can recognize three significant elements. Firstly St. Cyril speaks of baptism as illumination.[6] It is an experience of coming from darkness into light: although we have eyes we are unable to see. Secondly, there is a strong emphasis on the anamnetic function of the initiatory rites: we recall what Christ has done for us. It is through this anamnesis that we can grow in recognition of how we can become like Christ—imitators of Christ. Finally, the third element emphasized is that of the gift of the Holy Spirit. In all three of these elements we see a certain harmony with our analysis above. Illumination is very much the initial step of growth in the likeness. It is when the person is able to be reasonable, understanding and judicial that the person can truly make decisions and grow in the likeness. Furthermore, being able to recall a past action anamnetically entails recognition of another beyond the self; it entails recognition of an historic community. Finally, the third element of the Holy Spirit's self-gift is clearly an invitation to the synergic relationship. After all, a gift implies the ability to receive. In other words, God's self-gift is a most profound statement about humanity: it means that we are able to receive the transcendent. The ultimate potential of the human person is an openness to the ultimately transcendent.

In Nicholas Cabasilas (Byzantine theologian exact dates uncertain, active 1345-65) we see a similar understanding of the anthropological implications of the initiatory rites. For Cabasilas baptism is the image of Christ's resurrection and it is in this new resurrection that our human nature is restored.[7] Cabasilas proclaims:

> ... "New birth" and "new creation" mean nothing else then that those who are born and created have been born previously and have lost their original form, but now return to it by a second birth.[8]

Baptism is certainly an illumination not only in terms of the faculties of reasoning, but also, for Cabasilas it is a direct perception of God.[9] This latter element is probably a result of Cabasilas' concord with the Palamite theology of a direct vision of the divine light. Further the synergic elements by which we are united to the divine is also evident in Cabasilas. In discussing the eucharist he sets aside an entire section "With regard to the co-operation required of us" (IV, 11, b). It is the eucharist that for Cabasilas demands the greatest human preparation, since it is in the eucharist that we receive the greatest gift—the incarnate divinity. However, it seems that because of Cabasilas' emphasis on Christ, the communitarian aspect of the initiatory rites is not very evident. The approach of this Byzantine theologian stresses the person-Christ relationship above all else and so unfortunately the intersubjective aspects are not evident at all.

The contemporary Orthodox theologian Alexander Schmemann is the one who most clearly supports our analysis of the initiatory rites. For Schmemann baptism is first and foremost a first step in a new life: "Baptism is above all the restoration of man precisely as wholeness, the reconciliation of the soul and body."[10] Baptism (restoration of the image) is thus a recognition of the true meaning of human wholeness. As a result, it implies the harmonization of the psychological, the physical and the spiritual in the person. According to Lonergan this wholeness can only be achieved through attentiveness to the transcendental precepts which govern our process of human knowing.[11] Secondly, if we move to the communitarian aspect we recognize this most strongly in the three titles most often associated with chrismation: King, Priest and Prophet. All three of these titles imply of necessity a community—chrismation calls the person to live in harmony with others. It is in and through this life of community, a life in relationship that we are brought to its fullest expression: the eucharistic banquet. It is the eucharist which expresses the bond of the human and the divine. It is "the sacrament which fulfills the Church as presence and the gift in 'this world' of the Kingdom of God."[12] For Schmemann baptism especially, but as we have seen the other two sacraments also, are

> the sacrament of regeneration, as re-creation, as the personal Pascha and the personal Pentecost of man, as the integration into the *laos,* the people of God, as the "passage" from an old into a new life and finally as an epiphany of the Kingdom of God.[13]

Although in our analysis we have for the sake of clarity tended to isolate the three elements of our anthropology to one of the three sacraments they in fact are found in some degree in each of the three.

We conclude by returning to our hypothesis that in the Byzantine initiatory rites we have developed an anthropology wholly compatible with a modern view of the human person. We have seen that this anthropology contains three elements. Fundamentally, an image and likeness theology signifying the possibility in the human person to understand right and wrong, discern good from evil and act reasonably. This first element relates to the interior functioning of the human person and has perhaps its clearest formulation in the transcendental precepts outlined by Bernard Lonergan. Secondly, we have the need for attention to human intersubjectivity. The initiatory rites call the human person to recognize and develop human community. Finally, we have the third element—synergic relationship with God which is fulfilled ultimately in human divinisation. This third element is a recognition of the openness of the human to the ultimately transcendent—to the wholly beyond.

Clearly this anthropology is one which is in harmony with contemporary thought and needs to be studied more clearly and more precisely than this cursory study allows.

NOTES

1. *Baptism,* Introduction by Fr. P. Lazor (New York: Orthodox Church in America, 1972), p. 28.
2. *Baptism,* p. 32.
3. *Baptism,* p. 52.
4. *Baptism,* p. 33.
5. *Baptism,* p. 59.
6. *St. Cyril of Jerusalem's Lectures on the Christian Sacraments: The Protocatechesis and the Five Mystagogical Catecheses,* ed. F. L. Cross (London: SPCK, 1978), p. 40.
7. Nicholas Cabasilas, *The Life in Christ* (Crestwood, N.Y.: St. Vladimir's Seminary Press, 1974), p. 81—II, 10.
8. Cabasilas, p. 67—II, 2.
9. Cabasilas, p. 99—II, 21.
10. Alexander Schmemann, *For the Life of the World: Sacraments and Orthodoxy* (Crestwood, N.Y.: St. Vladimir's Seminary Press, 1974), p. 53.
11. Bernard Lonergan, *Method in Theology* (New York: Seabury Press, 1979), p. 11 and p. 53.
12. Schmemann, p. 115.
13. Schmemann, p. 10.

COMMENT

CONTEMPORARY ESSAYS IN ORTHODOX TRADITION AND LIFE

by *Robert Slesinski, Ph.D.*

Father Slesinski, a priest of the Byzantine rite diocese of Passaic, received his doctorate in philosophy from the Gregorian University. At present he is pastor of St. Nicholas of Myra Byzantine Catholic Church, Yonkers, N.Y.

For both the serious student and devoted enthusiast of the Eastern Christian scene, the publishing efforts of St. Vladimir's Seminary Press, one of the few publishing houses regularly offering new titles and both new and reprinted translations of classical works by the Greek Fathers of the Church, win unqualified approval, and merit a truly justified esteem. Among other titles, this past year has yielded two important collections of essays and addresses, Father John Meyendorff's *The Byzantine Legacy in the Orthodox Church* and Father Thomas Hopko's *All the Fulness of God.* In these essays, their respective authors not only treat aspects of venerable Orthodox tradition, but, more importantly, focus attention on this tradition's applicability to the changed conditions of today's world, suggesting, at the same time, the need for a fresh and critical review of it in order to secure it from the related dangers of ossification and irrelevance.

These essays equally deserve extended consideration from another point of view. Ecumenically speaking, they are of unquestionable value insofar as they afford privileged glimpses into the soul of contemporary Orthodox life through the eyes of two of its foremost theologians. Only by sufficiently understanding the Orthodox on *their* terms can one expect a profitable, ecumenical meeting of minds. On this score, it is especially important to note both the overt and implied criticisms of Orthodox thought and praxis offered by Fathers Meyendorff and Hopko, themselves. Paradoxically, it is precisely a sympathetic understanding of sectarian vulnerabilities that permits the ecumenical movement to capitalize on its true strengths. Ecumenical *rapprochement* is not fostered by the arrogant casting of aspersions by one Church upon another. It is rather only the mutual confiding and discussion of internal difficulties as well as common aspirations for the future that one can really hope for the sorely needed ecclesial healing without which the unfortunate misunderstandings and wounds of the past can only continue to fester.

THE BYZANTINE LEGACY IN THE ORTHODOX CHURCH

Fr. Meyendorff introduces us to the mind of contemporary Orthodoxy by showing its strict dependence on the heritage bequeathed it by Byzantium. He does not thereby insinuate that it was Byzantium that determined the forms of Orthodoxy. Quite to the contrary, he explicitly asserts (p. 9) the opposite. His only concern is to underscore the *consistency* of tradition in Orthodoxy. To learn valuable lessons for today one must return to historical sources in order to ensure a truly faithful adherence to original value and inspiration and not a merely mechanical and outward observance of forms.

Part I of his collection, entitled simply **The Byzantine Church,** offers an important compendium, notable both for its scope and incisiveness, regarding the essential make-up and ethos of the Church in the Byzantine world and beyond, especially as typified by the "Great Church" of Constantinople. This essay is also noteworthy in that it places the central points of dispute between the East and West on the nature and role of authority in the Church into proper, historical perspective. Noting how in the West, particularly after the Gregorian reform of the eleventh century, doctrinal authority was concentrated in the person of the pope, he observes how in the East no comparable evolution of understanding is verified. Indeed, he affirms (p. 30) "the East never considered that truth could be formally secured by any particular person or institution, and saw no seat of authority above the conciliar process, involving the bishops but also requiring a popular consensus."

Part II bears the heading, **Church and State,** and consists of two essays devoted largely to a discussion of political structures. Its primary value lies in its elucidation of the true meaning of the Byzantine ideal of a "symphony" between the Empire and the Church over and against all unfortunate caricatures connoted in the concept of "caesaropapism." As Fr. Meyendorff points out, the Byzantines never considered the emperor to be a divine being, but only as the representative and messenger of Christ, the one and only King. Analyzing the personality and imperial rule of Justinian, who, to his mind, best incarnates the Byzantine ideal of emperor, he notes (p. 49) how in Justinian's view there is no place at all for the Church as a society all to itself, but only for a society of the faithful, which is, at once, Empire and Church, and which is therefore conjointly administered by the emperor and the patriarch of Constantinople according to divine design. Fr. Meyendorff, of course, rightfully questions the theological legitimacy of Justinian's stance, pointedly asking (p. 8): "could the empire really be identified with the Kingdom of God?" He poignantly notes in conclusion (p. 64) not only did Justinian's dream of a universal empire based upon a single faith prove unworkable, but also that the problems of religious faith, themselves were proven to be irreducible to the legal structure of the state, as evidenced in the bitter struggles between the Chalcedonians and the Monophysites, whose division Justinian sought without lasting success to heal.

Various aspects of Byzantine culture are afforded treatment in the three essays comprising Part III of Fr. Meyendorff's book. The first considers a relatively infrequently treated topic, namely, the encounter between **Byzantium and Islam** in the sphere of religion. Two general observations of definite import were gleaned from this essay. The first concerns the mutual impenetrability of Byzantine and Islamic cultures, which gave rise only to most unfortunate polemics, possibly only slightly modified in the iconoclastic movement, which was, of itself more sensitive to Islamic objections to depictions of the divinity. It would seem that so much of the intractable, mutual misunderstanding was based solely on ignorance, fear, and prejudice. Another consequence of this impenetrability, as Fr. Meyendorff notes, is that the Byzantines were constantly kept on the defensive. "Islam," he writes (p. 114), "not only

153

obliged the Christians to live in a tiny enclosed world which concentrated on liturgical cult, it also made them feel that such an existence was a normal one." That this defensiveness has effected certain circles of Orthodoxy to this day, particularly as sometimes manifested in a persistent, even inexorable, conservatism, is important to bear in mind in ecumenical encounters with the Orthodox.

The second essay of this section also deserves explicit mention. Its title, *The Liturgy: A Lead to the Mind of Byzantium* speaks for itself, but its point needs to be brought home. The liturgy was (and is) the central focus of the Byzantine religious experience and outlook. Not only was it an expression of the life of Byzantium, it also gave cohesiveness to the remnants of the empire after Islamic domination, and was the chief sustenance for the missionary efforts among the Slavs. The liturgy is of such importance to the understanding of Byzantium and its legacy that it should not be the concern of professional liturgists and theologians alone, but also, as Fr. Meyendorff stresses, should become that of all historians of Byzantine civilization and its own peculiar art, literature, and political and social thought.

Part IV of Fr. Meyendorff's collection is devoted to a consideration of two representative issues of Orthodox theology, the doctrine of the *Holy Spirit* and *Hesychasm.* His selection is most apt, since both serve as central points of reference in Orthodox theological reflection. They both also relate to integral aspects of Orthodox religious experience.

As to the former, we find that the Godhead in the East has characteristically been known in the living experience of the three Divine Persons from which their essential unity among themselves has been affirmed. The personal character of the Spirit has thus been taken for granted in the East. Indeed, as Fr. Meyendorff remarks (p. 156), the prayer, "O Heavenly King," which opens every Byzantine liturgical office and rite, is addressed to the Spirit. In the Byzantine consciousness, it is precisely life in the Spirit that allows for the engrafting of the Christian into God, thus effecting his deification or *theosis.* In this perspective, sanctification is viewed as a personal communion with God, for which reason, in the eyes of the East, saints also serve as authentic witnesses of truth in addition to the magisterium of episcopal ministry. The charismatic leadership of holy men and women accordingly plays an important role in the Eastern Church. But the *charismata* of the holy do not supplant the exercise of episcopal authority; they only complement it. The Holy Spirit or Comforter not only seals the just in their holiness, but also imbues the full Body of the Church, under the caring tutelage of the hierarchy. Thus, for the East, all authentic pneumatology, as Fr. Meyendorff notes in conclusion (p. 165), must provide both a trinitarian and an ecclesial framework for properly understanding the "gifts of the Spirit," which otherwise become mere vagaries of passing fad.

One of Orthodoxy's most characteristic—and controversial—doctrines is the subject of Fr. Meyendorff's second theological essay, which offers a synoptic account of hesychasm and the life and teaching of its chief architect and proponent, St. Gregory Palamas (1296-1359). The central theme of this essay is a defense of hesychasm's one basic truth, namely, that "the living God is accessible to personal experience because He shared His own life with humanity (p. 167)." Palamas' profound conviction of this truth steered all his treatises dealing with the subject of hesychasm, and animates all his attempts to rebut the arguments of hesychasm's chief opponent, Barlaam the Calabrian, who even accused the hesychasts of Messalianism for their claim of a real and conscious experience of God. The chief merit of Fr. Meyendorff's elaboration lies in his isolation of the true problem—that of theological method. Barlaam, basing himself on the Aristotelian view that all human cognition is based in sense perception, favored a *mediate* knowledge of God through creation, while Palamas sought to vindicate man's capabilities for a more immediate, *experimental* knowledge of God. It was in the working out of the nature and properties of this experiential knowledge that led Palamas to make his classic, essence-energies distinction that permitted him to maintain God's absolute transcendence, hence unknowability, in his essence and, at the same time, uphold God's immanence in the world of concrete experience through his energies.

In the final part of his collection, Fr. Meyendorff, turns his attention to the problem of authority and ecclesial structure. In his first essay in this section, *St. Basil, the Church, and Charismatic Leadership,* he reiterates some of the points previously made in his chapter on the Holy Spirit regarding the presence in Byzantine Christianity of a certain confluence of institutional, hierarchical authority and charismatic or spiritual leadership in the Church. The whole issue is certainly a crucial one in ecumenical dialogue, for the resolution of many issues rests on the way in which the nature, role, and range of authority in the Church are conceived. The point of view of the East, as related by Fr. Meyendorff, is a positive contribution to this dialogue.

Fr. Meyendorff's next essay, *Ecclesiastical Regionalism: Structures of Communion or Cover for Separatism?,* is also of direct relevance for ecumenism, even though it limits itself as such to a peculiarly Orthodox dilemma: the traditional value of regionalism, which is given its fullest, canonical expression in autocephaly, often seems to be merely a pretext for the promotion of nationalism. Fr. Meyendorff forthrightly deplores this situation labeling it the "metamorphosis of regionalism into nationalism" (p. 229) and suggesting that it is nothing but a perfect description of that process giving rise to the heresy of "phyletism" as defined by the Council of 1872 held in Constantinople. What Fr. Meyendorff bemoans along with this council is the divisiveness wrecked upon the universal Orthodox Church by unilateral, unbridled nationalism effectively rendering the essential, confederated fellowship of Orthodoxy in true catholicity a mere formality. While Fr. Meyendorff most adeptly locates the crux of the matter for ecclesiology in the adoption of proper, determinant criteria for genuine regionalism, he is much less expansive on *what* these might actually be. But he is certainly both objective and searching when he boldly asserts that Orthodox must confront this internal matter squarely *before* any worthwhile dialogue with Rome on the question of authority and primacy in the Universal Church can be initiated.

In this regard, Fr. Meyendorff is to be commended for isolating the most critical issue for ecumenical discussion: the theological issue of the role of the Holy Spirit in history, specifically in the guidance of the growth and differentiation of the concept of authority in the Church. In critical fashion, Fr. Meyendorff poses (p.

230)—without answering*—the crucial question whether the Holy Spirit may not have guided the Roman Church in the evolvement of its historical consciousness of its peculiar authority as a legitimate response to the concrete demands of its history. Continued efforts to settle this question will also do much to unravel and explicate the antinomy of universalism and localism in the Church.

Fr. Meyendorff's final essay can, in a certain sense, be considered a variation on this same theme. Entitled *The Ecumenical Patriarchate, Yesterday and Today,* it poses the question of the role of the Patriarchate of Constantinople at the helm of universal Orthodoxy. Scolding his fellow Orthodox for their uncritically negativistic view toward the papacy, which stands out before *all* Christians as a symbol for world Christian witness, Fr. Meyendorff further chides them for not putting forth credible alternatives. However the Orthodox may ultimately conceive the role of the Ecumenical Patriarchate in their own future Church, we may only hope that attending this internal issue for Orthodoxy will also be a deepening of consciousness and respect for the mission of the Roman Pontiff in the Universal Christian Church.

ALL THE FULNESS OF GOD

Fr. Hopko's title is a reference to Ephesians 3:19 ("that you may be filled with all the fulness of God"). As its author notes (p. 7), all the essays contained therein "witness to the conviction that human beings are made, together with everything that exists, to be filled with all the fulness of God." As is the case with Fr. Meyendorff's collection, the essays also span a wide range of topics, all currently effecting contemporary Orthodoxy with some urgency.

Noting (p. 15) that it has become characteristic in our time to deny that the term *knowledge* can be applied in any real sense to our consciousness of God, Fr. Hopko in his essay explores the contrary affirmation of Orthodoxy that not only can God be known by human beings but, indeed, knowing God is the real purpose of life

---

*In his following essay, Fr. Meyendorff does indeed state that he does not believe that the Roman primacy ever enjoyed an indelible character. Furthermore, he adds (p. 244): "It was *conditioned* by the pope's doctrinal orthodoxy and was not the source of that orthodoxy."

itself. He writes (p. 14): "the Orthodox Church proclaims that God is not only to be believed in, worshipped, loved and served; He is also to be *known.*"

In fashioning a response to *how* Orthodoxy conceives this knowledge to be possible, Fr. Hopko places his reflection (without labeling it as such though) within the context of the traditional Slavophile theory of integral knowledge, which holds that man's cognition is not the product of one faculty alone, namely the mind, but is also that of his heart and will. In his discussion, it becomes evident that this is also a biblical and patristic teaching. That knowledge in its fullest sense is the work of the *whole* person is an illuminating truth to which one can readily lend assent. This truth aptly justifies the scriptural insight that "the pure of heart shall see God" (Mt 5:8), an affirmation implying the need for proper volitional and emotive effort supportive of the mind's sheer intellectual perspicacity in order that God truly be known.

But we would not agree with everything that Fr. Hopko has to say on the subject. Specifically, when he says (p. 17) that the way to the knowledge of God is not by reasoning, but rather by faith, repentence, purity of heart and poverty of spirit, and love and adoration, not only do we think he mistakenly conceives the true role of reasoning in this process, but also seems guilty of inconsistency in citing passages both from the Fathers (cf., e.g., p. 14) and Sacred Scripture (cf., e.g., his quotation of Rm 1:18-21, 28 on p. 20) in which appeals are made to an, at least, implicit reasoning process in order to justify our knowledge of God. Reasoning alone, of course, can never give us full access to the Divine Reality, which necessarily transcends both fallen and redeemed human nature. Philosophically speaking, however, it does enable us to affirm the existence of God as the transcendental condition of the possibility of all our determinate knowledges having ultimate meaning and justification and of our faith having more than just irrational, fideistic value. Nonetheless, Fr. Hopko is correct in his observation that rational "proofs" of the existence of God alone cannot sustain that state of *conviction* arising from a truly *experiential* knowledge of God, the sole access to which is given by faith, purity of heart, poverty of spirit, etc.

Fr. Hopko is also incisive—and clearly once again in the line of the tradition of integral knowledge—in drawing out the deepest implications of the view that a true knowledge of God entails spiritual communion and not just communication. And thus conceived, it must, as Fr. Hopko stresses, take place *in the Church,* in which all, he adds (p. 31), are necessarily "members one of another" (Eph 4:25). For this reason, the Church truly becomes the "key issue of our time" (p. 41), a thought, which resonates the message of Fr. Pavel Florensky as found in his now classic work, *The Pillar and Foundation of Truth,* published in 1914 prior to the Revolution of 1917 in a period well-known as a time of serious, spiritual reawakening for many of the Russian intelligentsia. Fr. Hopko rightfully sees the need for an analogous renewal of spirit in our own times. He writes (p. 35): "There is an urgent need today for Christians to rediscover the Church. There is a critical need to go beyond all the rhetoric about theologies and traditions, beyond all claims about the contributions and enrichments of the many sects and denominations, and to discover again the reality of the 'household of God, which is the Church of the living God, the pillar and bulwark of the truth' (1 Tim. 3:15)."

The truth about the Church is indeed central to the Orthodox vision of God and man. If "God became man that men might become Gods," as St. Athanasius said, then we cannot avoid the question about the Church. God's redemptive activity through his Son and the resultant *theosis* and, therefore, salvation of human beings upon their cooperation with divine grace are themselves intelligible realities only within the larger context of the Church. Thus, Fr. George Florovsky's maxim, *"Salvation is the Church,"* to which Fr. Hopko appeals (p. 30), not only poignantly captures the most basic soteriological insight of Orthodoxy, but also serves as the net conclusion of both venerable and contemporary Orthodox, *theocentric* anthropological reflection. Our only point of disagreement with Frs. Florovsky and Hopko is their labelling this maxim a "tautology"; it is rather, more profoundly, a real *plenitude of synthesis.*

Fr. Hopko's next essay fills a void frequently encountered in Orthodox theological literature. It treats the Bible and its meaning and role in the Orthodox Church. At the very outset of his study, he states (p. 49) the fundamental, guiding principle of all Orthodox thought on the Bible, namely that the "Bible is the book of the Church," and, accordingly, is "not a thing-in-itself which can be isolated from its organic context within the church community, in which and for which and from which it exists." More positively stated, the Bible has "its proper meaning only within the life and experience of the people of God." The Bible is also the Revealed Word of God, and it is through it that the Church teaches that one can encounter God. Because it is a mode of divine revelation, it is truly the Word of God. And yet it is also a human word, because it was written by human beings according to divine design and election. To clarify this antinomy, Fr. Hopko appeals to the formulation of Chalcedon to intimate "how the divine and the human can be united together and permeate each other and yet each remain essentially what it is in itself" (p. 56). Specifically in the instance of the Bible, "the divine Word becomes truly human without ceasing to be divine. And the human words become by the grace of the Spirit the Word of God without ceasing to be human" (p. 58). Thus the Bible, in analogy with the Incarnate Son of God himself, is truly a *theandric* reality.

It is, indeed, through it that God manifests himself to human persons so that they may respond and enter into a covenant relationship with him. As Fr. Hopko forcibly notes (p. 60), "the deepest meaning of the Bible lies not merely in what it tells about God, but in how it yields true knowledge of God by bringing man into loving communion with Him." But this knowledge, it bears repeating, is always gained within the context of the Church and her worship and in line with her interpretation and understanding of the Bible. Such a conception of Biblical exegesis Fr. Hopko labels (p. 68) "spiritual" or "churchly exegesis," and to his mind it is the only really relevant type of exegesis for the believing Christian.

The next five essays in Fr. Hopko's book all have definite ecumenical value and import. The first of these is entitled *Catholicity and Ecumenism,* and in it Fr. Hopko remarks (pp. 91f) how the Orthodox Church is necessarily "catholic" by nature, since "the Church . . . is the fulness of Him who fills all in all" (Eph 1:23). This existential reality of the Church's catholicity—be it in the Orthodox Church of Fr. Hopko or any true Church—should never be obscured or minimalized by acceptance of, or resignation, to various denominationalist or sectarian positions (as he calls them), which foster restrictive localism at the expense of true universalism, and, more gravely, in practice, if not in word, deny that there is One Lord of all in One Body.

Fr. Hopko's next essay considers the question of the "Uniate" or Eastern Catholic Churches. For the moment, we shall prescind from a treatment of it, only to return to it shortly to give it closer scrutiny.

In the brief, yet careful study that follows, he delves into the frequently misunderstood and neglected topic of *Infant Communion.* Fr. Hopko takes great care to explain the Eastern point of view vis-à-vis the practices of other denominations, limpidly setting forth the East's organic understanding of the sacraments as participations in the great Mysteries of the Christian dispensation.** Since baptism is a personal participation in Christ's death and resurrection and chrismation a personal experience of Pentecost, itself the constitutive moment of the Church, it is only natural that the full incorporation into the Church, which comes with one's personal pentecost, allow also for the possibility of sharing the full fruits of ecclesial membership, namely, the partaking of the Holy Mysteries, i.e. Holy Communion. For this reason, if infants are to be baptized, not only should they be chrismated (confirmed), but also communed. Otherwise—at least in the eyes of the East—the unitary process of Christian initiation is unexplainably fragmented. Fortunately, the theological profundity of this traditional Byzantine, pastoral point of view is now receiving a new hearing by theologians and liturgists, as indicated by the sympathetic, ecumenical studies found in both Roman Catholic and even Protestant literature.

The concluding two reflections of Fr. Hopko deal with Orthodoxy's place in contemporary American society. While the first one, *Orthodox Christianity and the American Spirit,* chides

---

**For another detailed discussion of this point, cf. our own "Infant Communion: A Pastoral Note" in *Diakonia,* XIV (1979), 128-37.

Orthodox who uncritically adopt the "common faith" of Americans, the best of American secular wisdom, which holds that religion is merely a private affair with no bearing or competence in the public sphere, the second, bearing the title, **Witness and Service in Orthodox Christian Life,** openly challenges those Orthodox Christians—here Fr. Hopko would have had no trouble in generalizing his criticism to many, if not the majority, of Christians—who have not rendered the degree of social witness entailed by their faith's mission to the *whole* world. If Orthodox renew their efforts in this regard, however, it should not be at the price of surrendering to the American, secularist prejudice as manifested in the discredited and vacuous "common faith" of Americans. Their contribution rather should be felt as that of *believing* Orthodox. And this view does not connote sectarian fanaticism, but only the type of public stance that should be that of *all* believing Christians. Fr. Hopko's hope is that the Christian life "will be neither the peacefully-coexisting conglomeration of relativistic individual and corporate opinions, nor the crusading confrontations of self-righteous and closed-minded sectarians, but the free and gracious life of spiritual communion and conflict revealed to the world in Christ who offers 'all the fulness of God' to those who seek Him" (p. 161). He is not alone in his hope.

REFLECTIONS ON EASTERN RITE CATHOLICISM

As a contribution to ecumenical dialogue, this essay by Fr. Hopko bears separate and more extended consideration. In one sense, considering its primarily negative outlook, this particular essay, first published in 1968 in *Diakonia* (III, 3, 1968), could well have been omitted from the present collection, or, at least, been reworked and given a more positive cast. The only updating seems to be the passing reference (cf. p. 120) to Pope John Paul II. On the other hand, its re-issuance indicates that the deeply set suspicions of the Orthodox toward all attempts of Unia have in no way abated. It is also clear that there is still a need for a truly understanding and irenic dialogue over this sensitive matter before the Orthodox apprehensiveness towards it can begin to dissipate.

Fr. Hopko begins by briefly stating the common Orthodox

attitude on the question of "Uniatism." His summary (p. 116) includes the following points: (1) unfaithfulness to Orthodoxy, (2) betrayal by Rome, and (3) inward impotency to retain and cultivate authentic self-identity. Of these objections, the first two we would—with certain serious reservations—be willing to concede. Obviously, by professing a Catholic identity, the "Uniates" have left the visible Orthodox fold. But whether in its inward depths this move truly constitutes infidelity is another question. At any rate, no *conversion* was ever involved, but only the conscious desire to profess publicly existent, internal bonds of faith and ecclesial solidarity. Similar caution must also be expressed regarding the accusation that Rome has failed to live up to its promises. One can readily admit that there has been a regrettable discrepancy—it is not necessary to delve into the well-known, historical particulars—between the highly laudatory, Roman magisterial theory concerning the equal dignity of the Eastern Churches, and the decretal exercise of the authority rendered possible by this theory, which, in practice, has, at times, bespoken both condescension and the alleged superiority of the Roman Church. Empathy, nonetheless, must still be shown those Catholics, both in officialdom and in the ranks, who have espoused (and, regrettably, some still do!) these misguided and outright erroneous views. One must never forget that there were truly complex theological and especially psychological reasons underlying and conditioning these unfortunate attitudes. These, in turn, seemingly could not but provoke the host of ill-advised, canonical and sacramental, administrative decisions abhorred by so many Eastern Catholics. One must remember that the "Uniate movement" arose more or less simultaneously with the counter-Reformation movement within the Roman Church. The legitimate preoccupation of the post-Tridentine Church with combating Protestantism and the avoidance of its excesses within the Catholic fold almost inevitably gave rise to the doctrine of *integralism*, the categories of which only naturally suggest strict uniformity as the exclusive model of ecclesial unity. That the Eastern Catholic Churches were made to suffer needlessly on its account is without a doubt the most tragic by-product of the integralist point of view. In sum, all these factors considered, the charges of apostasy and betrayal both seem to be unduly severe and unilateral assessments of a much more problematic ecclesial situation.

But it is with Fr. Hopko's third accusation that one really enters into the heart of the contemporary debate. Indeed, it particularly has real relevance for the one who professes a belief in the legitimacy and value of Eastern Rite Catholicism. Granted that the Catholic Church is not the monolithic institution it used to be, still, if the inner mutation of Eastern Churches according to Latin structures is a necessary, and not merely accidental, consequence of union with Rome, then all discussions about real unity not reducible to uniformity are only moot issues, as Fr. Hopko, himself suggests.

It is precisely at this juncture that we come to the heart of Fr. Hopko's misgivings about "Uniatism," and it is here, to his great merit, that he manages to formulate the crucial question of the whole debate. "Can the Eastern Rite Christian find," he queries (p. 120), "in his church the full possibility of coming to the knowledge of the truth in the most perfect communion with the living God through Christ in the Spirit in the Church?" Or, transposing this question into negative terms, he asks *(ibid.)*: "are there not formal and essential obstacles which belong to the official spirit and truth of Uniatism which, if pursued to the end, will inevitably lead to a deformed and imperfect experience of the Christian faith?" His question thus inexorably posed, how does he answer it? A close examination of what remains to his text only reveals that he manages to skirt the whole issue now that he has so succinctly formulated it. Thus our respectful challenge to Fr. Hopko: Let us seek together a plausible response to this question.

Most perceptively, Fr. Hopko admits that in the present world situation in general, and in the Christian world in particular, the former, time-honored distinctions between the East and West are gradually becoming less sharp, and may even now be deprived of any genuinely real meaning. Indeed, he bluntly asks (p. 121) whether the terms, "Eastern" and "Western" have any real significance at all in the souls of men? In this perspective, is there any sense at all to the proposal that the Eastern Rite Churches serve as a "bridge" between the East and the West? As for Fr. Hopko, he, himself remarks (p. 123): ". . . in such a situation, where the significations of the East and West are being emptied of their meaning in theory and in fact, the very idea of the Eastern Rite as 'bridge' or as 'obstacle' becomes proportionately devoid of serious application." In other words, is not the need for "Uniate" Churches thus obviated?

Fr. Hopko, himself gives (pp. 123f) an affirmative response to this question:

> In our opinion, therefore, the only conclusion can be that, given the continued growing together of the entire Christian world, with increased mutual borrowings and progressive disregard and disinterest in one's own past as something valuable in itself, Eastern Rite Catholicism as a particular institution will be really negligible.

But, it must be objected, his conclusion in no way necessarily follows from his premise. Nor need his ancillary conclusion (p. 124) obtain either, namely, that the "Uniates will be lost in the stream of events because the questions of cultures and customs and rituals and traditions and jurisdictions and authorities will be simply not interesting." If the point is, indeed, compelling in the instance of "Uniates," it will be so only because it equally will bespeak the analogous conditions of both Roman Catholics and Orthodox. Furthermore, when Fr. Hopko adds *(ibid.)* that in the present situation of ever-expanding Christian horizons, the only real question that soon will need to be asked is: "'What do you think of Christ, whose son is He?'", it does not follow, short of becoming disincarnate, that the subordinate issues of ecclesial tradition will, of their own accord, fall into harmonious place. And thus, it is simply utopian to imply that the *experience* of Eastern Rite Catholics will not have any significant bearing in that process of growth in the understanding of the faith, which will help foster a truly united response, in full symphony, to the admittedly primary question: "What do you think of Christ, whose son is He?"

Granted that the sometimes wearisome preoccupation of Eastern Rite Catholics for ritual and cultural purity and formal authority is not a consideration of the first importance as such, the explicit concern for them is also not, as Fr. Hopko stresses (p. 125) a "vain striving, a striving after the wind." They only reflect a heart-felt conviction that a definitive reconciliation not only is possible, based upon a mutual and respectful acceptance of the differing *forms* of expression of a common faith *experience,* but, more radically, that such an experience is already *shared,* making the continued division between Orthodox and Catholics woefully unnecessary. Ritual integrity has never been the primary motivation in the mission of Eastern Rite Catholicism; it has rather been the Eastern Catholic's sometimes impugned, faith experience that there indeed *are* one Lord, one baptism, and one faith that has been his real wellspring of sustenance throughout decades of suspicion and mistrust.

And, of course, no Eastern Rite Church has ever remained "inwardly untouched," as Fr. Hopko notes (p. 126). Nor should they have been! Fr. Hopko is simply unrealistic in his expectations on this matter. No Christian Church should ever remain completely untouched by the others. Nor should a dislike for syncretism discourage or prohibit a tasteful commingling of Rites, if circumstances counsel it. Even less does such a blend imply that strange anomaly of "Eastern Rite *Roman* Catholicism" of which Fr. Hopko, himself speaks (p. 134) in his article on infant communion.

As a priest serving a Byzantine Rite parish, this reviewer himself was once edified by the frank comment of a parishioner, of equally mixed Roman-Byzantine/Orthodox background, who stated his need of many years previous to reconcile himself to the co-existence of statues and icons in his home in order to maintain the familial peace and harmony expected of any true Christian. Had he not had an experience of the One Lord and Savior, the One God and Father of us all?

Ironically, Fr. Hopko would not disagree with us. As he, himself concludes his reflection, he notes (p. 127) that the great hope of true Christian unity lies not in the "so-called 'purification' of the Eastern Rites or in any privileged 'autonomy' or 'independence' for 'Oriental churches' which accept some sort of Vatican connection," but rather "in the common discovery of one faith, one Lord, one baptism, one God and Father of us all." And curiously, he adds that the "situation at present seems capable of feeding that hope more than the centuries of union councils and decrees." But those marks of the present era which he lists that do indicate the realization of

Christian unity in our time, are only analogous to those that coun-
seled the development of Eastern Rite Catholicism in the first place.
Indeed, the state of affairs that to Fr. Hopko seems to obviate the
need for Eastern Rite Catholicism in our day only gave rise to
it—along with other factors—in years gone by.

To conclude our analysis to Fr. Hopko's reflection, we would
like to express our firm agreement with him on his choice of pre-
mises. We would only disagree on the conclusions to be drawn from
them. Thus to respond to his own initial set of questions, we would
affirmatively answer the first one concerning the possibility of the
Eastern Rite Catholic finding the true faith and Lord in his Church,
and respond with an emphatic negative to the second one implying a
necessary deformity of Christian experience in Eastern Rite
Catholicism.

To sum up our observations concerning these latest in Orthodox essays, we again express our appreciation to their authors,
Fathers John Meyendorff and Thomas Hopko, for making the
fruits of their scholarship more widely accessible, and acknowledge
our debt to them. They have rendered an educational and forma-
tional service that extends well beyond Orthodoxy, and we can only
hope that their studies receive a wide and sympathetic audience.
And if we have indicated a divergent estimation of the "Uniate"
question as offered by Fr. Hopko, it is only because we think we
share and cherish a common experience and vision of the Christian
faith.

PURPOSE, SCOPE AND METHOD OF THE DIALOGUE BETWEEN THE ORIENTAL ORTHODOX AND ROMAN CATHOLIC CHURCHES

The following statement was prepared and approved, as a guide for their work, by the members of the joint commission for dialogue between the Oriental Orthodox (non-Chalcedonian) and Roman Catholic Churches in the United States.

Introduction

The Oriental Orthodox and Roman Catholic Church share in the same Spirit, the Incarnate Son and the Father through saving faith. For this profound reason our churches have much to contribute to one another from the spiritual treasures which they derive from their holy traditions. The responsibility to open channels of communication which may serve to facilitate this spiritual exchange derives from the Gospel command given to all Christians to love one another both in word and act after the example of the Father who "gave His only Son" (Jn 3:16) and Jesus Christ who "loved his own . . . to the end" (Jn 13:1). To share our lives with one another, ourselves and our spiritual and material riches, in the cause of strengthening the faith of those who are in Christ, this is the only adequate response to the one who calls us to "love one another as I have loved you" (Jn 15:12).

It is in this spirit that we begin our dialogue. We recognize that the church is called to be the community of those who live a common life like the Trinity; a world-wide community in which no single member or local church is foreign to any other member or local church but rather one in which each have their measure to receive and give. Hence this dialogue aims at contributing to the establishment of the conditions which make possible the visible manifestation of the love which already exists between our churches. The goal of the dialogue, therefore, is to work toward the realization of a mutually acceptable profession of faith which embraces the whole range of the life of faith and a corresponding communion of ecclesial life which respects the freedom of Christian communities in all things which do not pertain to the essentials of the life of faith.

As a step in this direction this dialogue intends to promote 1) mutual growth of our churches through the reciprocal sharing in doctrinal and spiritual traditions as well as liturgical life; 2) cooperation in their common responsibility for the furthering of the unity of all Christian churches and the preaching of the Gospel to the world; 3) unity of action between the churches in responding to the various problems and questions which arise in the numerous Christian communities and the world at large.

In brief, since the main concern of this dialogue is the fostering of conditions which favor full communion between our churches, it has both a practical and doctrinal orientation. It looks to ways of deepening unity in Christ through both concrete acts of love and theological discourse. For the dialogue in love which nourishes unity includes both word and act.

I. Dialogue in Love—Practice of Love

As a consequence of the estrangement between our churches which took place many centuries ago, and the accompanying insensitivity toward the ecclesial status of one another, both churches have attempted to proselytize individual members and particular local communities of the other church. Such activity has been especially detrimental to the stability and growth of certain Oriental Orthodox churches. Moreover this practice is contrary to the demands of an ecclesial dialogue in love which assumes that both churches, as churches of Jesus Christ, should live in a communion which respects the ancient traditions and styles of life of one another.

The long history of estrangement, intensified by well-meaning though at times self-serving ecclesiastical activity, must come to an end. This can only be achieved through a dialogue in love which leads us to seek new ways to remedy the effects of actions of the past which do not harmonize with the new experience of the ecclesial status of both churches; concrete acts of love, especially when costly, demonstrate that both churches recognize one another as true churches of Jesus Christ deserving of the right to life, respect, and support. Therefore the daily life of the two churches commands our attention. We intend to consider what practical means of cooperation are possible in the social, moral, and political spheres; whatever means can be employed to afford the faithful of both churches the experience of their oneness in Christ. Beyond this the dialogue intends to respond, where possible, to the needs of other churches, especially in lending support to heal schisms wherever they exist. Finally it accepts the task of developing practical suggestions for ways by which the two churches can effectively cooperate in common witness to the Gospel before the world.

II. Dialogue in Love—Theological Dialogue

Theological dialogue is a requirement of the dialogue in love. For one of the aspects of the dialogue in love is the mutual commitment to seek the truth together in order that both partners may live more fully in the truth.

This mutual commitment to seek the truth is not based on speculation concerning the possibility of arriving at knowledge of God and the mystery of the human person. It is grounded on the conviction that divine revelation of these mysteries has occurred in history, reaching its fullness in Jesus Christ; that the Holy Spirit was sent to make this revelation accessible to all people until Christ's Second Coming by sustaining and nourishing the church of Jesus Christ in the truth.

The church is the place where God's word always remains present and affirmed. But it is the "tent of the word of God" and, in its proper activity, sacrament of the truth: the way which gives all people access to God. This means that the dogmas, by which the church formulates its experience of the mystery of God acting in history, function as introduction into the mystery of faith: God the Father who reveals self in Jesus Christ through the Spirit. The totality of the mystery cannot be expressed adequately in any of its dogmatic formulations. Dogmatic statements are historically conditioned expressions of the divine truth. Although affirming divine truth, they remain in need of continual reinterpretation so as to be made more fully intelligible in changing historical and cultural contexts. Therefore Christian theology has the task of continually re-reading dogmas in the light of Scripture and Tradition as well as the newer insights and expressions of the life of the church. Just as in the early undivided church, so now the written Scripture is accepted as our norm of faith in the context of the living church which interprets it in the light of the past and present ecclesial self-understanding. Since we believe that our churches possess the Spirit of God, we are also convinced that our mutual witness of faith in dialogue can contribute to a deeper knowledge of the divine truth.

However this dialogue can only be carried on in the atmosphere of love. For charity furnishes the insight that the Spirit dwells in each of us and that we can only expect the other to accept the witness of faith insofar as he is convinced in faith, and this means in the Spirit. This conviction of the presence of the Spirit in the partners in dialogue, grounded on the experience of mutual love, determines the style of the dialogue. It is only properly conducted in a non-authoritarian, open and discoursive way. Since there exists in all truly Christian dialogue the presence of Christ in the Spirit the partners should maintain an openness to receive from one another the liberating power of the Gospel and share with one another their personal understanding of the truth as the Spirit reveals it.

1. Conditions for Theological Dialogue

The word *dialogue* means a speaking together with the accent on togetherness. By its very nature it aims at broadening areas of mutual agreement. Consequently it is imperative that the partners be open to one another *(reciprocity)* and ready to learn from one another and change ways of thinking and acting when the truth discovered through the conversations leads in a new direction *(mutual commitment)*. In brief, dialogue aims at mutual enrichment and unity at as many levels as possible: communication of self to the other on all levels (human relations, truth, practical collaboration).

What is demanded of dialogue in general must be found in this dialogue between members of the churches of the Oriental and Roman Catholic traditions. The partners of the dialogue should consider each other as "equals." This means that 1) each should view the other as faithful to the Gospel according to his lights; 2) each should regard the other as possessing the Spirit and so capable of teaching or learning in speaking or listening through the Spirit; 3) both partners share in common the fundamental spiritual goods which are the mutual possession of both churches.

2. Differences Between Churches and Theological Dialogue

While the principle of equality between the members of the dialogue must be affirmed, the churches which they represent have developed characteristic theological approaches to the Christian economy of salvation to which correspond differences in the organizational form of church life, liturgy and spirituality. Many of the differences are clearly superficial but others are more substantial. Since we reject that form of doctrinal indifferentism which claims that all positions held by the churches of Jesus Christ have equal validity, the partners of this dialogue are committed to seek together resolutions to those seemingly incompatible divergencies in content and expression of doctrine and the variations in the concrete style of ecclesiastical life which derive from them.

In this connection we recognize the existence of a hierarchy of truths within the diverse formulations of Christian faith. The partners of this dialogue, therefore, accept the task of articulating this hierarchy of truths and explaining the relationships between these truths as they see it. Here the problem of language inevitably arises. Since it is a question of establishing communication between two theological traditions, it is clear that the partners must submit the language they use to critical study. To avoid traveling along parallel lines wherein the same thing is meant by different words, the mutual effort must be made to discover the mentality, the genius of the culture, the philosophical outlook, traditions and styles of life which lie behind what is being said.

3. Methodology of the Theological Dialogue

The method of the dialogue involves several elements which can operate in succession or concurrently: 1) exchange of ideas where each one presents a point of view on the subject under discussion; 2) comparison of ideas to bring out differences and likenesses; 3) further investigation of shared positions; 4) highlighting aspects of the subject previously unnoticed which lead to further investigation.

Concerning the subjects of the dialogue a distinction must be made between 1) truths confessed in common; 2) truths obscured in one community but developed in the other; 3) religious insights even in areas of divergence (e.g., particular forms of worship; emphasis on certain aspects of Christian life).

Once this distinction is established, the following approach is recommended:

1) Begin the dialogue with elements which unite the two churches. This will foster a positive spirit which, it may be hoped, will prevail when dealing with areas of disagreement. Moreover it will afford a yardstick by which the partners are in a better position to evaluate differences and make changes where necessary.

2) An exposition of doctrine should be made in a constructive way which avoids defining by opposition, a process which leads to overstressing or hardening of certain positions.

3) In the discussion of doctrine an effort should be made in the direction of a constructive synthesis which attempts to take into account the whole scope of revealed truth.

4) In examining theological problems which exist between the Oriental Orthodox and Roman Catholic Churches, the historical developments since the New Testament and Patristic periods, as well as the current theological developments and ecclesial practices in both churches, should not be ignored. Also account should be taken of the fact that the Spirit of the church is both a conserving and renewing Spirit.

5) In examining problems which exist between the two churches a distinction should be made between divergences which are compatible and those which are seemingly incompatible with reference to full communion.

4. Themes of the Theological Dialogue

The ways by which our knowledge of Christian faith come to us are varied. They parallel the ways in which we reach out for and allow reality to enter our consciousness. The world is laid open to us by our moods and feelings (sentient field), by our interaction with people (interpersonal field), by the personal and social stories which serve to organize our feelings and to form a sense of continuous identity (narrative field). In these primal fields the knowing subject is not consciously detached from the object known. However the subject may consciously detach himself from the object to be known and seek to know the real in itself (theoretic field).

Corresponding to these ways by which knowledge of the faith is obtained and expressed, theologians distinguish between two types of theological statement: 1) those which derive more directly from the experience of the life of faith and are expressed in self-involving language; 2) those which attempt to formulate in a scientific way the doctrinal content of the more direct expressions of faith. Since the liturgy, with its self-involving language, is the best expression of the ecclesial experience of the life of faith, it provides an indispensable source of the dogmatic statements of the official church and the theological reflection of scientific theology. Thus it is fitting that this dialogue begin with the study of the liturgies of the two churches and, in particular with the sacraments of the church.

Moreover since the Mystery of Christ, in which all Christian theology is grounded, is expressed and realized in the church most perfectly through the celebration of the Divine Liturgy, the Eucharist, it seems most appropriate that this dialogue begin with and continually return to this theme. For the value of particular theological positions and practices of the church can be measured by the harmony they display with the faith expressed in the celebration of the Eucharist.

In the discussions about the Eucharist, or whatever topic is singled out for analysis, the participants are resolved to adopt as a working principle the one which Pope John XXIII formulated in his opening address to the participants of Vatican Council II:

> For the deposit of faith itself, namely the truths contained in our venerable teaching, is one thing; the way of expressing them is another.

There already exists a concrete example of the application of this principle which has brought our churches closer together. The joint statement published by the Syrian Orthodox Patriarch Ignatius Jacoub III and Pope Paul VI at the end of the Patriarch's visit, October 1971, reads in part:

> Pope Paul VI and the Patriarch Mar Ignatius Jacoub III are in agreement that there is no difference in the faith they profess concerning the mystery of the Word of God made flesh and become really man, even if over the centuries difficulties have arisen out of different theological expressions by which this faith was expressed.

This agreement provides us with a solid base for the hope that in "speaking the truth in love" (Eph 4:15a) this dialogue will make a contribution to our further growth together "into him who is the head, into Christ, from whom the whole body, joined and knit together by every joint with which it is supplied, when each part is working properly, makes bodily growth and upbuilds itself in love" (Eph 4:15b-16).

DOCUMENTATION

JOINT INTERNATIONAL COMMISSION FOR THE THEOLOGICAL DIALOGUE BETWEEN THE ROMAN CATHOLIC CHURCH AND THE ORTHODOX CHURCH

SECOND PLENARY SESSION
Munich, 30th June - 6th July, 1982

PRESS RELEASE

From June 30th to July 6th, the International Mixed Commission for Theological dialogue between the Roman Catholic Church and the Orthodox Church held its second plenary session at the Exerzitienhaus Schloss Fürstenried, Munich (Germany).

The Commission established in December 1979, had held its first meeting in May, 1980 at Patmos-Rhodes where it had approved a general plan for this theological dialogue, chosen the first themes for discussion and established its structure for carrying on its work. That meeting accepted as the general method of the commission to start with what both Churches have in common and, by developing this, to touch upon from inside and progressively the points upon which agreement does not yet exist.

The theme of this second plenary session, therefore, was The Mystery of the Church and the Eucharist in the Light of the Mystery of the Holy Trinity. Serving as a basis for discussion was a document which had received ample preparation during the period following the meeting in Rhodes. In fact, three joint subcommissions meeting separately in 1980 and early 1981 at Chevetogne (Belgium), Rome and Beograd had prepared their written reflections and common papers on the theme. A coordinating committee composed of eight Catholics and eight Orthodox met in Venice in May 1981 to bring together the results of this work and prepare a written synthesis for the consideration of the entire commission.

The discussions in Munich centered around questions of the nature of the Eucharist, its expression of the activity of the Holy Trinity in the economy of salvation, the relationship of the Eucharist to the Church and the centrality of the Eucharist for an understanding of communion within the local Church and for communion among the local Churches in the Universal Church. Large areas of agreement were outlined and foundations were laid for further consideration of questions about which there remain differences.

The results of these discussions have been brought together in a document which will be submitted to the Churches for their information and will be published in the near future, as a means of informing the Churches of these deliberations and of soliciting reactions to the work already accomplished.

While considering the theoretical questions connected with Eucharist and the Church, the Commission was conscious of the great significance these questions have for Christian life in the modern world, for communion among peoples and nations and for peace and justice among men. This concern was underlined by the absence of four of its members, prevented from coming to the meeting from Lebanon because of the painful events which are still in course in that war-torn country. A message of prayers and solidarity was sent to them.

The discussions were carried out in an atmosphere of openness and fraternal cooperation. Contributing to this were the spiritual activities which accompanied them. The meeting began on the evening of June 30th with solemn vespers in the Frauendom, presided over by the Bishop of Würzburg Msgr. Paul-Werner Scheele, chairman of the Ecumenical commission of the Bishops' Conference of Germany. On Saturday, July 3rd all assisted at a Solemn Mass presided over by Cardinal John Willebrands at which the Catholic members of the Commission concelebrated. On Sunday, all assisted at the Solemn Liturgy celebrated by Archbishop Stylianos of Australia and the Orthodox clergy. On July 6th, the tenth anniversary of the death of the Ecumenical Patriarch Athenagoras I, a service was held in the chapel of Schloß Fürstenried, during which a commemoration was made of this great contributor to the Orthodox-Catholic Dialogue. This possibility for close familiarity with each others liturgical traditions and spirituality was an important factor in helping all to discuss the central theme of the Eucharist with a spirit of fidelity to ones own tradition joined to a sincere openness to other traditions.

Before closing its meeting, the Commission decided that, in agreement with the plan for theological dialogue approved at Rhodos, the theme of its next meeting will be Faith, Sacraments and Unity. Under this heading, consideration will be given to questions of Faith and Communion in the Sacraments as well as to particular questions connected with the Sacrament of Baptism, Christmation (Confirmation) and the Eucharist and the unity of the Church.

During their stay in Munich, the members of the Commission were the guests of the Archdiocese of Munich and Freising. Every effort was made by the authorities of the archdiocese and their lay and religious collaborators to provide all that was necessary for the efficient working of the sessions and to show a personal attention to each of the participants.

The Commission is particularly grateful for these efforts since they contributed in a significant way towards creating the atmosphere of fraternal openness and trust already mentioned. The Commission is also grateful to the civil authorities of Bavaria for its help and encouragement especially through the reception offered on June 30th.

The next plenary meeting will be held at a place and date which are yet to be decided. It will be proceded by meetings of the subcommissions and coordinating committee, following the procedure which proved so helpful for conducting the present meeting.

In carrying out its work, the Commission was conscious of the responsibility Christians have for divisions among persons and nations. It considers its own deliberations a very positive contribution to the work for reconciliation and peace in the world, and it invites the members of the Churches it represents to aid this work for peace and mutual collaboration by their own prayer, reflection and common activity.

Schloss Fürstenried, July 6, 1982

The following is the text of the document approved by the Commission (translation from the French original)

THE MYSTERY OF THE CHURCH AND OF THE EUCHARIST IN THE LIGHT OF THE MYSTERY OF THE HOLY TRINITY

Faithful to the mandate received at Rhodes, this report touches upon the mystery of the church in only one of its aspects. This aspect, however, is particularly important in the sacramental perspective of our churches, that is, the mystery of the church and of the eucharist in the light of the mystery of the holy Trinity. As a matter of fact the request was made to start with what we have in common and, by developing it, to touch upon from inside and progressively all the points on which we are not in agreement.

In composing this document we intend to show that in doing so we express together a faith which is the continuation of that of the apostles.

This document makes the first step in the effort to fulfill the program of the preparatory commission, approved at the first meeting of the commission for dialogue.

Since there is question of a first step, touching upon the mystery of the church under only one of its aspects, many points are not yet treated here. They will be treated in succeeding steps as has been foreseen in the program mentioned above.

I

1. Christ, Son of God incarnate, dead and risen, is the only one who has conquered sin and death. To speak, therefore, of the sacramental

178

nature of the mystery of Christ is to bring to mind the possibility given to man, and through him, to the whole cosmos, to experience the "new creation," the kingdom of God here and now through material and created realities. This is the mode *(tropos)* in which the unique person and the unique event of Christ exists and operates in history starting from Pentecost and reaching to the Parousia. However, the eternal life which God has given to the world in the event of Christ, his eternal Son, is contained in "earthen vessels." It is still only given as a foretaste, as a pledge.

2. At the Last Supper, Christ stated that he "gave" his body to the disciples for the life of "the many," in the eucharist. In it this gift is made by God to the world, but in sacramental form. From that moment the eucharist exists as the sacrament of Christ himself. It becomes the foretaste of eternal life, the "medicine of immortality," the sign of the kingdom to come. The sacrament of the Christ event thus becomes identical with the sacrament of the holy eucharist, the sacrament which incorporates us fully into Christ.

3. The incarnation of the Son of God, his death and resurrection were realized from the beginning, according to the Father's will, in the Holy Spirit. This Spirit, which proceeds eternally from the Father and manifests himself through the Son, prepared the Christ event and realized it fully in the resurrection. Christ, who is the sacrament *par excellence,* given by the Father for the world, continues to give himself for the many in the Spirit, who alone gives life (Jn. 6). The sacrament of Christ is also a reality which can only exist in the Spirit.

4. The Church and the Eucharist:

a. Although the evangelists in the account of the Supper are silent about the action of the Spirit, he was nonetheless united closer than ever to the incarnate Son for carrying out the Father's work. He is not yet given, received as a person, by the disciples (Jn. 7:39). But when Jesus is glorified then the Spirit himself also pours himself out and manifests himself. The Lord Jesus enters into the glory of the Father and, at the same time, by the pouring out of the Spirit, into his sacramental *tropos* in this world. Pentecost, the completion of the paschal mystery, inaugurates simultaneously the last times. The eucharist and the church, body of the crucified and risen Christ, become the place of the energies of the Holy Spirit.

b. Believers are baptized in the Spirit in the name of the holy Trinity to form one body (cf. 1 Cor. 12:13). When the church celebrates the eucharist it realizes "what it is," the body of Christ (1 Cor. 10:17). By baptism and chrismation (confirmation) the members of Christ are "anointed" by the Spirit, grafted into Christ. But by the eucharist the paschal event opens itself out into church. The church becomes that which it is called to be by baptism and chrismation. By

179

the communion in the body and blood of Christ, the faithful grow in that mystical divinization which makes them dwell in the Son and the Father, through the Spirit.

c. Thus, on the one hand, the church celebrates the eucharist as expression here and now of the heavenly liturgy; but on the other hand, the eucharist builds up the church in the sense that through it the Spirit of the risen Christ fashions the church into the body of Christ. That is why the eucharist is truly the sacrament of the church, at once a sacrament of the total gift the Lord makes of himself to his own and as manifestation and growth of the body of Christ, the church. The pilgrim church celebrates the eucharist on earth until her Lord comes to restore royalty to God the Father so that God may be "all in all." It thus anticipates the judgment of the world and its final transfiguration.

5. The mission of the Spirit remains joined to that of the Son. The celebration of the eucharist reveals the divine energies manifested by the Spirit at work in the body of Christ.

a. The Spirit prepares the coming of Christ by announcing it through the prophets, by directing the history of the chosen people toward him, by causing him to be conceived by the Virgin Mary, by opening up hearts to his word.

b. The Spirit manifests Christ in his work as savior, the Gospel which is he himself. The eucharistic celebration is the *anamnesis* (the memorial): Truly, but sacramentally, the *ephapax* (the "once and for all") is and becomes present. The celebration of the eucharist is *par excellence* the *kairos* (proper time) of the mystery.

c. The Spirit transforms the sacred gifts into the body and blood of Christ *(metabole)* in order to bring about the growth of the body which is the church. In this sense the entire celebration is an *epiclesis,* which becomes more explicit at certain moments. The church is continually in a state of *epiclesis.*

d. The Spirit puts into communion with the body of Christ those who share the same bread and the same cup. Starting from there, the church manifests what it is, the sacrament of the Trinitarian *koinonia,* the "dwelling of God with men" (cf. Fv. 21:4).

The Spirit, by making present what Christ did once for all—the event of the mystery—accomplishes it in all of us. The relation to the mystery, more evident in the eucharist, is found in the other sacraments, all acts of the Spirit. That is why the eucharist is the center of sacramental life.

6. Taken as a whole, the eucharistic celebration makes present the Trinitarian mystery of the church. In it one passes from hearing the word, culminating in the proclamation of the Gospel—the apostolic announcing

of the word made flesh—to the thanksgiving offered to the Father and to the memorial of the sacrifice and to communion in it thanks to the prayer of *epiclesis* uttered in faith. For the *epiclesis* is not merely an invocation for the sacramental transforming of the bread and cup. It is also a prayer for the full effect of the communion of all in the mystery revealed by the Son.

In this way the presence of the Spirit itself is extended by the sharing in the sacrament of the word made flesh to all the body of the church. Without wishing to resolve yet the difficulties which have arisen between the East and the West concerning the relationship between the Son and the Spirit, we can already say together that this Spirit, which proceeds from the Father (Jn. 15:26) as the sole source in the Trinity and which has become the Spirit of our sonship (Rom. 8:15) since he is also the Spirit of the Son (Gal. 4:6), is communicated to us particularly in the eucharist by this Son upon whom he reposes in time and in eternity (Jn. 1:32).

That is why the eucharistic mystery is accomplished in the prayer which joins together the words by which the word made flesh instituted the sacrament and the *epiclesis* in which the church, moved by faith, entreats the Father, through the Son, to send the Spirit so that in the unique offering of the incarnate Son, everything may be consummated in unity. Through the eucharist believers unite themselves to Christ, who offers himself to the Father with them, and they receive the possibility of offering themselves in a spirit of sacrifice to each other, as Christ himself offers himself to the Father for the many, thus giving himself to men.

This consummation in unity brought about by the one inseparable operation of the Son and the Spirit, acting in reference to the Father in his design, is the church in its fullness.

II

1. If one looks at the New Testament one will notice first of all that the church describes a "local" reality. The church exists in history as local church. For a region one speaks more often of churches, in the plural. It is always question of the church of God but in a given place.

Now the church existing in a place is not formed, in a radical sense, by the persons who come together to establish it. There is a "Jerusalem from on high" which "comes down from God," a communion which is at the foundation of the community itself. The church comes into being by a free gift, that of the new creation.

However, it is clear that the church "which is in" a given place manifests itself when it is "assembled." This assembly itself, whose elements and requirements are indicated by the New Testament, is fully such when it is the eucharistic synaxis. When the local church celebrates the eucharist, the event which took place "once and for all" is made present and manifested. In the local church, then, there is neither male nor female, slave nor free, Jew nor Greek. A new unity is communicated which overcomes divisions and restores communion in the one body of Christ. This unity transcends psychological, racial, sociopolitical or cultural unity. It is the "communion of the Holy Spirit" gathering together the scattered children of God. The newness of baptism and of chrismation then bears its fruit. And by the power of the body and blood of the Lord, filled with the Holy Spirit, there is healed that sin which does not cease to assault Christians by raising obstacles to the dynamism of the "life of God in Christ Jesus" received in baptism. This applies also to the sin of division, all of whose forms contradict God's design.

One of the chief texts to remember is 1 Corinthians 10:15-17: one sole bread, one sole cup, one sole body of Christ in the plurality of members. This mystery of the unity in love of many persons constitutes the real newness of the Trinitarian *koinonia* communicated to men in the church through the eucharist. Such is the purpose of Christ's saving work, which is spread abroad in the last times after Pentecost.

This is why the church finds its model, its origin and its purpose in the mystery of God, one in three persons. Further still, the eucharist thus understood in the light of the Trinitarian mystery is the criterion for functioning of the life of the church as a whole. The institutional elements should be nothing but a visible reflection of the reality of the mystery.

2. The unfolding of the eucharistic celebration of the local church shows how the *koinonia* takes shape in the church celebrating the eucharist. In the eucharist celebrated by the local church gathered about the bishop, or the priest in communion with him, the following aspects stand out, interconnected among themselves even if this or that moment of the celebration emphasizes one or another.

The *koinonia* is eschatological. It is the newness which comes in the last times. That is why everything in the eucharist as in the life of the church begins with conversion and reconciliation. The eucharist presupposes repentance *(metanoia)* and confession *(exomologesis),* which find in other circumstances their own sacramental expression. But the eucharist forgives and also heals sins, since it is the sacrament of the divinizing love of the Father, by the Son, in the Holy Spirit.

But this *koinonia* is also kerygmatic. This is evident in the synaxis not only because the celebration "announces" the event of the mystery, but also because it actually realizes it today in the Spirit. This implies the proclamation of the word to the assembly and the response of faith given by all. Thus the communion of the assembly is brought about in the kerygma, and hence unity in faith. Orthodoxy (correct faith) is inherent in the eucharistic *koinonia.* This orthodoxy is expressed most clearly through the proclamation of the symbol of faith which is a summary of the apostolic tradition of which the bishop is the witness in virtue of his succession. Thus the eucharist is inseparably sacrament and word since in it the incarnate Word sanctifies in the Spirit. That is why the entire liturgy and not only the reading of holy scriptutes constitutes a proclamation of the word under the form of doxology and prayer. On the other hand, the word proclaimed is the Word made flesh and become sacramental.

Koinonia is at once ministerial and pneumatological. That is why the eucharist is its manifestation *par excellence*. The entire assembly, each one according to rank, is *leiturgos* of the *koinonia*. While being a gift of the Trinitarian God, *koinonia* is also the response of men. In the faith which comes from the Spirit and the word, these put in practice the vocation and the mission received in baptism: to become living members, in one's proper rank, of the body of Christ.

3. The ministry of the bishop is not merely a tactical or pragmatic function (because a president is necessary) but an organic function. The bishop receives the gift of episcopal grace (1 Tm. 4:14) in the sacrament of consecration effected by bishops who themselves have received this gift, thanks to the existence of an uninterrupted series of episcopal ordinations, beginning from the holy apostles. By the sacrament of ordination the Spirit of the Lord "confers" on the bishop, not juridically as if it were a pure transmission of power, but sacramentally, the authority of servant which the Son received from the Father and which he received in a human way by his acceptance in his passion.

The function of the bishop is closely bound to the eucharistic assembly over which he presides. The eucharistic unity of the local church implies communion between him who presides and the people to whom he delivers the word of salvation and the eucharistic gifts. Further, the minister is also the one who "receives" from his church, which is faithful to tradition, the word he transmits. And the great intercession which he sends up to the Father is simply that of his entire church praying with him. The bishop cannot be separated from his church any more than the church can be separated from its bishop.

The bishop stands at the heart of the local church as minister of the Spirit to discern the charisms and take care that they are exercised in harmony, for the good of all, in faithfulness to the apostolic tradition. He puts himself at the service of the initiatives of the Spirit so that nothing may prevent them from contributing to building up *koinonia*. He is minister of unity, servant of Christ the Lord, whose mission is to "gather into unity the children of God." And because the church is built up by the eucharist, it is he, invested with the grace of priestly ministry, who presides at the latter.

But this presidency must be properly understood. The bishop presides at the offering which is that of his entire community. By consecrating the gifts so that they become the body and blood the community offers, he celebrates not only for it, nor only with it and in it, but through it. He appears then as minister of Christ fashioning the unity of his body and so creating communion through his body. The union of the community with him is first of all of the order of *mysterion* and not primordially of the juridical order. It is that union expressed in the eucharist which is prolonged and given practical expression in the "pastoral" relations of teaching, government and life. The ecclesial community is thus called to be the outline of a human community renewed.

4. There is profound communion between the bishop and the community in which the Spirit gives him responsibility for the church of God. The ancient tradition expressed it happily in the image of marriage. But that communion lies within the communion of the apostolic community. In the ancient tradition (as the *Apostolic Tradition* of Hippolytus proves) the bishop elected by the people—who guarantee his apostolic faith, in conformity with what the local church confesses—receives the ministerial grace of Christ by the Spirit in the prayer of the assembly and by the laying on of hands *(chirotonia)* of the neighboring bishops, witnesses of the faith of their own churches. His charism, coming directly from the Spirit of God, is given him in the apostolicity of his church (linked to the faith of the apostolic community) and in that of the other churches represented by their bishops. Through this his ministry is inserted into the catholicity of the church of God.

Apostolic succession, therefore, means something more than a mere transmission of powers. It is succession in a church which witnesses to the apostolic faith, communion with the other churches which witness to the same apostolic faith. The see *(cathedra)* plays an essential role in inserting the bishop into the heart of ecclesial apostolicity. On the other hand, once ordained, the bishop becomes in his church the guarantor of apostolicity and the one who represents it within the communion of churches. That is why in his church every eucharist can only be celebrated in truth if presided over by him or by a presbyter in communion with him. Mention of him in the anaphora is essential.

Through the ministry of presbyters, charged with presiding over the life and the eucharistic celebration of the communities entrusted to them, those communities grow in communion with all the communities for which the bishop has primary responsibility. In the present situation the diocese itself is a communion of eucharistic communities. One of the essential functions of presbyters is to link these to the eucharist of the bishop and to nourish them with the apostolic faith of which the bishop is the witness and guarantor. They should also take care that Christians, nourished by the body and blood of him who gave his life for his brethren, should be authentic witnesses of fraternal love in the reciprocal sacrifice nourished by the sacrifice of Christ. For, according to the word of the apostles, "if someone sees his brother in need and closes his heart against him, how does God's love abide in him?" The eucharist determines the Christian manner of living the paschal mystery of Christ and the gift of Pentecost. Thanks to it there is a profound transformation of human existence always confronted by temptation and suffering.

III

1. The body of Christ is unique. There exists then only one church of God. The identity of one eucharistic assembly with another comes from the fact that all with the same faith celebrate the same memorial, that all by eating the same bread and sharing in the same cup become the same unique body of Christ into which they have been integrated by the same baptism. If there are many celebrations, there is nevertheless only one mystery celebrated in which all participate. Moreover, when the believer communicates in the Lord's body and blood, he does not receive a part of Christ but the whole Christ.

In the same way, the local church which celebrates the eucharist gathered around its bishop is not a section of the body of Christ. The multiplicity of local synaxes does not divide the church, but rather shows sacramentally its unity. Like the community of the apostles gathered around Christ, each eucharistic assembly is truly the holy church of God, the body of Christ, in communion with the first community of the disciples and with all who throughout the world celebrate and have celebrated the memorial of the Lord. It is also in communion with the assembly of the saints in heaven, which each celebration brings to mind.

2. Far from excluding diversity or plurality, the *koinonia* supposes it and heals the wounds of division, transcending the latter in unity.

Since Christ is one for the many, so in the church which is his body, the one and the many, the universal and local are necessarily simultaneous. Still more radically, because the one and only God is the communion of three persons, the one and only church is a communion of many communities and the local church a communion of persons. The one and unique church finds her identity in the *koinonia* of the churches. Unity and multiplicity appear so linked that one could not exist without the other. It is this relationship constitutive of the church that institutions make visible and, so to speak, "historicize."

3. Since the universal church manifests itself in the synaxis of the local church, two conditions must be fulfilled above all if the local church which celebrates the eucharist is to be truly within the ecclesial communion.

a) First, the identify of the mystery of the church lived by the local church with the mystery of the church lived by the primitive church—catholicity in time—is fundamental. The church is apostolic because it is founded on and continually sustained by the mystery of salvation revealed in Jesus Christ, transmitted in the Spirit by those who were his witnesses, the apostles. Its members will be judged by Christ and the apostles (cf. Lk. 22:30).

b) Today mutual recognition between this local church and the other churches is also of capital importance. Each should recognize in the others through local particularities the identity of the mystery of the church. It is a question of mutual recognition of catholicity as communion in the wholeness of the mystery. This recognition is achieved first of all at the regional level. Communion in the same patriarchate or in some other form of regional unity is first of all a manifestation of the life of the Spirit in the same culture, or in the same historical conditions. It equally implies unity of witness and calls for the exercise of fraternal correction in humility. This communion within the same region should extend itself further in the communion between sister churches.

This mutual recognition, however, is true only under the conditions expressed in the anaphora of St. John Chrysostom and the first Antiochene anaphoras. The first condition is communion in the same kerygma, and so in the same faith. Already contained in baptism this requirement is made explicit in the eucharistic celebration. But it also requires the will for communion in love *(agape)* and in service *(diakonia),* not only in words but in deeds.

Permanence through history and mutual recognition are particularly brought into focus in the eucharistic synaxis by the mention of the saints in the Canon and of the heads of the churches in the dyptichs. Thus it is understood why these latter are signs of catholic unity in eucharistic communion, responsible, each on its own level, for maintaining that communion in the universal harmony of the churches and their common fidelity to the apostolic tradition.

4. We find then among these churches those bonds of communion which the New Testament indicated: communion in faith, hope and love, communion in the sacraments, communion in the diversity of charisms, communion in the reconciliation, communion in the ministry. The agent of this communion is the Spirit of the risen Lord. Through him the church universal, catholic, integrates diversity of plurality, making it one of its own essential elements. This catholicity represents the fulfillment of the prayer of Chapter 17 of the Gospel according to John, taken up in the eucharistic epicleses.

Attachment to the apostolic communion binds all the bishops together, linking the *episkope* of the local churches to the college of the apostles. They too form a college rooted by the Spirit in the "once for all" of the apostolic group, the unique witness to the faith. This means not only that they should be united among themselves by faith, charity, mission, reconciliation, but that they have in common the same responsibility and the same service to the church. Because the one and only church is made present in his local church, each bishop cannot separate the care for his own church from that of the universal church. When, by the sacrament of ordination, he receives the charism of the Spirit for the *episkope* of one local church, his own, by that very fact he receives the charism of the Spirit for the *episkope* of the entire church. In the people of God he exercises it in communion with all the bishops who are here and now in charge of churches and in communion with the living tradition which the bishops of the past have handed on. The presence of bishops from neighboring sees at his episcopal ordination "sacramentalizes" and makes present this communion. It produces a thorough fusion between his solicitude for the local community and his care for the church spread throughout the world. The *episkope* for the universal church is seen to be entrusted by the Spirit to the totality of local bishops in communion with one another. This communion is expressed traditionally through conciliar practice. We shall have to examine further the way it is conceived and realized in the perspective of what we have just explained.

Munich, Schloss Fürstenried, July 6, 1982

BOOKS RECEIVED

CHRISTIANITY AND POLITICS: Catholic and Protestant Perspectives, Carol Friedley Griffith (Ethics and Public Policy Center, Wash., D.C., 1981) pp. 116, $5.00.

THE MAKING OF THE OSTRIH BIBLE, Robert Mathiesen (Ukrainian Research Institute, Harvard Univ., Cambridge, Mass., 1982) pp. 110.

UKRAINIAN CHURCHES, Photographed by William Brumfield (Ukrainian Research Institute, Harvard Univ., Cambridge, Mass., 1982).

AN EARLY SLAVONIC PSALTER FROM RUS', Moshe Altbauer (Ukrainian Research Institute, Harvard Univ., Cambridge, Mass., 1982) pp. 179.

TAUFLITURGIE DES SYRO-MALABARISCHEN RITUS, Francis Chirayath (Augustinus-Verlag Wurzburg, Germany, 1982) pp. 179.

IN ESSENTIALS, UNITY, An Ecumenical Sampler, Edward A. Powers (Friendship Press, N.Y., 1982) pp. 119, $4.95.

CHRISTIAN UNITY: Matrix for Mission, Paul A. Crow Jr. (Friendship Press, N.Y., 1982) pp. 119, $4.95.

COME TO MY PLACE: MEET MY ISLAND FAMILY, Esiteri Kamikamica (Friendship Press, N.Y., 1982) pp. 32, $4.95.

PACIFIC PEOPLE SING OUT STRONG, William L. Coop (Friendship Press, N.Y., 1982) pp. 96, $4.95.

UKRAINIAN CATHOLICS IN AMERICA, Bohdan P. Procko (University Press of America, 1982) pp. 170.

MOLCHANIE, THE SILENCE OF GOD, Catherine De Hueck Doherty (Crossroad, New York, 1982) pp. 100, $8.95.

FAKHRUDDIN 'IRAQI (Divine Flasher), William C. Chittick and Peter Lamborn Wilson (Paulist Press, N.Y., 1982) pp. 178.

JACOPONE DA TODI, Serge and Elizabeth Hughes (Paulist Press, N.Y., 1982) pp. 296.

DIAKONIA

Devoted to promoting a knowledge and understanding
of Eastern Christianity
edited by Rev. John F. Long, S.J.

MANAGING EDITOR
Rev. Richard d. Lee

ORTHODOX ASSOCIATE EDITORS
Dr. Johm E. Rexine
Bohdan Demczuk

CIRCULATION MANAGER
Mrs. Rita Ruggiero

Editorial and Business Correspondence: Manuscripts should be typed double-spaced, with footnotes separate. Authors should retain a carbon copy and enclose return stamps. All manuscripts, subscriptions and correspondence should be sent to the following address: DIAKONIA, John XXIII Center, 2502 Belmont Avenue, Bronx, N.Y. 10458.

Published by the John XXIII Center
2502 Belmont Avenue
Bronx, N.Y. 10458

Subscription price:

USA:	$ 9.00
CANADA and Foreign:	$10.00
Single Numbers:	$ 3.00

DIAKONIA

Published by the John XXIII Center

2502 Belmont Avenue

Bronx, New York 10458

diakonia

DEVOTED TO PROMOTING A KNOWLEDGE AND UNDERSTANDING OF EASTERN CHRISTIANITY

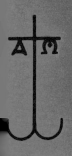

VOLUME XVII
NUMBER 3
1982

DIAKONIA   Volume XVII   Number 3
                              1982

EDITORIAL 189
   SANCTIFICATION AND DEIFICATION
     Eleuterio F. Fortino 192

   THE QUESTION OF INFANT BAPTISM IN THE
   BYZANTINE CATHOLIC CHURCHES OF THE U.S.A.
     Robert Taft, S.J. 201

   ST. BASIL'S COSMOLOGY
     Emmanuel Clapsis 215

   BYZANTINE ART AND THEOLOGY
     Russel Becker, O.F.M. 224

   PROBLEMS IN THE STUDY OF EARLY MONASTICISM
     John Blake More 233

COMMENT
   THE BEGINNING OF THE THEOLOGICAL DIALOGUE
   BETWEEN ORTHODOX AND CATHOLICS
     Metropolitan Chrysostomos of Myra 243

   THE CHRISTIAN TRADITIONS OF LEBANON
     Charles A. Frazee 251

JERUSALEM AND FRATERNITY AMONG HER
   THREE RELIGIONS
     Stephen Bonian, S.J. 265

DOCUMENTATION
   THE VISIT OF HIS HOLINESS PATRIARCH PIMEN
   TO NEW YORK 275

BOOKS RECEIVED 281

DIAKONIA INDEX 283

EDITORIAL

THE CHURCH IS FIRST OF ALL PEOPLE

As is noted elsewhere in this issue, Jerusalem has been at the center of the religious feelings and yearnings of Christians, Jews and Moslems for many centuries. This religious significance for each group has been at the basis of political and military struggles which continue until the present day and which make a mockery of the city's name.

Jerusalem's history is filled with instances of religious intolerance in which the dominating religious group has restricted and even oppressed the other religions. We Christians must recognize the grave responsibilities we have had for this in the past. Most recently, from 1948 to 1967, the Jordanian authorities suppressed the Jewish quarter in East Jerusalem and refused to permit Jews to visit and care for the monuments of their faith there. The government of Israel, on the other hand, has frequently stated its commitment to guaranteeing the existence of the holy places of the various religious communities and of access to them. Up to the present it has fulfilled this commitment.

And yet, developments in and around Jerusalem have become a source of increasing concern to the leaders of the various Christian communities for some time now. Pressure is being exerted by the Israeli government to force Christian teachers and religious leaders to take political stands dictated by that government for reasons of "national security." Some teachers of Bethlehem University are among those expelled from the country for refusing to do so, and there is a strong probability that this policy will be extended to all clergymen and religious who wish to serve the Christian people in the country. The assistant archbishop to the Armenian patriarch of Jerusalem has been denied the renewal of his residence permit despite the requests and protests of the leaders of his own and the other Christian communities.

The stated aim of this policy is to counteract what the government authorities call terrorism. Christians and Moslems in the Holy Land see in it but another step in a process of reducing their influence there and of eventually eliminating their presence.

The sad fact of the last thirty five years is that there has been a steady drain on the Arab community in general and on the Christian community in particular. Church leaders are very deeply concerned about this phenomenon. People whose families have lived in the land for centuries find themselves strangers in their own homeland. Those with intellectual and other talents see little hope for developing them or using them at home. If they go outside for higher education, most often they are refused re-admittance. Permanent emigration seems to be the only solution. Towards this they are encouraged by the Israeli government and public opinion.

For those of us who have a particular concern for the Christian churches of the East—Catholic and Orthodox—this development is an increasingly tragic one. Buildings, no matter how magnificent their exteriors and how sumptuous their decorated interiors, are not, and never will be, the Church. This is as true of the churches of Jerusalem as of the local churches anywhere else in the world. It is living communities which form the People of God, the Church.

Catholic and Orthodox leaders in the Holy Land are seeking to maintain their communities as living entities. In many different ways the Catholic Church contributes to these efforts. As an example, through its sponsorship of Bethlehem University, directed by the Christian Brothers, the Holy See is seeking to contribute to the intellectual and moral formation of an Arab elite in the Holy Land. The university serves the general community; sixty percent of its students are Moslems. It hopes that its graduates will be able to take their rightful place in the political, intellectual and economic life of their homeland. The university also seeks in a particular way to keep the Christian presence alive by forming the religious and lay leaders who will serve all the Christian churches in the Holy Land and be the nuclei of the living Christian communities mentioned above. These efforts, and others like them, are being threatened by the policies of the Israeli government.

It is in the context of these developments that we can legitimately raise the question of the value for the future of any unilateral guarantee of the existence of the Christian holy places and of free access to them. Local Christian communities are already suffering from restrictions upon their life and development. What is to prevent future restrictions—all in the name of "national security" or "the needs of new settlers to recover their 'historic' homeland"—both on the places and on those persons from outside who may be caring for them and serving the Christian people living around them.

History has shown that, in the past, domination of Jerusalem by one religious group has inevitably led to restrictions on the others. For thirty five years the Holy See has insisted that Jerusalem and its surroundings enjoy a special international status protected by international guarantees and safeguards. Recent developments only go to emphasize the need for giving renewed and serious attention to this position of the Vatican.

Our interest in this question here is essentially religious. For centuries, Christian communities of many traditions have found their home in Jerusalem, the birthplace of the Christian Church. Christians from every country and clime have journeyed there as to the source of their Christian faith. Pope Paul VI and the Ecumenical Patriarch Athenagoras I made their pilgrimage to embrace on the Mount of Olives and give a new impetus to the movement for Christian reconciliation. Even the reverence for physical places takes its roots from the realization that they are the memorials to the faith of the living people of God "who are living stones making a spiritual house" (1 Peter 2,5). The growing developments between Christians and Jews in many parts of the world will certainly be affected more by the way our Christian communities are able to maintain themselves in the Holy Land than by our ability to keep open shrines of stone and wood.

For the future, then, Christians who have the privilege of visiting the Holy Land should be assured that they will not merely be wandering through the museum pieces of a past civilization, conducted by disinterested guides of another faith and finding in the grotto of Bethlehem an interesting variant on the monasteries of the Dead Sea. They should be able to be received by their brothers and sisters of the Church of God which is in Jerusalem and, in the union of prayers and sacramental worship, give witness as a people to the saving acts done in that land by Our Lord and Savior Jesus Christ.

J.F.L.

ARTICLES

SANCTIFICATION AND DEIFICATION

by Eleuterio F. Fortino

Msgr. Fortino, an official of the Vatican Secretariat for Promoting Christian Unity, is a priest of the Italo-Albanian Byzantine community of southern Italy. He is rector of the Greek Catholic Church of St. Athanasius in Rome.

"The Lord Jesus Christ will give a new form to this lowly body of ours and remake it according to the pattern of his glorious body, by his power to subject everything to himself."[1] This carries with it the duty to "stand firm in the Lord as you have learned" as well as the necessity for the faithful to forget the past and to push on towards the future towards the goal which is "the prize to which God calls me—life on high in Christ Jesus."[2] This all is to be done not through some utopian flight, but in the heavy experience of daily life, made up of temptation, of death, of suffering "by being formed into the pattern of his death in the hope of arriving at resurrection from the dead."[3] This thought, upon which Paul makes some reflections to the Christians of Philippi based on his personal experience, summarizes an important aspect of the entire Christian experience which is based on these fundamental elements, the vocation, the being drawn by Christ, the being conquered by Him (*katalampten ypo Christou,* as St. Paul puts it), the assuming of His form, being conformed to Him (*symmorphizomenos*) and the being transfigured by Him (*metaschematizei to soma*).

This implies a process, a continuous tension: "it is important that we continue on our course, no matter what stage we have reached."[4] This vision of change is fully taken up by Saint Gregory of Nyssa when he proposes Moses as a type of the person called by God and of the experience of every person who arrives at a knowledge of God and

192

at his own renewal: "No one is ignorant of the fact that every being, subject to change by nature, does not remain identical with itself but continually passes from one condition to another."[5]

Furthermore, according to Saint Gregory, no limit can hem in the perfect life and can halt its progress. Perfection consists in progress. Sanctification, which is nothing other than conformation to Christ, the perfect visible image of God, expresses this mysterious process of transfiguration which the Spirit of God works in every person, transforming him into the image of God.

Human Healing

Saint John Damascene (7th Century), whose thought represents a solid theological and spiritual current which has strongly influenced the development of Christian thought in the east, presents an anthropological vision of extreme interest, even for the present day. He takes off from the biblical data which he keeps proposing under various forms but which make up a fundamental and unchanging basis. Man is "created a rational being, intelligent and free, in the image of God."[6] To follow this nature, therefore, is to live according to God's will and to live according to virtue. Nonetheless, John is very careful not to attribute perfection to a purely human force, because it is God who sustains us in this effort: "without his cooperation and his assistance we are powerless either to will good or to do it."[7] This *synergia,* this human-divine cooperation, guarantees the authentic progress of man who, as a free being, can always not cooperate and also deviate from the vocation to which he is called: "it depends upon ourselves whether we are to persevere in virtue and follow God who invites us into ways of virtue, or to abandon it and thus dwell in wickedness.

When we persevere in what is according to nature, we are in a state of virtue; but, when we abandon what is according to nature, that is to say, virtue, we come to what is contrary to nature and dwell in wickedness."[8] The affirmation of human liberty is therefore fundamental for understanding Christian behavior. The identification of acting according to nature and following virtue and, conversely, of acting contrary to nature and working evil presupposes the biblical conception (*Gen.*1,26) of man created in the image and likeness of

God. It is an anthropological vision which is radically positive despite the creaturely condition of man who is thus subject to many limitations of intellect and will. Consequently, when John Damascene will speak of the divine economy in what regards our salvation and must explain what is the healing work (*kedemonia*) of God in favor of man, he finds himself on the level of ethical correction and therefore of conversion, just as the "fall" of man is put on the level of "disobedience." Man failed to keep the Creator's commandment and was stripped of grace (*charis*), deprived of that familiarity (*parresia*) which he enjoyed with God and was clothed with the roughness of his wretched life . . . and put on death."[9]

Maintaining the parallelelism nature-virtue, Damascene presents conversion as a passing from the devil to God, a changing of tendency and consequently of behavior: "Repentance is a return through discipline and toil from that which is against nature to that which is according to it, from the devil to God."[10]

Nevertheless, he speaks of the necessity that nature be renewed (*anakainisthenai*), joining it immediately with the other necessity "to learn the way of virtue which turns back from corruption and leads to eternal life."[11]

This state of evil, however, is mysterious and more obscure than even reason itself understands. It was necessary for the one who was to effect redemption from sin to be without sin.[12] Man has need of a deeper healing. If this first act is exclusively the work of God who, through Christ, redeems humanity, the rest requires the full participation of man, beginning with a renewal of his understanding of his own alienation from his own "natural" vocation. "Conversion," this intellectual and moral change of direction (*metanoia*), consequently imposes itself as the primary and essential act of sanctification as the process of assimilation to God.

Participation in the Divine Life

"One alone is holy, one alone is Lord, Jesus Christ." This hymn, which is repeated in every eucharistic celebration in the Byzantine Church, keeps in proper view the fact that *holiness is of the nature of God* and that Jesus Christ is true God of true God, as the Creed proclaims. It also underlines the unicity of the nature of the Triune God. The sanctity which is attributed to human beings, to the saints, can only be through participation. St. John Damascene, in speaking of the saints and of the reasons which permit and even require their veneration, applies to them by analogy the titles of "gods, kings and lords" titles which are, above all, due in a unique way to God. "I say that they are gods, kings and lords not by nature, but because they have ruled over and dominated their passions, because they have preserved a truthful likeness to the divine image to which they were made (for the image of a king is also called a king), and because they have freely been united to God and, receiving Him as a dweller within themselves, have through association with him become by grace what He is by nature."[13] In this conception of Damascene there is maintained clearly the necessary distinction between God and deified man, overcoming the permanent temptation of man to put himself in the place of God (*Gen.* 3,5,22, sin of the first parents; *Gen.* 11,4, tower of Babel), the temptation of every paganizing humanism. Nonetheless, the participation in the divine nature and life is real. In the same chapter Damascene quotes various texts of Scripture to show that God dwells in man and transforms him: "I will make my dwelling in them";[14] "Are you not aware that you are the temple of God and the Spirit of God dwells in you?"[15] This all comes from the ancient divine plan which destined men to be in the image of Christ. God the Father "predestined those whom he foreknew to share the image of His Son" true image of the invisible God, "that the Son might be the first born of many brothers."[16]

The process of this transformation comes about by participation in the divine nature through the good will of God. "The divine power of his has freely bestowed on us everything necessary for a life of genuine piety, through knowledge of God himself who called us by his own glory and power; by virtue of them he has bestowed on us the great and precious things he promised, so that through these you who have fled a world corrupted by lust might become sharers of the divine nature."[17]

This participation is realized through faith and by means of sacramental insertion into Christ. Saint John Damascene in the

Orthodox Faith speaks only of two sacraments: baptism and eucharist.

One Baptism

"We confess one baptism unto remission of sins and life everlasting, for baptism shows the death of the Lord. Indeed, through baptism we are buried with the Lord, as the divine Apostle says."[18] The immersion in the water (death of Christ) is a radical event. "Therefore, just as the death of the Lord happened but once, so also must we be baptized only once." And further on: "by the three immersions baptism signifies the three days of the Lord's burial in the tomb."[19] The assimilation to death carries with it the aspect of resurrection to life.

"If the Spirit of him who raised Jesus from the dead dwells in you, then he who raised Christ from the dead will bring your mortal bodies to life also, through his Spirit dwelling in you."[20] Following Saint Paul, Saint John Damascene makes this synthesis: "Since man is twofold, being of body and soul, the purification he gave us is also twofold, through water and the Spirit, with the Spirit renewing in us what is to His image and likeness and the water, by the grace of the Spirit, purifying the body from sin and delivering it from corruption —the water completing the figure of the death and the Spirit producing the guarantee of life."[21] It is not the religious rite which effects this "psychic regeneration" (as Damascene expresses it) as if by some magical operation, but the mysterious action of the Spirit who acts through the rite, because of the redemptive and regenerative work of Christ.

"Becoming like us, He redeemed us from corruption by His own suffering; He made a fountain of forgiveness gush out for us from His sacred and immaculate side, both water unto regeneration and the washing away of sin and corruption, and blood as drink productive of life everlasting."[22] Baptism inserts one into Christ, with whom is formed a "mysterious body," through whom there is communicated life, new life, divine life. "We receive the first fruits of the Holy Spirit through baptism, and this rebirth becomes the beginning of another life for us, a seal, a safeguard and an illumination."[23]

Here we are at the heart of the Christian mystery: the reestablishment of communion between God and man by means of the *incarnation* of God and the *deification* of man.

In the same chapter, Damascene speaks of the anointing received during baptism and which renders one conformed to Christ. He does not distinguish from baptism this "chrismation" which forms part of the entire baptismal event (death, resurrection, conformation to Christ, new life). "Oil (*elaion*) is used at baptism to show our anointing (*chrisin*), making us anointed (*christous*) and proclaiming God's mercy (*eleon*) on us through the Holy Spirit, since the dove had also carried an olive branch to those who had been delivered from the flood."[24] Flood—baptism—purification; oil—olive branch—salvation; anointing which transforms into Christs (anointed ones)—anointed who are conformed to Christ. The thought is brought into focus by means of the theological and mystical concept of incorporation into Christ. At the conclusion of the Byzantine rites of baptism there is sung a verse of the letter of Paul to the Galations which sums up this concept: "All you who have been baptized into Christ have clothed yourselves with him . . . you are all one in Christ Jesus."[25]

In the Eucharist

This process is completed in the Eucharist. Once purified, by participating in the eucharist we are united to the body of the Lord and to His Spirit and become body of Christ. Damascene explains this process by analizing the terms participation and communion. "Participation (*metalepsis*) is spoken of because through it we partake of the divinity of Jesus. Communion (*koinonia*) is also spoken of, and it is truly that, because through it we have communion with Christ and partake of His flesh and of His divinity; we also have communion with and are united to one another. For, since we partake of one bread, we are all become one body of Christ and one blood and members one of another, being of one body with Christ."[26]

Finally, Damascene explains why the bread and the wine of the eucharist are sometimes also called "symbols, antitypes" of future goods and states: "not because they are not really the body and blood of Christ, but because it is through them that we participate in the divinity of Christ now, while then we shall participate through the intellect and by vision alone."[27] Participation in the sacrament is participation in the body of Christ; through it one takes part in the very divinity of Christ.

Such a participation implies an interior purification. Saint John Damascene uses the image of the burning coal, taken from the prophet Isaiah: "Let us approach it with burning desire, and with our hands folded in the form of a cross, let us receive the body of the Crucified one. With eyes, lips, and faces turned toward it let us receive the divine burning coal, so that the fire of the coal may be added to the desire within us to consume our sins and enlighten our hearts, and so that by this communion of the divine fire, we may be set on fire and deified."[28] The element of purification thus reappears. The process of sanctification in man always has these two poles: liberation from sin and assimilation to Christ. The saint is one who has arrived at the condition of "new creature," the living image of Christ. Furthermore, the saint is one who, liberated from the slavery of sin, has arrived at the "full measure" of Christ.

Deified Creature and Ethical Expression

"God is life and light and in Him the saints are in the light and life."[29] This definitive result almost always implies a passing through the darkness and the fear of death. The provisional nature of things, the ambiguities, the oppositions with which daily life is lived establish the context in which there is developed the "new creature," the saint.

The "newness" of the person must be expressed in ethical behavior. This newness, determined by the incorporation into Christ and by the dwelling of the Spirit in the human person, is described by Saint Paul in this way: "The fruit of the Spirit is love, joy, peace, patient endurance, kindness, generosity, faith, mildness and self control";[30] he sums up the whole with the lapidary expression: "Since we live by the Spirit, let us follow the Spirit's lead."[31] In this way to the *image* of God, in which man was created, there is added the *likeness*. A person himself becomes "light and life" for others. The gospel counsel is categoric: "So your light must shine before men so that they may see goodness in your acts and give praise to your heavenly Father."[32]

Concluding Remark

The Saint is one in whom there has been realized the redemption, the deified man. He is therefore the living testimony to the saving work of God who acts and is efficacious. As such the Saint can be proposed as example to imitate and venerate. He is sign of hope because he certifies that every human being can realize his vocation and all of human society can be transformed into a new creation. The Christian community, called to sanctification and deification, already incorporated into Christ, is seed and instrument of this transformation for all humanity.

Romanos the Singer (6th century) in his *kontakion* for the feast of All Saints, sums up this vision in song: "Earth has become heaven. The fiery bodies in the firmament and the martyrs in the body of the Church shine forth and illumine the whole universe so that David can say with us: your flashes of lightning have been reflected on the earth, O you who are rich in mercy."

NOTES

This is a translation of the Italian text which first appeared in *Echi d'Oriente,* Rome, 1982.

1. *Phil.,* 3, 21
2. *Phil.,* 3, 14
3. *Phil.,* 3, 11
4. *Phil.,* 3, 16
5. St. Gregory of Nyssa, *The Life of Moses.*
6. St. John Damascene, *The Orthodox Faith* II, p. 12. Two English editions have been consulted in making this translation: St. John Damascene, *Writings, The Fathers of the Church,* vol. 37 and the *Nicene and Post Nicene Fathers,* second series, vol. 9.
7. *op. cit.,* II, 30
8. *ibid.*
9. *op. cit.,* III, 1
10. *op. cit.,* II, 30
11. *op. cit.,* III, 1
12. *ibid.*
13. *op. cit.,* IV, 15
14. *Lev.* 26, 12

15. 1 Cor., 3, 16
16. *Rom.*, 8, 29
17. *2 Pet.*, 1, 3-4
18. *De Fide Orthodoxa*, IV, 9
19. *ibid.*
20. *Rom.*, 8, 11
21. *op. cit.*, IV, 9
22. *ibid.*
23. *ibid.*
24. *ibid.*
25. *Gal.*, 3, 27-28
26. *op. cit.*, IV, 13
27. *ibid.*
28. *ibid.*
29. *op. cit.*, IV, 15
30. *Gal.*, 5, 22
31. *Gal.*, 5, 27
32. *Mt.*, 5, 16

ON THE QUESTION OF INFANT COMMUNION IN THE BYZANTINE CATHOLIC CHURCHES OF THE U.S.A.

by Robert Taft, S.J.

Father Taft is Ordinary Professor of Oriental Languages and Liturgy at the Pontifical Oriental Institute, Rome; Visiting Professor of Liturgy at the Graduate School of the University of Notre Dame. He is on the editorial staff of many scholarly journals and is the author of over 50 scholarly publications especially in the area of Byzantine liturgy.

In modern times it has been the constantly reiterated will of the Holy see that Eastern Catholics: 1) avoid Latinization, 2) preserve their own tradition *in its purity,* 3) and return to their tradition where they have departed from it. The Vatican II decree *On the Eastern Churches* reaffirms this:[1]

> 6. All members of the Eastern Churches should be firmly convinced that they can and ought always preserve their own legitimate liturgical rites and ways of life, and that changes are to be introduced only to forward their own organic development. They themselves are to carry out all these prescriptions with the greatest fidelity. They are to aim always at a more perfect knowledge and practice of their rites, *and if they have fallen away due to circumstances of time or persons, they are to strive to return to their ancestral tradition.*

> 12. The holy ecumenical council confirms and approves the ancient discipline concerning the sacraments which exist in the Eastern Churches, and also the ritual observed in their celebration and administration, *and wishes this to be restored* where such a case arises.

In harmony with this unambiguous will of the Church, the commission preparing the new Code of Eastern Canon Law has prepared new legislation (not yet approved) restoring the ancient discipline of infant communion:[2]

The traditional discipline of the Eastern Churches prescribes the communion of newly baptized infants as the completion of initiation . . . The commission has not ignored a problem so important as the communion of neophytes, for which reason it was obliged to reestablish the ancient common discipline by composing a new canon in the following terms: "Sacramental initiation into the Mystery of Salvation is perfected through the reception of the Most Holy Eucharist. Therefore let it be administered as soon as possible after Baptism and Chrismation with the Sacred Myron, according to the discipline proper to each Church."

Such a decree would warm the hearts of western Catholic experts on Christian Initiation, who for some time now have been arguing for the restoration of the integrity of the threefold rite of initiation in the Roman Rite.[3] Unfortunately, proposals of this sort have met with less than enthusiastic acceptance in Byzantine Catholic communities that long ago abandoned in favor of the Latin discipline their ancient tradition of infant communion immediately following baptism and chrismation. The reason usually given for this opposition is that this reform would greatly disturb laity and clergy alike. As usual in such matters, this is only the surface of the problem. The real roots of opposition go much deeper, and involve hidden theological prejudices and questions of group identity which must be attended to if the pastoral issue is ever to be resolved satisfactorily. Let us look at these problems.

1. The Proposed Reform Would Disturb the Faithful:

I think this is a red herring. My own suspicion is that the main reason for opposition to the change has less to do with the laity than with the clergy. Most lay persons will accept legitimate change except when the clergy has failed to prepare them properly. I have made a few discreet inquiries and according to the (admittedly limited) information I have received, there has been no major problem with the faithful in those parishes where the custom of infant communion has been restored. There may have been some complaints, but aren't there always? What would have become of the recent Roman-Rite renewal if every such complaint had brought the process to a halt? Of course some pastors may have been imprudent in restoring traditional discipline without sufficient preparatory catechesis. The solution in such cases is to counsel pastoral prudence in implementing the reform, not its abandonment.

2. The Change could be Disruptive among the Clergy:

So I believe the real issue has little to do with disturbing the consciences of the faithful. It is the clergy who are divided on the question. It is no secret that some clergymen have resisted the liturgical reforms promulgated by the Holy See, and still celebrate the liturgy in a way that bears little resemblance to the Byzantine Rite. On the other hand the reform initiated by the Holy see over forty years ago[4] has made progress especially in recent years. There is now a group of priests and religious who, following the teaching of the Holy See, wish to be both Catholic and Byzantine in spirit, not just in name. They are acquainted with the new Roman recension of the liturgical books, and with the teaching of the Holy See, and are simply trying to obey the clear and express will of the Church regarding fidelity to their liturgical traditions.

However, it would be superficial to view the problem exclusively in terms of obedience to Church authority. For if we penetrate beneath the surface of rite and discipline and obedience we shall see, I think, that the problem is a much deeper one involving group identity and its symbols.

3. Symbols of Identity:

I suspect that the real issue is not ritual practice at all. Many of the rubrical niceties that divide the clergy—the size and shape of a veil or discos, the cut of a vestment, the breadth of one's sleeves, where to put the antimension—are of little significance in themselves. But these divergent ritual uses have become symbols of religious identity, much as was true of the Ritualist Movement in late nineteenth century Anglicanism in England. At issue were not mere differences of rubric, but symbolic affirmations of the conviction that Anglicanism was not "Protestant" but "Catholic."

At bottom, then, what we are faced with is two different interpretations of the community's past, two different historical visions. This is possible because history, of course, is not a shared past, but one's *view* of that past seen through the lens of present concerns. This vision is not a passive view of the past as an objective reality, but a pattern formed through a process of selection determined by one's present outlook.

Some Eastern-Catholic clergy see their history as a progress from schism and spiritual stagnation to a life of discipline, renewal, and restored religious practice in the Catholic communion. For this group the adoption of certain Latin—they would say "Catholic"—devotions and liturgical uses is a sign of this new identity.

Others, while not at all denying their commitment to Catholic communion nor underestimating the obvious spiritual benefits it has brought their Churches, see themselves somewhat as Orthodox in communion with Rome, distinguished from their Orthodox Sister Churches in nothing but the fact of that communion and its doctrinal consequences. They see the latinisms that have crept into their tradition as a loss of identity, an erosion of their heritage in favor of foreign customs with which they can in no wise identify themselves.

So for some, latinization is a *sign* of their identity, for others its *negation,* and *both* are right because they perceive themselves differently. In such a situation there is no way to please everyone. To reintroduce the custom of infant communion would upset those who oppose the liturgical restoration mandated by Vatican II. On the other hand, to impede the restoration of this traditional usage, or to suppress it where it has been successfully reintroduced, *is already* causing bitterness, disillusionment, and mistrust in the sincerity and obedience of the hierarchy among those who are striving to further the will of the Holy See in this matter and meet only with opposition for their pains.

Underlying the particular issue, then, is the more serious question of Rome's credibility: is the Holy See to be believed in what it says about restoring the Eastern Catholic heritage? The morale of some of the younger clergy has of late been deeply affected by this cul-de-sac: they feel mandated to do one thing by the Holy See, and then are criticized or even disciplined if they try to obey.

When faced with such a stalemate it is difficult to avoid the conclusion that justice demands a verdict in favor of those who are right. In Catholic practice that should mean those trying to do what the Holy See has rightly been telling them to do for years. Now that is all well and good in theory, but disciplinary decisions are of little avail unless what is commanded is both right and perceived to be right, and unless those so commanded are prepared to obey.

The problem, as usual, is one of leadership, without which the hesitant or reluctant have no one to follow. What is needed is not just discipline and obedience, but also a clergy education loyal to the clear policy of the Church on this question, and prudent pastoral preparation. This is the only way out of the vicious circle that has been created: the proposed reforms are resisted because the clergy and people are not prepared to accept them—yet little or nothing has been done to prepare the clergy and people for a renewal that is not understood and hence not accepted.

Although I cannot pretend to read minds, I would guess that there are two main reasons behind this deep-rooted reluctance to welcome the policy of Rome: 1) the proposed change seems to be a pointless archaism; 2) its opponents are convinced in their hearts that the practice of infant communion is just not "Catholic," and hence not "right."

Let us look at these two issues to see if we can dispel some of the anxiety by an analysis of the facts.

4. Antiquarianism?

Can one fairly accuse the Catholic Church of promoting a liturgical reform from sheer archaism? Is the restoration of infant communion just the resurrection of a fossil, a return to the past for its own sake, a closing of the door on change, evolution, progress, in the name of some abstract, static principle of purity of rite, divorced from history and real life? If so it would be a novelty. The Catholic Church has never been ruled by a retrospective ideology. For her, tradition has never meant the past, but the present living reality of the Church in continuity with that past. Indeed, far from clinging blindly to a dead past, the Catholic Church has evolved so much that other Christian communions have accused her of all sorts of innovations and corruptions of the pristine tradition!

No, the interests of the Church in this matter are far more serious than some sort of antiquarian estheticism or immobile ritualism. The Eastern traditions of the Church are not the property of any one group but the heritage of all, and the Church is bent on protecting them not from organic evolution and growth, but from decline and abandonment through prejudice, misunderstanding, and ignorance. It is no secret that in the past, liturgical latinization was carried out, against the will of the Holy See, not for legitimate motives of pastoral adaptation, but in slavish imitation of the dominant Latin tradition.

The proposed restoration is, then, not a blind imitation of a dead past, but an attempt to free Eastern Catholics from a period in which, severed from the roots of their own tradition, they were deprived of any organic development and could conceive of growth only as sterile servility to their neighbors. Can one seriously propose this as a program to be preserved in our day?

The orientation of liturgical reform, therefore, is never toward the past but toward present pastoral needs. Of course the liturgical scholar studies the past, but the purpose of this historical research is not to discover the *past*—much less to imitate it—but to recover the integrity of the pristine *tradition* which the *past* may well have obscured. The aim is not to *restore* the past but to *overcome* it. For history is not the past, but a genetic vision of the present, a present seen in continuity with its roots. It is precisely those who do not know their past that are incapable of true, organic change. They remain victims of the latest cliché, prisoners of present usage because they have no objective standard against which to measure it.

Now in the case of Christian Initiation, modern historical research and theological reflection have shown that the universal primitive tradition of both East and West viewed the liturgical completion of Christian Initiation as one integral rite comprising three moments of baptism, chrismation, and eucharist, and without all three the process is incomplete.[5] In Christian antiquity, to celebrate initiation without eucharist would have made about as much sense as celebrating half a wedding would today. For this reason, contemporary Western Catholic experts on the liturgy and theology of Christian initiation have insisted on the necessity of restoring the integrity of this process which broke down in the West only in the Middle Ages.[6]

Hence the irony of those critics of the Byzantine Catholic liturgical restoration who accuse its promoters of fostering a return to the Middle Ages. As we shall see in the next section, it is precisely in the Middle Ages that the practice of infant communion in the Roman Rite is first called into question for typically medieval motives that no one with any sense would heed today. So it is not the proponents of restoration but its opponents that are behind the times, stuck in a medieval rut out of which the major scholarly voices in this field have been trying to lead the Church for over twenty years.

5. Infant Communion contrary to Catholic Tradition?

I suspect that some of the Eastern Catholic clergy, educated in Latin seminaries or at least in Latin categories of a previous epoch, are convinced that the practice of infant communion is not "Catholic"— or at least not as Catholic as the Latin practice of delaying first communion until children have attained the use of reason. Why they might think this is no mystery. The prevailing Latin thesis was that the use of reason was necessary to receive the eucharist fruitfully. If this is so, then what could be the point of infant communion?

These findings are betrayed by the fact that proponents of renewal are ridiculed as *"vostochniki"* ("orientals"), and accused of being "Russian" or "Orthodox." Indeed, the fear is expressed that the introduction of authentic Byzantine (they call them "Orthodox") practices and spirit will lead young seminarians and priests to defect to the Orthodox Church. (The truth of the matter is that Orthodoxy becomes attractive *precisely for the opposite reason,* when young candidates for the ministry are led to believe that in spite of the explicit orders of the Holy See, their heritage continues to be progressively diluted by latinization, and is preserved only among the Orthodox.)

Perhaps this problem, too, can be dissipated by a glance at the facts.

a) The Traditional Integrity of the Rites of Christian Initiation, East and West:

From the beginning of the primitive Church in East and West the process of Christian Initiation, for both children and adults, was one inseparable sequence comprising catechumenate, baptism, confirmation, and eucharist. Note that "eucharist" here does not mean just "receiving communion." It means crowning the process of entrance into the ecclesial communion of Christ's Body by celebrating with that Body the sacrament of this communion, the common eucharistic sacrifice and banquet. History is unmistakably clear in this matter: every candidate, child or adult, was baptized, confirmed, and given communion as part of a single initiation rite. This is the universal ancient Catholic tradition. Anything else is less ancient and has no claim to universality.

So for centuries this was also the tradition of the Church of Rome. In 417 Pope Innocent I in a doctrinal letter to the Fathers of the Synod of Milevis, teaches that infant initiation necessarily includes communion:

> ... to preach that infants can be given the rewards of eternal life without the grace of baptism is completely idiotic. For unless they eat the flesh of the Son of Man and drink His blood, they will not have life in them.[7]

From the text it is obvious that Innocent I is teaching principally that without baptism infants cannot be saved. But the argument he uses from John 6:53, which refers to the necessity of *eucharist* for salvation, shows he simply took it for granted that communion was an integral part of Christian Initiation even for infants.

That this was the actual liturgical practice can be seen, for example, in the seventh-century *Ordo romanus XI*[8] and in the twelfth-century Roman pontifical, which repeats almost verbatim the same rule (I cite the later text):

> Concerning infants, care should be taken lest they receive food or be nursed (except in case of urgent need) before receiving the sacrament of Christ's Body. And afterwards, during the whole of Easter week, let them come to mass, offer, and receive communion every day.[9]

So until the twelfth century this was the sacramental practice of the Roman Church. It was also the doctrinal teaching of the Latin theologians: Christ Himself said it was necessary for eternal life to receive His Body and Blood (Jn. 6:53 "Unless you eat the flesh of the Son of Man and drink His blood, you shall not have life in you"), and this was applied to all, including infants.[10]

The practice was called into question in the same century not because of any argument about the need to have attained the "age of reason" *(aetas discretionis)* to communicate. Rather, the fear of profanation of the host if the child could not swallow it led to giving the precious blood only. And then the forbidding of the chalice to the laity in the West led automatically to the disappearance of infant communion too. This was not the result of any pastoral or theological reasoning. When the Fourth Lateran Council (1215) ordered yearly confession and communion for those who have reached the "age of reason" *(annos discretionis)* it was not affirming this age as a *requirement* for reception of the eucharist.[11] Even the 1910 decree *Quam singulari* issued under Pius X mentions the age of reason not as required before communion *can* be received, but as the age when the *obligation* of satisfying the *precept* of annual confession and communion begins.[12] Nevertheless the notion eventually took hold that communion could not be received until the age of reason, even though infant communion in the Latin Rite continued in some parts of the West until the sixteenth century. For the Byzantine Rite, on December 23, 1534, Paul III explicitly confirmed the Italo-Albanian custom of administering the eucharist to infants.[13]

The Fathers of Trent (Session 21, 4)[14] denied the *necessity* of infant communion but refused to agree with those who said it was useless and inefficacious—realizing undoubtedly that the same arguments could be used against infant baptism, because for over ten centuries in the West the exact same theology was used to justify both!

I have gone into this matter at some length in order to provide a firm basis in tradition for theological judgments. We may draw the following conclusions.

1. For 1200 years the universal practice of the entire Church of East and West was to communicate infants.

2. This practice was not only permitted; at one time the ordinary magisterium taught that it was *necessary*.

3. The practice was not suppressed by a doctrinal or pastoral decision of the Church. It simply died out.

4. Only later (thirteenth century) was the "age of reason" theory advanced to support the *innovation* of baptizing infants *without* also giving them communion.

5. Hence to advance *doctrinal* arguments against infant communion is to assert that the sacramental teaching and practice of the Roman Church was in error for 1200 years.

6. Since for Catholics, at least, this is an unacceptable conclusion, then it is clear that the "age of reason" requirement for communion is a medieval western *pastoral* innovation, not a *doctrinal* argument.

7. Decrees concerning Latin pastoral practice such as *Quam singulari* of Pius X can in no way be interpreted as affecting Eastern-rite usage.

b) Vatican II and the New Roman Initiation Rites:

The universal tradition of the *integrity* of Christian Initiation was abandoned by the West only in the twelfth century. The traditional *order* of initiation (baptism, confirmation, communion) was maintained until *Quam singulari* in 1910, when in some countries first communion began to be given before confirmation. But the Holy See has in the official *praenotanda* to the new Roman *Rite of Christian Initiation* promulgated May 15, 1969, reaffirmed the traditional order and interrelationship of these rites:

1. Through the sacraments of Christian initiation men and women are freed from the power of darkness. With Christ they die, are buried and rise again. They receive the Spirit of adoption which makes them God's sons and daughters *and, with the entire people of God, they celebrate the memorial of the Lord's death and resurrection.*

2. Through baptism men and women are incorporated into Christ. They are formed into God's people, and they obtain forgiveness of all their sins. They are raised from their natural human condition to the dignity of adopted children. They become a new creation through water and the Holy Spirit. Hence they are called, and are indeed, the children of God.

Signed with the gift of the Spirit in confirmation, Christians more perfectly become the image of their Lord and are filled with the Holy

Spirit. They bear witness to him before all the world and eagerly work for the building up of the body of Christ.

Finally they come to the table of the eucharist, to eat the flesh and drink the blood of the Son of Man so that they may have eternal life and show forth the unity of God's people. By offering themselves with Christ, they share in his universal sacrifice: the entire community of the redeemed is offered to God by their high priest. They pray for a greater outpouring of the Holy Spirit so that the whole human race may be brought into the unity of God's family.

Thus the three sacraments of Christian initiation closely combine to bring the faithful to the full stature of Christ and to enable them to carry out the mission of the entire people of God in the Church and in the world.[15]

Thus the Church reaffirms the normative value of the ancient tradition of initiation—a renewal that has been received with enthusiasm by all experts in the field.

c) Conclusion:

The conclusion is ineluctable: both universal early tradition and the present teaching of even the Latin Church show Eastern practice to be not a strange exception that should be abandoned, but a traditional ideal that should be preserved or restored.

Some Pastoral Considerations:

I have been working in the field of liturgical scholarship long enough to have lost all illusions about the possibility of effecting change through academic argumentation alone. But since my ultimate aim in this article has been pastoral, perhaps the reader will bear with me if I presume to suggest a possible plan of action for implementing the instructions of the Holy See in the matter of liturgical restoration:

1. In parishes where the custom of infant communion has not yet been restored, pastors, regardless of their own feelings, can not refuse communion at baptism or at other times *to children whose parents*

request it. This is their right, and pastors are servants of the Church and not of their own personal prejudices.

2. In all parishes it is desirable that the custom of infant communion *at least at baptism* be restored gradually. This could be done unobtrusively by beginning with the young parents, who are generally flexible, open to change, and often quite desirous of fostering their own heritage. They can be instructed as to why their children should receive the Precious Blood of Christ at baptism, and be told that they may also bring their children to communion afterwards, if they wish.

3. If parents do not wish to bring their children for communion again *after* the first baptismal eucharist, the issue need not be forced.

4. The reasons supporting this tradition should be introduced into the new catechetical books prepared by the respective Offices of Religious Education.

5. Seminary instruction must teach the reasons for, and binding nature of, the liturgical restoration in this and all other aspects of the tradition, so that young priests will not be trained in a way contrary to the will of the Holy See.

6. The custom of "First Communion" at the age of reason, borrowed from the Latin Rite, may be maintained by calling it "First Solemn Communion," when the eucharist is received for the first time after catechesis and first confession. In this way one can (a) avoid the social problems caused by suppressing this popular festivity; (b) assure that first confession be made at the proper time; (c) avoid creating divisions, during the transition period of renewal, between those children who have and those who have not already received communion.

NOTES

1. A. Flannery (ed.), *Vatican Council II. The Conciliar and Post Conciliar Documents* (Collegeville MN: The Liturgical Press, 1975) pp. 443, 445 (emphasis added).

2. My translation from the report of Bishop Miroslav Marusyn, *Nuntia* 2 (1976) 20:

"La disciplina tradizionale nelle Chiese Orientali prescrive la comunione dei fanciulli neobattezzati come completamento dell'iniziazione ... Il coetus non ha trascurato un problema così importante come la comunione dei neofiti, per la quale era obbligato a ripristinare la disciplina antica unica, componendo un canone nuovo del seguente tenore: Initiatio sacramentalis in Mysterium Salutis receptione SS. Eucharistiae perficitur; ideoque ea post Baptismum et Chrismationem Sancti Myri administretur quamprimum iuxta disciplinam unicuique Ecclesiae proprium."

3. See for example such representative studies as those by two major Catholic experts in the field, professors of liturgy respectively at Yale and Notre Dame Universities: A. Kavanagh, O.S.B., *The Shape of Baptism: The Rite of Christian Initiation* (Studies in the Reformed Rites of the Catholic Church, vol. 1, N.Y.: Pueblo 1978); M. Searle, *Christening. The Making of Christians* (Collegeville MN: The Liturgical Press 1980).

4. For the major Byzantine Catholic traditions the work of restoration was begun in 1938 by the Oriental Congregation, with the establishment of the commission for the reform of the "Ruthenian" liturgical books used by the Byzantine Catholic Ukrainians, Carpatho-Russians or Rusyns, Slovaks, Croats, and others. This enormous undertaking reached fruition with the publication of the "Ruthenian recension" of the *Liturgikon* (1942) and *Malyj Trebnik* (1947) or Ritual, and the promulgation in 1944 of the *Ordo celebrationis vesperarum, matutini et Divinae Liturgiae iuxta recensionem Ruthenorum*, which later appeared also in English. M. A. Berko, *The Order for the Celebration of Vespers, Matins and the Divine Liturgy according to the Ruthenian Recension* (Washington D.C. 1958). This work prescribes the correct way to celebrate these services in the restored rite.

5. See the works referred to in note 3.

6. The major study in English of this disintegration is J.D.C. Fisher, *Christian Initiation. Baptism in the Medieval West. A Study in the Disintegration of the Primitive Rite of Initiation* (Alcuin Club Collections 47, London 1965).

7. *Ep.* 30, 5 *PL* 20, 592: . . . praedicare parvulos aeternae vitae praemiis etiam sine baptismatis gratia posse donari, perfatum est. Nisi enim manducaverint carnem Filii hominis et biberint sanguinem eius, non habebunt vitam in semet ipsis.

8. Ed. M. Andrieu, *Les "ordines romani" du haut moyen âge*, II: *Les textes* (Spicilegium sacrum lovaniense, études et documents 23, Louvain 1948) pp. 446-7.

9. Ed. M. Andrieu, *Le pontifical romain au moyen âge*, vol. 1 (Studi e testi 86, Vatican 1938) p. 248: 37. Illud autem de parvulis providendum est, ne postquam baptizati fuerint, ullum cibum accipiant nec ablactentur, sine summa necessitate, antequam communicent sacramento corporis Christi. Et postea per totam hebdomadam paschae omnibus diebus ad missam procedant, offerant, et communicent.

10. See for example Regino of Prüm (*PL* 132, 205); Radulphus of Ardens (*PL* 155, 1850); William of Champeaux (*PL* 163, 1039).

11. Denzinger, *Enchiridion* p. 437.

12. *AAS* 2 (1910) 582 = Denzinger, *Enchiridion* 2137-2144. However nn. 2138-9 could be interpreted as implying that the age of reason is required for first communion. But constantly repeated papal approval of Eastern usage, and ancient Latin practice itself, show that this can only be a disciplinary decree restricted to the Latin rite.

13. *New Catholic Encyclopedia* 7:748.

14. Denzinger, *Enchiridion* p. 933.

15. *The Rites of the Catholic Church as Revised by Decred of the Second Vatican Ecumenical Council and Published by Authority of Pope Paul VI.* English translation prepared by ICEL (N.Y.: Pueblo 1976) vol. 1, pp. 3-4; official Latin text in R. Kaczynski, *Enchiridion documentorum instaurationis liturgicae I (1963-1973)* (Rome: Marietti 1976) nn. 1777-8 (emphasis added).

ST. BASIL'S COSMOLOGY

by Rev. Emmanuel Clapsis

Father Clapsis is pastor of the St. George Greek Orthodox Church in Kingston, N.Y. and is currently completing doctoral studies at Union Theological Seminary in New York.

The cosmological view of St. Basil (330-370 A.D.) can be found in his celebrated homilies of *Hexaemeron*,[1] which are an extensive commentary on the narrative of the "six days" of creation in Genesis 1:1-26. He delivered them before 370 A.D. while still a presbyter and in 440 the African Eustathius translated them into Latin. Ever since St. Basil's work has influenced the Greek and Latin Fathers of the Christian church.[2]

Our study will examine the relation of God to the Cosmos, what the Creation reveals about God and finally the doxological and ethical implications of cosmology. It is my belief that theology, anthropology and cosmology are inseparably related.[3] In the formation of man's consciousness theology, cosmology and anthropology co-inherently and simultaneously influence man's understanding of existence.

Basil wrote his *Hexaemeron* as a Christian response to a philosophical debate about the nature of the world. The Greek philosophers, despite the richness of their thought on the subject, were causing confusion and uncertainty because their theories did not remain unaltered and firmly established but "the later account always overthrew the preceding one."[4] The *Hexaemeron* does not have scientific value as we understand science today.[5] Basil wanted to give a religious explanation of what is the nature and the destiny of the world.[6] He claims that "his words of truth" are not identical with the "persuasive language of human wisdom" but they are the expression of the teaching of the Spirit whose end is the salvation of the people.[7] The "persuasive language of human wisdom" can only be accepted if it helps us to deepen our faith in God.[8] Basil leaves freedom to his

215

listeners to accept as plausible some rational explanations about the place of the earth in the universe and its immobility, but he wants the people to transfer their admiration from nature to God Who has ordered the universal system. He states: "Our amazement at the greatest phenomena is not lessened because we have discovered the manner in which a certain one of the marvels occurred. But if this is not so, still let the simplicity of faith be stronger than the deductions of reason."[9] In summary, Basil's purpose is to present to the extent that it is possible a coherent religious picture of the origin and the destination of the world. His primary goal is the edification of the church through the understanding of God's wonders in creation. Human wisdom is integrated in his cosmology to the extent that it furthers the faith of the people. The study of God's wonders in creation presupposes also the spiritual preparation of the people so they can receive a worthy concept of God.[10] Basil relies on the authority of Moses and he takes literally his words as they are found in Genesis 1:1-26 in order to elaborate his religious understanding of the Cosmos without ignoring the philosophical thought of his age.[11]

The World

Basil accepts as divinely inspired the Mosaic cosmology that "In the beginning God created the heaven and the earth."[12] This is a radical proposition that contradicts the cosmological assumptions of Greek philosophy.[13] The philosophers in their godlessness moved to assert that the Universe was guideless, eternally existing without a rational cause.[14] Basil based on Gen. 1:1 defines the world as a created entity which has a beginning in time, despite the fact that creation is a timeless act of God. It is important to refute and discredit the assumption "of the existence of a world without beginning and without end"[15] because if this is affirmed, then matter as an uncreated and eternal entity would be of equal rank with God, worthy of the same honors.[16] God created the world *ex-nihilo*. "Everything by the command of God was brought forth from non-existence into existence."[17] God created the substance and the form of the world (heaven and earth) and whatever the world potentially and actually contains.[18] In this creative process God is free from all limitations of time sequence:

"God, however, before any of the objects now seen, existed, having cast about in His mind and resolved to bring into being things that did not exist, at one and the same time devised what sort of a world it should be and created the appropriate matter together with its form."[19] The origins of time coincide and begin with the beginning of the created world which is the foundation of time. All created things are enveloped by time.[20] It is because time began with the created order that it must end with the consummation of the world. There is a close proximity between the nature of the created world and the progress of time; for they both follow the divine ordained course.[21] The difference between time and eternity is not quantitative but qualitative. Whatever lives in time and with time will have an end, but whatever lives in eternity is God without beginning and end, free of time successions, unchangeable. Thus the concept of time and eternity is used to define the ontological difference between God who lives in eternity and the created, in time, Cosmos.[22] God is infinite in His nature and all created entities are finite.

God's involvement in the created world does not stop with His initial timeless and instantaneous act of creation. Basil considers that it is an inseparable part of the thought of true religion the belief that "all things are kept under control by the power of God."[23] God's providential activity comprises the whole creation and reaches even to the smallest, irrational entities, for God has foreseen all and neglected nothing.[24] The interest of God in his created world, today, continues to preserve and secure, by certain natural law, all the creatures during the course of their existence, in a way which proves that "His eyes never sleep and He watches over all."[25] God the creator relates with His creation the world not only by his initial act of creation, but by his continuous providence, manifested in the orderly life of the created world.

The ontological distinction of God as uncreated, and Cosmos as created is an important Patristic concept that defines the Ontological difference between God and the world. The world as a created entity with a beginning is subject to the logical rule that whatever has a beginning must also have an end.[26] Thus the world is subject to motion, change and an end. The end of the creation in Basil's thought, is not its ultimate annihilation but its radical regeneration to an eternal, by participation, world totally and constantly immersed in God's Grace.[27] The changeability of the world must be accepted as a necessary precondition of the belief that man will experience another form of life depending on the Just Judgment of God on the final consummation of the World. Basil, finally, referring to I Cor. 8:31 and Matt. 24:35, insists that the passing away and the renewal of the world is a fundamental element of the Christian faith and has thus already been declared in the opening verses of the Bible through the affirmation that the world has a beginning.[28]

The Nature of the World

Reflecting upon creation we will discover that the world is not an accidental, meaningless production of an irresponsible God. "The world was not devised at random or to no purpose, but to contribute to some useful end and to the great advantage of all beings, if it is truly a training place for rational souls and a school for attaining the knowledge of God, because through visible and perceptible objects it provides guidance to the mind for the contemplation of the invisible as the Apostle says: 'Since the creation of the world his invisible attributes are clearly seen . . . being understood through the things that are made.' (Rom. 1:20)."[29] What made the orderly arrangement of visible things possible in creation was the operation of some "systematic reason" in it.[30] Basil considers God as the source of all reason and the supreme reason itself.[31] Thus the order of Cosmos reveals God's reasonableness and wisdom.[32]

The Creation of the world can be called an act of creative art in which although the action of Creation ceased, the work remains even if the craftsman is not present. This gives us the opportunity to admire the work of the creative artist and attempt to grasp his creative wisdom. "The world is a work of art, set before all for contemplation, so that through it the wisdom of Him who created should be known."[33] In viewing the world as a work of creative art we must be aware that the logical certainty that "the arts come into being later than the materials,"[34] cannot be applied in God's creative artistic acts because "God at one and the same time devised what sort of a world it should be and created the appropriate matter together with its forms."[35] The wisdom of the great Artist can be also appreciated by the unity and harmony of the world. "The whole world, which consists of diverse parts, He (God) bound together by an unbroken bond of attraction into one fellowship and harmony, so that objects which are farthest apart from each other in position seem to have been made one through affinity."[36] God Judges that His creation is good.[37] Basil finds the goodness of the world, in its final goal, its purpose of existence "the goodness (of creation) is determined by the purpose of God's creative activity."[38] Any attempt to use the world against its God-given purpose creates natural evil and we fail to appreciate the essential nature of the world.

The world serves as the medium by which man gets to know God: "From the beauty of the visible things let us form an idea of Him who is more beautiful; and from the greatness of these perceptible and circumscribed bodies let us conceive of Him who is infinite and immense and who surpasses all understanding in the plenitude of His power."[39] It is also true that in Basil's thought we know the essential nature of the world from God's qualities: "He created as one good, something useful; as one wise, something beautiful; as one powerful, something mighty."[40] The assumption about the nature of the world as the medium by which we know God and the essential belief about the goodness of the world as the reflection of God's qualities are founded in Basil's strong belief that God is the creator of the world and creation is good because it owes its origins to God and "nothing contrary is produced by the contrary."[41] If this is the case what is the origin of evil that we witness in our world?

Evil

Basil finds the source of all corruption and evil in "the changes of conditions which are transitions from one condition to the contrary."[42] He refuses to conceive evil as a living and animated substance. It is a condition of the soul which is opposed to virtue and which springs up in the people when they fall away from God. Basil states: "Do not contemplate evil from without and do not imagine some original nature of wickedness, but let each one recognize himself as the first author of the vice that is in him."[43] In reference to disease, poverty, ignominy, death and whatever else causes men sorrow, he does not think that we should classify them as evils, because "we don't count among our greatest blessings what is opposed to them. And some of them are, according to the nature and others seem to be for the advantage of many."[44] Finally, he rejects as a "source of impious fabrication" the belief that darkness is an evil power or evil itself resisting and opposing the goodness of God.[45] Basil makes the point that if we presume that light (God) and darkness (evil) are two equal powers in opposition to each other, then they will be entirely and mutually destructive of their nature, and they will continuously have and unceasingly provide troubles for each other when engaged in war. But, if One of the opponents excels the other in power, he altogether annihilates the conquered one.[46] The dualistic conception of historical existence as the realm of an eternal struggle between two equal opposing divine beings is rejected as contradictory both to Basil's understanding of the nature of God, and of the destiny of man to live eternally, by participation, with God, and to Basil's refusal to attribute to evil any substantial or ontological existence.[47]

The evil that we experience in our world is caused by distorted sinful relations of man with Cosmos and God. These sinful conditions are radically opposed to God's purpose and will concerning the destiny of the world. This deviation from God's goals concerning the Creation can be sometimes conscious or even unconscious ignorance of God's plans. Man needs to study God's wisdom in order to discover his proper relation with Cosmos and God.

Conclusion

In summary, we have seen that in Basil's cosmology the author of all creation is the eternal, uncreated and limitless God who created the world ex-nihilo. The essential goodness of the world is very strongly affirmed to the extent that the cosmos serves God's purpose to become the manifestation of His wisdom and to bring man closer to God. Man, reflecting upon the beauty and goodness of the created world, will relate doxologically to God. The praise of God is the proper response of man to God's infinite love and majestic creation.[48]

Evil, for Basil, is the result of human change and deviation from God's ultimate design about the destiny of the world. It will be consistant with Basil's thought to assume that the world has been created by God in order to facilitate man's relationship with God. Basil adopts literally the biblical view that man has been created by God according to His image and Likeness (Gen. 1:26-27). He, unfortunately, does not materialize his promise to explicate systematically in what respect man is the Image of God and how he shares in His Likeness.[48] Finally, Basil believes that men should study the nature of Cosmos because cosmology gives moral lessons to men about their life on earth. For example, He speaks about social injustice, taking as an example the fact that the majority of fishes eat one another, and the smaller among them is food for the larger. Basil with great eloquence states: "If it ever happens that the victor over a smaller becomes the prey of another, they are both carried into one stomach of the last. Now, what else do we do in the oppression of our inferiors? How does he differ from the last fish, who with a greedy love of riches swallows up the weak in the folds of his insatiable avarice? That man held the possessions of the poor man; you, seizing him made him a part of your abundance. You have clearly shown yourself more unjust than the unjust man and more grasping than the greedy man. Beware, lest the same end as that of the fish awaits you—somewhere a fishhook or a snare, or a net. Surely, if we have committed many unjust deeds, we shall not escape the final retribution."[49]

NOTES

1. S. Giet, *Basile de Cesaree: Homelies sur l'Hexaemeron,* Texte grec, avec introduction et tradiction (sources Chretiennes, 26), Paris, Edition du Cerf, 1951; the most recent English translation of *Hexaemeron* that we use in our study is by Agnes Clare Way, *Saint Basil Exegetic Homilies* (Washington, D.C.: The Catholic University of America Press, 1963).
2. St. Ambrose writing on the same subject imitates St. Basil and inserts passages directly translated from the Greek of St. Basil in his own treaty. St. Gregory of Nazianzus says: "When I take his Hexaemeron in my hand and read it loud I am with my Creator, I understand the reasons for creation, and I admire My Creator more than I formerly did . . . (Migne, P.G. 44 col, 61); Johannes Quasten

in his *Patrology* (vol. III p. 217) writes: "There is no work in late Greek literature which could be compared with these homilies in rhetorical beauty."

3. For the relation between theology, cosmology and anthropology in early christian literature see: Richard A. Norris, Jr., *God and World in Early Christian Theology,* (New York: The Seabury Press, 1965).

4. *In Hex.* hom. 1.2. He also attacked the Gnostic and manichean view of Cosmos.

5. Markos A. Orphanos, *Creation and Salvation according to St. Basil of Caesarea* (Athens 1975), p. 41.

6. John F. Callahan, Greek Philosophy and the Cappadocian Cosmology, *Dumbarton Oaks Papers* 12 (1958) pp. 31-57; Markos A. Orphanos, *Creation and Salvation according to St. Basil of Caesaria* (Athens 1975); E. F. Robbins, *The Hexaemeral Literature: A Study of the Greek and Latin Commentaries on Genesis* (Dissertation), (Chicago: The University of Chicago Press, 1912); Olympia Papadopoulou-Tsanana, *The Anthropology of Basil the Great* (In Greek), (Thessaloniki: Patriarchal Institute for Patristic Studies, 1970).

7. Hom. 1:1.

8. The Christian attitude toward pagan literature and learning is a topic of a special treatise written by Basil. For an English translation see: F. M. Padelford, *Address to young Men on the Right Use of Greek Literature: Essays on the Study and Use of Poetry by Plutarch and Basil the Great,* (New York, 1902) pp. 97-120.

9. Hom. 1:10.

10. Hom. 1:1.

11. For the Greek sources of Basil's cosmology see the introduction in the book of Stanislas Giet, *Basile de Cesaree, homelies sur l'hexaemeron* (Paris, 1950), pp. 47-69.

12. *Gen.* 1:1.

13. The opposition of Biblical cosmology to Greek philosophy is ably presented in Fr. Georges Florovsky's article: "St. Athanasius' Concept of Creation," in *Studia Patristica,* ed. F. L. Cross (Berlin: Akademie Verlag; Texte und Untersuchungen Zur Geschichte de altchristlichen Literatuz, Band 81, 1962) pp. 36-55.

14. Hom. 1:2.

15. Hom. 1:3.

16. Hom. 2:2.

17. Hom. 8:7.

18. Hom. 2:3.

19. Hom. 2:2; 1:6.

20. John F. Callahan, "Greek Philosophy and the Cappadocian Cosmology," *Dumbarton Oaks Papers* 12 (1958) p. 36.

21. Hom. 1:5.

22. Hom. 1:3.
23. Hom. 1:9.
24. Hom. 7:5; 9:5.
25. *In Hex.* Hom. 7:5; *Hom. In Psalm* 32:3; Markos A. Orfanos, *Creation and Salvation according to St. Basil of Caesaria,* p. 51.
26. *In Hex.* Hom. 1:3.
27. For the eschatology of St. Basil and the destiny of the world see: Olympia Papadopoulos-Tsanana, *The Anthropology of Basil the Great,* In Greek (Thessaloniki: Patriarchal Institute for Patristic Studies, 1970).
28. *In Hex.* Hom. 1:3; *Hom. on Psalm* 32:2.
29. *In Hex.* Hom. 1:6.
30. *Ibid.*
31. Hom. 1:2.
32. Hom. 2:3; 3:10; 7:7; 7:11.
33. Hom. 1:7.
34. Hom. 2:2.
35. *Ibid.*
36. Hom. 2:2; 1:7.
37. *Gen.* 1:4 etc.
38. *In Hex.* Hom. 4:6; 4:1; 2:7; 3:10.
39. Hom. 1:11.
40. Hom. 1:7.
41. Hom. 2:4.
42. Hom. 2:4. Basil also wrote a small treatise against the assumption that God is the source and the origin of evil.
43. Hom. 2:5.
44. *Ibid.*
45. Hom. 2:4.
46. *Ibid.*
47. In other parts of his work, Basil accepts the existence of Devil or Satan as a spiritual and incorporeal being who through his free will became an evil spirit. This is due not to his nature but to his corruption and his rejection of Divine grace. This proves that even the archtype of evil Satan emerges as the result of distorted relation between him and God. For Basil's thought on this subject see: Markos Orfanos, *Creation and Salvation according to St. Basil of Caesaria* (Athens 1975) pp. 27-37; for the concept of Satan in early Christian literature see: Jeffrey B. Russell, *Satan: The Early Christian Tradition,* (Ithaca: Cornell University Press 1981).
48. Hom. 2:4.
49. Hom. 7:2; for an excellent presentation of Basil's sociology see: Panagiotis Christou, "The Sociology of Great Basil," *Theologica Meletimata* vol. 2, (Thessaloniki: Patriarchal Institute for Patristic Studies, 1975) pp. 71-158. (In Greek).

BYZANTINE ART AND THEOLOGY

by *Russell Becker, O.F.M.*

Father Becker is a Lecturer in Theology at the John XXIII Institute of Eastern Christian Studies and is a consultant of the Byzantine Catholic Diocese of Passaic for Adult Religious Education.

This study will briefly look at the role of art in Byzantine culture. It will speak only of the icon, one aspect of that art. Besides the icon, architecture and music play no small part in the world-view of the Byzantine Church. I have noticed in the course of reading that there is a very strange movement or rather tension in the Byzantine Church. This is caused by the presence of Hellenic influences and Semitic influences. Art and theology cannot really be spoken of apart in this area, even though one may want to examine each one alone. There is no strictly Byzantine art apart from theology and there is no Byzantine theology that can be spoken of apart from art. In the west it is possible to distinguish secular and religious art but I do not think that this is possible in the east. I believe that this is due to the Iconoclast heresy which had as a positive result the melding of Byzantine art and theology. They have become inseparable.[1] Byzantine art, then, is always religious and always theological.

Man's Search for Meaning

Art and theology both express man's inner feelings. Theology speculates and contemplates, learns to know and love, reveals and teaches man's ultimate goal and the source of his meaning. Art does this in a visible, plastic way. This is hopefully an integrative process which will lead man to wholeness, harmony and peace.

Twentieth century art does not always do this. It is very often a wrenching experience; it fools, confuses and disturbs what little integrity is left to man. It is the product of the fragmentation and atomization which humanity experiences after seventy-five years of materialism, war, assassination, revolution, torture, and nuclear proliferation.

This art can be instant, satirical, cynical and often violent. It assaults the person and as a result destroys what little peace, wholeness and harmony he has left. I think that it also discourages him from even attempting to seek these out. Theology these days often does the same thing. Rather than leading one to the source of his meaning and his ultimate goal, it tends to confuse and shock him. I am not meaning to write off this century and its contributions but hopefully just stating the extreme to point up the need for help that Byzantine art and theology can give to us.

Matter Articulates

The Byzantine conception of the essential function of all forms of religious art, especially the icon, lies in the mystery of creation, incarnation and redemption. St. John of Damascus in responding to the iconoclastic controversy emphasized the change which occurred in the relationship between God and the visible world when he became flesh. By God's own will he became visible by assuming a material existence and giving to matter a new function and dignity.[2] Already following the teaching of St. Gregory of Palamas the divine energies, the deifying grace penetrates matter and transfigures it.[3] Central in the scheme of creation and incarnation was man, who was the bridge between matter and God, between the world of mind (*noetos*) and the world of material things (*aisthetos*).

> Gregory of Nyssa conceived man as the bridge between the two worlds in which all Being was divided . . . a crucial text was Gen. 2:7; God had formed man from the dust of the earth and breathed into his nostrils the breath of life. By reason of his body man belongs to the world of matter; by reason of his soul he belongs to the world of the mind. In him alone Mind and Matter, the worlds of noetos and aisthetos, intermingle and interpenetrate; through man alone the material becomes articulate in praise of God: without him, mind and sense remained distinct within their boundaries, bearing within themselves the Magnificence of the Creator Logos, but praising silently . . . Nor was there any mingling between them; nor yet were the riches of God's goodness manifested . . . till Man was placed on the earth as a kind of second world, a micro-cosm, a new angel, a mingled worshipper . . . visible, yet intelligible . . . to be the husbandman of mortal plants *[these last phrases are from Gregory of Nazianzen].*[4]

Since man is body he shares in the material world around him, which passes within him through his sense perceptions. Because man is mind he belongs to the world of higher reality and pure spirit. Cyril of Alexandria saw man as God's crowned image because he is both. It is man who moulds and manipulates matter and renders it articulate. "The sound in a Byzantine hymn, the gestures in a liturgy, the bricks in a church, the cubes in a mosaic are matter made articulate in the Divine praise."[5]

In the light of these things art could not be neutral for the Byzantine Church. It was entirely dedicated to God. Byzantine art is an integral part of religion, one of the instruments of the knowledge of God and one of the means of communion with him.[6]

The Icon

The icon is a picture of a sacred subject which is painted on a panel of wood of varying size. The surface beneath is prepared with a mixture of powdered alabaster and glue beneath which linen is sometimes stretched and colors are laid on using the yolk of an egg as medium.[7] It was the defense of the icon that produced the great understanding of the role of art in the theology of the Byzantine Church, and also refined the Christological doctrine of the early Church. Icons are possible because of the humanity of Christ, a new humanity which was fully restored to communion with God; it was deified in virtue of the communication of idioms, fully bearing again the image of God.[18] This fact is reflected in iconography as a form of art. The icon is a further instance of the Divine Presence revivifying matter:

> In an icon all the elements of nature are represented and transformed into a vision of God. The mineral world is represented by chalk and alabaster which is covered by paint and by the jewels and precious metals which adorn the icon. The plant world is represented by the wood on which the icon is painted. The animal world is represented by the egg with which the paint is mixed. And even the human world is represented by the relics of the saints which are added to the paint. This amalgamation of all the elements of creation in the icon is an assertion of and emphasis upon the indwelling holiness of the entire created world which participates and shares in the redemption of Christ.[9]

Theodore the Studite sees the art of iconography reflecting the work of God: "The fact that God made man in his own image and likeness shows that iconography is a divine action."[10]

Icon and Theology

The Byzantine Church sees art as a visual interpretation of dogma; the goal of this art is sophisticated and metaphysical. Nowhere is the Orthodox faith more visibly expressed than in the icon. The icon demonstrates the fundamental truth of the faith.[11]

The seventh Ecumenical Council says that icons express the approved legislation and tradition of the Catholic Church and that the conception and tradition of the icon is derived from the Holy Fathers.[12] Uspenskii as quoted by Ware says that the dogma presented is an objective reality, clearly defined and in accordance with Orthodox doctrine; icons do not present individual interpretations nor abstract conceptions but the fundamental truths of the Church.

This is not the primary function of the icon i.e. to teach, nor is this the primary function of theology in the East. The icon is a mystery which leads the beholder to something beyond itself.

Mystery-Presence

This understanding of the icon reminds one of the liturgist from Maria Laach, Odo Casel. His theory of mystery-presence and the Eucharist are usually passed over very quickly in most seminaries. Here is where I believe the icon should be placed. It is more than a picture, more than a teacher, more than a window to another world. It is for the believer an inscape, a leading into a fuller participation or at least experience of the Incomprehensible One. When one stands before the icon with the right disposition of heart and mind one is really in touch with the presence of the subject which the icon represents.

> According to Orthodox belief an icon is a place of gracious presence. It is the place of an appearance of Christ, of the Virgin, of the saints, of all those represented and hence serves as a place for prayers to them.[13]

The doctrinal basis for the icon is the fact of the Incarnation of Christ. In assuming a human body he used matter as a vehicle of spirit, rescued it from corruption and consecrated it to share in his redemptive purpose. What is true of Christ's material body is true of other forms of matter such as the material elements in the sacraments, the scriptures and the icon. It is in these three that Christ witnesses to a God who is in our midst.

The Council of Constanople (869-870) says that the icon is to be venerated with the same honor as the book of the Gospels:

> Just as we all attain salvation through the letters written in the Book of the Gospels, so all alike, whether learned or uneducated, benefit from the colours painted in the icons. What the written word proclaims through letters, iconography proclaims and represents through colours *(Canon 3).*

Christ who is present to us through the Scriptures is present to us through the icon. St. John of Damascus says that the icon is *a memorial or remembrance.*

The idea of the icon as a presence, a memorial recalls the biblical concept of *memorial.* When one remembers in the bible, it is not just a theoretical recollection. What is recalled becomes a present reality. It is not a subjective, psychological act of returning to the past, but an objective reality destined to make someone or something perpetually present before God. Memorial in the biblical mode is a sacred sign from God to his people who preserve it as a spiritual treasure, and it implies a continuity of the mysterious permanence of divine action. Biblical people recalling, remembering, proclaiming the saving acts of God were able to become partakers in those saving acts, for God is mysteriously present, acting on behalf of very generation.[14] Just as the Eucharist and the Scriptures proclaim the good news about God becoming man, about his presence among us with a glorified and deified humanity first in Christ but also through him and the Spirit in the Virgin and the saints, so too the icon.

This sacramental presence in wood and color and lines is brought about by the prayer of the Church. The connexion between the icon and what it depicts is created by the Church. Through the blessing wood and color and lines become truly an icon, and a link between the human and the divine through which the worshipper comes into contact with "the other world".[15] This blessing establishes the connexion between the image and the prototype; it is a mystical meeting.[16] Now under visible signs (colors and lines) the eyes of faith can unfailingly discern and comprehend the transcendant reality truly present.[17] Through this presence we co-participate in the mystery and the Lord is then continually present in his church giving it life and healing. Through the icon we intimately come in touch with God.

Icon and Prayer

The cult of icons rests above all on prayer. Before the icon man can come close to the mystery of God. Man can pray before the icon for the Spirit to fill him with the gifts God has given to his saints. The icon helps man to become transparent to the divine life and rediscover the lost image of God in himself. The icon itself becomes the channel through which our prayer reaches God and God's grace touches us.

> When the faithful pray before an icon, their prayer does not stop at the icon-object. It orients itself with it and directs its thought, its movement, its fervor toward the person of whom the icon is the image.[18]

For the simple faithful the veneration of icons is a real experience, and a source of the life-giving grace of God. Through the contemplation of the icon man is transfigured by the Light of grace which shines through it.

Icons and Time

In our prayer and liturgical life we confront the mystery of God. This life is not a static thing but a movement, a movement from time to timelessness. While the Office sanctifies the day the Eucharist takes us into the "eighth day," where there is no time. The icon assists in this journey to eternity and helps us to experience and strengthen us so that we may once again go back into time to live our lives as deified creatures. Aslanoff writes:

> We venerate the icon in the same manner in which we venerate Sacred Scripture. When we listen to the reading of the Gospel at the Office of Christmas, it is not the text read at the precise time of December twenty-fifth which strikes our intelligence. It is not a commemoration of a past historical event. The proclamation of the Nativity read at office

transports us outside our spatial-temporal reality to the time which is already eternity and the place which is already the Kingdom of God realized for all men at Bethlehem.[19]

In worship every temporal sign of the Lord's saving work is relived. Events of our religious history are not mere past events but mystically happening even to this day. In worship time ceases to exist in the form of past, present and future and is changed into a mystical life experience in which all is condensed and experienced mystically as something living and present before our eyes.

> Byzantine iconography reflects this meaning of time.... In iconography time in the mathematical sense is abolished, the sacred events and persons are represented in such wise that they are made contemporary and appear as belonging to the eternal present, or, to put it in another way, to eternity—introduced and lived in the present and in every moment of time.[20]

The icon becomes our Tabor. We experience through it the eternal realities; we have our inscape into a deeper more profound experience of eternity. Just as the Transfiguration strengthened the apostles so that they could continue on their way to Jerusalem for the fulfillment of Christ's earthly time our experience of eternity which we receive in our encounter with the mystery-presence of the icon strengthens us as we wait in joyful hope for the fulfillment of all time in the Parousia.

Conclusion

Gibbon thought that the icon was superstition, ignorance, false-hood and folly. This could not be farther from the truth. We do not boldly face the icon and proclaim our righteousness as the Pharisee did but we come to the icon with reverence and silence. We know that it is here that the Lord continues to reveal himself to us and it is here that we discover who we are. We encounter the Lord and our souls find salvation. Before the icon we cannot speak because we are confronted with the awesomeness of God. We are not worshipping idols but letting God touch us through the matter he created and redeemed.

Just as the theology of the East is best described as apophatic so too the art of the east. Truth is there, it is not demonstrated. It is there for us to contemplate and experience in love, not to dissect and analyze. The Scriptures are the word of God made language and the icon is the word of God made picture. Both reveal to us the Glory of God.

St. John of Damascus speaks of the icon as a revelation and a song of triumph. This it is. It is a grace and the life of God which penetrates and purifies. Archbishop Raya remarks:

> From the icon properly venerated emanates a power that inspires hope and gives consolation . . . it is a bearer of the Spirit, a concrete example of matter restored to its original harmony and beauty, a first fruit of the transfigured cosmos. By the contemplation of a sacred representation the mind becomes filled with its meaning and mystery. The Divinity represented takes possession of the viewer. It is a basic psychological principle that the contemplative becomes transformed into what he beholds: "You become what you contemplate."

NOTES

1. Stephanou, Eusebrus, *Belief and Practice in the Orthodox Church,* New York: Minos Publishing Co., 1966, p. 108.
2. Meyendorff, John, *Byzantine Theology,* New York: Fordham University Press, 1976, p. 45.
3. Aslanoff, Catherine, "The Veneration of Icons," in *Diakonia,* vol. 6, no. 4, 1971, p. 336.
4. Mathew, Gervase, *Byzantine Aesthetics,* New York: Viking Press, 1963, p. 24.
5. *ibid.*
6. Ware, Timothy, "Theology of Icons," *Eastern Churches Review,* vol. 7, no. 1, 1976, p. 5.
7. French, R. M., *The Eastern Orthodox Church,* New York: Hutchinson University Library, 1953, p. 130.
8. Meyendorff, *op. cit.,* p. 48.
9. Raya, Joseph, *The Face of God,* Denville, N.J., Dimension Books, 1976, p. 153.
10. Meyendorff, *op. cit.,* p. 48.
11. Stephanou, *op. cit.,* p. 108. Cf. Alexei Hackel, *The Icon,* Freiberg, Herder, 1954, p. 7.
12. Ware, *op. cit.,* p. 7.

13. Bulgakov, Sergius, *Orthodox Church,* London, 1935, p. 162.
14. Bouyer, Louis, *Eucharist,* South Bend: University of Notre Dame Press, 1968, p. 104.
15. French, *op. cit.,* p. 133.
16. Bulgakov, *op. cit.,* p. 162.
17. Florovsky, Georges, introduction to *The Icon* by Joseph Myslevic, Charleston: Walker, Evans and Cogswell, 1957, p. 4.
18. Aslanoff, *op. cit.,* p. 334.
19. *ibid.*
20. Kalokyris, Konstantinos, "Byzantine Iconography and 'Liturgical' Time," *Eastern Churches Review,* vol. 1, no. 4., 1968, p. 358.
21. Raya, *op. cit.,* p. 155.

PROBLEMS IN THE STUDY
OF EARLY MONASTICISM

by John Blake More

Mr. More is doing graduate studies at the John XXIII Institute of Eastern Christian Studies.

The rise of monasticism in the fourth century, both as a historical phenomenon and as a religious response to the newly established Christian society in the Roman Empire, has produced a great diversity of positions and opinions among modern scholars. This study reviews some salient contemporary work on early monasticism with a view to determining which areas of the general field would be most fruitful as avenues of further investigation. The areas of focus here will be as follows: the extent to which early monasticism can be considered a lay movement; its possible connection with the "martyrdom mentality" of the early Christians; monasticism as a reaction within (and perhaps *against*) the institutional church; whether the monastic movement was largely individualistic or communal.

If the Empire recognized Christianity in the fourth century, the Christian community also accepted Roman society. In doing so, the Christians not only deferred to a social system with which they had co-existed for some time, but they also sought accommodations with an infrastructure of values that was not always and everywhere compatible with the Gospel message. In particular, Roman social structure promoted injustice and the system of values operative at the time was essentially corrupt. There is a strong tendency to interpret the rise of Christian monasticism as a reaction to and withdrawal from what some early Christians saw as their faith's "compromise" with the Empire. These Christians considered that the Roman state and society, rather than being Christianised by the Church, was effectively introducing into the life of the Christian community elements of corruption, secularization, and worldliness that did not characterize it in its pre-Constantinian era. On this view, "monasticism became the 'salt' which does not allow the world to absorb Christianity and subject it to itself."[1]

Many writers conceive the rise of monasticism in terms of reaction or resistance to the developing social milieu, but there is another view according to which it can be seen as a natural result and outcome of certain features of primitive Christian life. Georges Florovsky points out that "even as an enduring historical society, the Church was bound to be detached from the world. An ethos of 'spiritual segregation' was inherent in the faith of ancient Israel."[2] A more specialized version of this view sees monasticism as an attempt to keep alive the martyr mentality of the earlier Christians. When the persecutions stopped, actual martyrdom ceased to be a viable expression of Christian witness and was replaced by monasticism:

> . . . it is in a way, for the sake of the Christian world, in order to keep alive the *martyria,* the testimony of the kingdom of God by which the world is saved, that monks left the world, undertaking their spiritual flight.[3]

Thus, monasticism is to the Church victorious what martyrdom was to the Church under persecution. It is a reasonable and perhaps necessary transformation of the earlier ideal which preserves the essential elements of seclusion and renunciation, brings the idea of community to the fore, and institutionalizes celibacy. In tracing the rise of monasticism, J. M. Besse writes:

> They were, however, numerous in the fourth century; one could say that, by their numbers they wished to offer to God a recompense for the glory which the heroism of the martyrs no longer rendered to Him. The witness the latter had given to the Lord by pouring out their blood, they (the monks) were going to render to him by a life which was one of total immolation, lived in separation from the world and far from its pleasures, in the practice of the most attractive virtues. The monks thus became the martyrs of the triumphant Church.[4]

However, a somewhat less approving interpretation of the connection between martyrdom and monasticism is offered by P. Schaff:

At the same time, however, monasticism afforded also a compensation for martyrdom, which ceased with the Christianization of the state, and thus gave place to a voluntary martyrdom, a gradual self-destruction, a sort of religious suicide ... the ascetics now sought to win the crown of heavenly glory, which their predecessors in the time of persecution had more quickly and easily gained by a bloody death.[5]

Monastic life is of course voluntary, but it is difficult to see why Schaff considers the monastic life any more "voluntary" than the martyrdom of the *earlier* Christians. Apart from the force of their ideals and convictions, the early Christians were in no way obliged to undergo the kind of death they did. It is precisely the freedom with which a martyr accepts his end that makes it a valid testimony to his faith. As to the easiness and quickness of the martyr's bloody death as compared to the protracted nature of the monastic commitment, Schaff is probably being unreasonable. A more balanced view is offered by Schmemann who quotes L. Bouyer:

The supernatural essence of Christian life has always required some absolute expression which would reveal the complete freedom of the Christian in relation to all the realities of this world. Martyrdom was the first response to this demand, born from outward conditions; when these conditions changed and the world ceased to struggle against Christianity, but, on the contrary, proposed an alliance which could and very often did become more dangerous for spiritual values, which were not susceptible to "naturalization," monasticism became a sort of affirmation of their independence.[6]

While Schaff prefers to interpret monasticism as a negative realization of their new freedom on the part of Christians (notice his words "suicide" and "self-destruction"), Schmemann/Bouyer stress that is was precisely in an attempt to maintain the independence of spiritual values that monastic life had its ontogenesis. On this reading monasticism is not a reaction at all, but a natural continuation of Christian life under altered conditions.

H. Chadwick speaks of a "double ethical standard" among primitive Christians and suggests that monasticism developed out of the way of life of those in the community who, unlike the majority, did more than the tenets of the Faith required, those who lived out the

Christian commitment more fully, those "individual Christians in local communities who renounced marriage and all but a minimum of possessions" . . . and . . . "held before themselves and the local congregation the ideal of renunciation with devotion to prayer and to works of mercy."[7] At least one writer chooses to disassociate the rise of monasticism from all notions of reaction, criticism, and social comment:

> Their choice of a life secluded from the world and devoted to a close union with God was not made because of fear of the persecutions . . . , nor because of disgust at the superficial culture of the times, nor because of the fact that they saw their brethren in the faith yielding to a growing lukewarmness; it was simply that they saw it as the only form of life in which they could adequately realize their ascetic ideals.[8]

Bihlmeyer is warmly sympathetic to the idea of monasticism, and therefore tends to smooth over what other historians of the period see as real problems. In actual fact the culture of the times was superficial, and to that extent contradicted the ideals of Christianity; further, there was a growing lukewarmness among Christians, fostered by the compromise with Roman society. While it would be comforting to accept Bihlmeyer's claim, it is also difficult to escape the conclusion that in some sense "average morality had created the authority of the Church and she in her turn legitimized average morality."[9]

Primitive Christianity was characterized by seclusion, renunciation, aesceticism, and idealism. Pre-Constantinian Christians kept themselves apart from their fellow citizens for several reasons. They feared persecution, they formed a spiritual community of believers whose creed required radical separation from things and persons of the world, and their inchoate sacramental system precluded attendance by the uninitiated. Renunciation became a feature of early Christian life as a witness to the entirely spiritual nature of the Christian's calling and as an outward expression of the greater transcendence of spiritual over material values. Asceticism was a scrupulous response to the evangelical counsels, and "idealism" is used here as a cover-term for a complex of attitudes of which the "chiefest" was a willingness to forgo self-interest for the sake of Christian faith, even to the extent of martyrdom.

The Christian community constituted a sub-culture within the Roman state in the sense that its values were different from and largely antagonistic to those of Roman society. Members of the Christian community could be divided into two groups, who for the purposes of discussion we will call *core Christians* and *outer Christians*. The core Christians will tend to live out their faith commitment more intensely than the outer Christians, who will always be the more numerous of the two groups. With continually increasing conversions to the faith, and births within the community, the number of outer Christians will increase correspondingly, since any increase in the membership of a value-sharing group diminishes the intensity of the group's commitment. With the passage of time the core Christians, living out the Gospel precepts with increasing intensity and in ever closer community, come to an understanding of the fullness of Christian life exclusively in terms of those features that have (not so exclusively) characterized the community at large from the beginning: seclusion, renunciation, aesceticism and idealism.

But as the number of the outer Christians increases, their morals and manners bear a growing similarity to those of the general society rather than to those of their Christian brothers. Thus, the social and moral complexion of the total Christian community changes over time and many members identify themselves indifferently as Christians or as members of secular society. If "all was not well" within the Christian community, this state of affairs can be attributed both to a growing luke-warmness produced by a natural increase in membership and a more indirect influence, at least in the outer Christians, from the larger society. An additional factor of important formal influence was the more or less constant effort at suppression of which the Christian community was the object.

In these terms, statements made earlier in this paper will have to be more finely nuanced, without at the same time diminishing the crucial importance of the Empire's recognition of Christianity in the IV century nor of the Church's accommodation to the realities of the Roman state and society. It would perhaps be more accurate, in searching for causative factor for the rise of monasticism to assign roughly equal importance to the internal development of the primitive

Christian community *and* to the public events of that period. In this way, the aescetic movement can be seen as a natural outgrowth and development of the life lived out by the core Christians, rather than exclusively as a reaction to the established conditions following those public events. We should remember that St. Anthony was born in 250 and went to live with an aescetic who had already been leading a form of monastic life for some time, a fact which shows that the impulse to monastic life clearly pre-dates the Constantinian accommodation.

In any event, the monastic movement shows precisely the four features that we have designated as radically characteristic of the life of the primitive core Christians: seclusion, renunciation, aesceticism and idealism. The idea of *community* was so much built into the very fibre of the primitive Christian ethos, that it seems pointless to include it here as an identifying feature, but it was precisely the sense of community that had to be artificially introduced into or imposed upon monasticism once it appeared to be developing an institutional dimension. This issue is the central topic of the remainder of the present discussion.

In her contribution to the *Cambridge Medieval History,* J. M. Hussey says that,

> Fourth century churchmen, particularly bishops, were not without their doubts and tried to bring the (monastic) movement within the diocesan framework.[10]

and Hussey writes later in the same work:

> In its very early days monasticism had threatened to develop outside diocesan control, but wise episcopal and imperial policy had brought it within the framwork of the Church. This was done by decrees in the general councils, supplemented by local church councils and by patriarchal and episcopal rulings.[11]

The fact that the church hierarchy had to take such measures suggests that at some point the monastic movement had diverged in a radical way from the spirit of primitive Christianity; and I would submit that all the concrete manifestations of this departure can be subsumed under the general heading of absence of community. While the early church was not entirely free of ambiguity in respect of the forms of its prayer life (private vs. collective), Pauline and other New Testament texts with their emphasis on the church as the body of Christ do seem to favor the corporate mode. But early Christianity was not just community; it was more importantly liturgical and eucharistic community. Christ prayed alone, it is true, but he also prayed with his disciples; in their presence he instituted the Eucharist.

> Now the new worship was indeed a spiritual sort; it was worship "in truth and in spirit." For it was worship paid God by men who were moved by the Holy Spirit. Yet its inwardness was not to debar all outward expression. This worship was not to consist exclusively of the individual's private prayer; it was not to be inimical to liturgy.[12]

In the context of eucharistic worship the young church saw itself primarily as the *New Israel* and the People of God. The monastic movement in its early stages enjoyed no clear mandate from the community of Christians as a corporate body, and the early monks, perhaps under Origenist or Gnostic influence, largely ignored the sacramental and liturgical life of the church. For these reasons early monasticism, however rich its later contributions to liturgy and theology may have been, stands out as an individualist, separatist, and essentially lay movement. Most historians of the movement agree on this point, as can be seen from the following citations:

> There was a class of hermits, the Sarabaites in Egypt, and the Rhemoboths in Syria, who lived in bands of at least two or three together; but their quarrelsomeness, occasional intemperance and opposition to the clergy brought them into ill repute.[13]

> At this time, most of the monks were not priests.[14]

> Monastic life and virginity were often joined together in the same individual. This double profession, no matter how noble it might be, could not be considered equivalent to the priestly dignity.[15]

> Inherent in eremitism was the danger of excessive individualism, unmitigated by obedience to rule or superior, owing its impetus to lay spirituality, and at times compounded by claims to a gift of prophecy. Cultivation of exaggerated mortification, frequently in a spirit of rivalry, engendered a feeling of pride or self-righteousness that could lead to a patronizing of clergy or fellow solitaries.[16]

It has to be born in mind that while these citations give an accurate general picture of early monastic life in regard to its connection with the clergy, there were significant exceptions, as indicated in Chitty's *The Desert a City*.[17] In any case, the fact that we are dealing with a movement essentially of laymen suggests that the earlier idea of Christianity as, above all, *community* was at some times and in some places tenuous. As John Meyendorff comments: "The very existence of a definite category of Christians practicing a distinct way of life and setting up their own organizations parallel to the existing community inevitably involved church unity itself."[18]

Apart from the issue of the essentially lay character of the IV century aesceticism, there is the problem of its highly individualistic stripe. Christian *community* in the first centuries, from which we are suggesting monasticism was at first a deviation (but to which we are *not* suggesting it constituted a serious threat) was a happy compromise to the conflicting claims of collectivism and radical individualism, polarities that seem not to have let up in their demands on the individual in *any* historical period. However, given the special status of the Christian community as the earthly repository of the Kingdom of God, it was a particularly unfortunate circumstance that, as Chadwick points out, the withdrawal of the aescetics from the larger community "unquestionably weakened the ordinary congregations, and was regarded by many bishops with a misgiving that individual extravagances did much to justify. Throughout the fourth century the monastic movement was straining to overcome the deep distrust of many of the bishops. Its spirit seemed too individualistic and separatist."[19]

It is probably accurate to say that the sense of community that had so characterized the primitive church was weakened by the large-scale exodus in the IVth century of core Christians who considered that they could best live out their faith commitment in the solitude of the desert. In the course of time, these were joined by other Christians whose objective was principally to give free rein to their own need for individualized expression, to engage in aescetical extravagance, and to externalize a sense of rebellion against the clerical establishment. The presence of these persons in the aescetical movement placed further stress on church unity and was sometimes the cause of open conflict with church and imperial authorities. Instances of conflict were, however, exceptional and unrepresentative of the movement as a whole; and unity was restored (if indeed it was ever seriously threatened) principally by action of the bishops, who succeeded in bringing the entire movement under firm ecclesiastical control. Eventually, monasticism takes on a largely institutional (and to a lesser degree, *clerical*) character, extravagances diminish, and what we have called "core" Christianity moves its center from the urban centers of the Empire to the desert.

In searching for the root causes of the rise of monasticism in the IVth century many writers place undue stress on the monk's dissatisfaction with the larger Christian community because of its presumed compromise with Roman secular values. This is an over-simplification that ignores some of the subtleties of primitive Christian life, an understanding of which can bring out the natural continuity between earlier Christianity and the rise of monasticism.

On the other hand, the rise of monasticism in the IVth century did have a limited effect on church unity, owing in the first instance to its lay character but also because it attracted many strong individualists. This problem was solved by action of the bishops and civil authorities. A rapid solution was made easy by the sense of community that was built into the fabric of Christian tradition.

NOTES

1. A. Schmemann, *The Historical Road of Eastern Orthodoxy,* (Crestwood, N.Y.: SVS, 1977), p. 109.
2. G. Florovsky, *Christianity and Culture,* (Belmont, Mass: Norland, 1974), p. 68.
3. A. Schmemann, *Church, World, Mission,* (Crestwood, N.Y.: SVS, 1979), p. 44.
4. J. M. Besse, *Les Moines d'Orient,* (Poitiers: Oudin, 1900), p. 96.
5. P. Schaff, *History of the Christian Church,* (Grand Rapids, Michigan: Aerdmans, 1910), p. 55.
6. A. Schmemann, *The Historical Road,* p. 107.
7. H. Chadwick, *The Early Church,* (Harmondsworth, England: Penguin, 1967), p. 175.
8. K. Bihlmeyer, *Church History,* revised by H. Tuchle, Vol. I, (Westminster: Newman, 1968), p. 158.

9. H. B. Workman, *The Evolution of the Monastic Ideal,* (Boston: Beacon, 1962, 1913), p. 6.
10. J. M. Hussey, *Cambridge Medieval History, Vol. IV,* Part 2. (1967), p. 163.
11. *Ibid.,* p. 167.
12. J. A. Jungmann, S.J., *The Early Liturgy,* (Notre Dame, Ind., 1959), p. 11.
13. P. Schaff, *op. cit.,* p. 157.
14. K. Bihlmeyer, *op. cit.,* p. 363.
15. J. M. Besse, *op. cit.,* p. 411.
16. Ernest W. McDonnell, *Monastic Stability,* chapter 8 of Angeliki E. Laiou— Thomadakis (ed), *Charanis Studies,* (New Brunswick, N.J., 1980), p. 126.
17. D. J. Chitty, *The Desert a City,* (Crestwood, N.Y.: SVS, 1966), throughout.
18. J. Meyendorff, *The Byzantine Legacy in the Orthodox Church,* (Crestwood, N.Y.: SVS, 1982), p. 199.
19. H. Chadwick, *op. cit.,* p. 176.

COMMENT

THE BEGINNING OF THE THEOLOGICAL DIALOGUE BETWEEN ORTHODOX AND CATHOLICS

by *Metropolitan Chrysostomos of Myra*

The Metropolitan of Myra, Chrysostomos, is a member of the Holy Synod of the Ecumenical Patriarchate and president of its commission for interreligious affairs. The following is a sermon he preached at Rhodes in June 1980.

The East and the West are already at work in a dialogue in truth so as to be reconciled in love. The theological dialogue between Orthodoxy and Roman Catholicism has begun. Inaugurated at the invitation of the Ecumenical Patriarch and on a territory within his jurisdiction, the Johannine Isle of Patmos, this dialogue has now made a beginning on the Pauline island of Rhodes.

Yes, the theological dialogue decided on some years ago, carefully prepared on both sides and announced to the world at the historic see of the Apostle Andrew by the Bishops of Old and New Rome, Pope John Paul II and the Ecumenical Patriarch Dimitrios I; the dialogue awaited everywhere, which became for some a great legend, which became and remains for them an object of expectation and for others a matter of contestations; this dialogue, as something demanded by our times and as an expression of the responsibility of the Churches, is now becoming a reality.

This is an event full of significance. Orthodoxy and Roman Catholicism have been led to meeting and discussion and are called to agreement and convergence. This is to be *in equality and in truth*. This was proposed and presented seventeen years ago on this very island of Rhodes by the second Panorthodox Congress. It is to be *in historical integrity and the objective justification* of the positions of yesterday and of today; this has been recognised as a fundamental condition of the dialogue. It is *to seek into and develop the common tradition of the Church* through careful verification of the points of convergence between the two sides, as also of the points that separate us. On this too both sides are already in agreement. Lastly, it is to be *in mutual understanding; and with a readiness for reconciliation, in humility and in love.* This is what has been decided and is intended by the commissions on either side.

These commissions, already set up as responsible groups of men with the mandate of their Churches, are ready "to give account for" their work (*Hebr.* 13:17) before God and men, to conduct a dialogue—nothing but a dialogue—and thus to prepare the day when the tunic of Christ will once more be woven without seam, that Christ who "works with us and confirms the message by the signs that attend it" (*Mark* 16:20).

From this sacred pulpit it is not my task today to speak about the facts of yesterday; still less to pass judgement on the "positions" of yesterday, this or that "position" regarding the dialogue now begun; nor to trace in advance the prospects for tomorrow. One has no such prophetic charism and no one can claim it for himself. After all, all belongs to the Lord.

Rather I wish to sketch the setting of this dialogue: first its *historical setting* which has, I think, fundamentally changed; then the setting of the *theological problematic* of the dialogue which is differentiated from that of the past; the setting of the *sociological conditions* of the dialogue which, I believe, urge us on today. And finally there is the setting of the *biblical precept* for the dialogue, the only one that has not changed, as if God had defined the distinctive signs and the principal characteristics of the dialogue we are undertaking today.

Historical Setting

My brothers, just now I spoke first of the historical setting of the dialogue, and I said this has fundamentally changed. This is true of both sides.

Orthodoxy, first of all, is no longer in the Middle Ages, is no longer simply Byzantium, is not a monocracy in a theocratic form. Orthodoxy today is one, undivided, coherent, but yet has its differentiations. It is not a unilateral and totalitarian juridical system; it is not uninational, a centripetal group in which the ecclesiastical authorities are centralised. It is far beyond all that. Through its unchangeable presuppositions Orthodoxy has acquired large, very large dimensions. Over and above the masses of population, the millions of faithful it represents; over and above the plurality of cultures and traditions it comprehends; over and above the canonical forms of structures it presents through its well known system of autocephalism, it is a new and living reality, full of vigour, a force in various Sees, a system of local churches in the one Orthodoxy, with full awareness of its ecclesial composition.

History has made it so. It has been truly said of the Church of Constantinople that it is "Byzantium after Byzantium". I would state unreservedly that the Orthodoxy of today is a reordered form of the Orthodoxy of yesterday. Every good thing—unchangeably good— inherited from yesterday has been assimilated by the traditional and contemporary dimensions of Orthodoxy, which is, and is today, the historical reality of our time in the system of contemporary Christianity. So the dialogue with her must take account of these new historical and realistic data of Orthodoxy.

Similar assertions hold true for the Roman Catholic Church as well—at least for those of us who see her from outside. History has carried out a transforming work in her regard also, and has made her what she is. Several historical contexts in which she once moved more easily have changed. The West is no longer a Latin Middle Ages, a dry scholasticism, an immutable Caesaropapism etc.

It is not my task in this orthodox pulpit to evaluate or describe the other side: such an attempt would be unjust, or at least maladroit.

In any case, history is decisive, penetrating and often inexorable.

This shows that between the second half of the thirteenth century (or the first half of the fifteenth) when the known procedures of dialogue and of attempts at union were started by one side or the other on the presuppositions and in the historico-political conditions then known—between those days and these closing decades of the twentieth century there is a recognised difference of historical setting, a difference in the historical scene of the theological dialogue between the Orthodox East and the Latin West.

Theological Problematic

Next, my brothers, I referred to the theological problematic of the dialogue: I said this was differentiated from that of yesterday. That is clear, beyond discussion.

It has been said on the Orthodox side, and admitted by the other side, that "the dialogue must start from the elements that unite the Orthodox Churches and the Roman Catholic Church."

But already this is the assertion of a crucial differentiation which makes itself felt. Let me explain. It is impossible, for instance, to forget the problematic of not so long ago, when the East and the West took cognizance of their differences, from the ninth century (perhaps even earlier) until the last years of the nineteenth century, just a few decades ago. Clearly the two worlds were built up on the points which divided them. The Orthodox, through minute and persistent examination of the smallest details, an examination justified by the patristic experience as well as by the demands of the Byzantinism of the time, on the one side, and, on the other side the Roman Catholics through their unchangeable "positions" inspired by the systematic dialectic of their scholastic and neo-scholastic schools, both insisted on the points, great and small, that separated them.

Thus conflict was nourished, the distance between them grew, hatred was perpetuated, helped it is true by non-theological factors, from politics to those expansionist tendencies of which the past knew so much.

And today? Can all this be blotted out, will it be blotted out, by the stroke of a pen? Certainly not. It has been said—once again by the Orthodox side and admitted by the other side—that study and research into the points that unite us "in no way means it is desirable or even possible to avoid the problems that divide the two Churches. It means only that the starting point of the dialogue should be in a positive spirit, a spirit that should prevail in the treatment of the problems that have accumulated during a division of several centuries."

These few examples suffice, I believe, to show that the problematic is no easier, and that it cannot be simplified, set aside or betrayed; it is simply differentiated, has been led towards a new scale of values in the assessment of differences, and has become more constructive.

Sociological Conditions

The third point I wish to speak of refers to the sociological conditions of the dialogue: these, as I have said, urge us on.

Here, in the East as in the West, we must give the first word to the People of God. Yes, the People of God is on the side of reconciliation, fraternization, the unity of our forces in a world divided in so many ways, secularized, shaken by the opposed forces that deny God. It is this People that prays the Lord day and night "for the peace of the whole world, for the stability of the holy Churches of God, and for the union of all."

This People must be kept informed, and this is true on both sides. It must be kept informed in a way that is not incomplete, and it must not be given an erroneous picture of the work undertaken. This is a definitive condition of our dialogue.

Over and above this, I do not think that there is anyone on either side who denies the need for the dialogue since, certainly, the conditions laid down will be observed, extreme positions will be avoided, agreed half-solutions and compromises will be excluded, and thus the obstacles to the dialogue and to its goals will be removed.

May I at this stage read a paragraph from the basic text, proposed by the Orthodox side and accepted by both sides, the Foundation-Text of the present dialogue. This text says: "The dialogue of love must continually accompany the theological dialogue in order to faciliate the solution of difficulties and to strengthen the deepening of brotherly relations between the two Churches at local as well as at the general level. To this end it will be desirable that unacceptable situations should be reconsidered, as for instance the question of 'uniatism', and 'proselytism' etc."

Generally speaking, the theological dialogue can bear fruit only in an atmosphere of love, humility and prayer.

That, my brothers, is why I consider that the sociological conditions of the dialogue urge us on today. Society is tired of the ambiguities of yesterday. Healthy societies have shown and are showing their preference for constructive dialogue in every realm, and certainly also in the realm of the churches.

At one time solutions were imposed from above, to be absorbed by the masses. Orthodoxy has a long experience of this. Today movements are demanded by the masses and imposed from below. To turn a deaf ear to such demands is unthinkable. This is why the sociological conditions of the contemporary dialogue between the Churches must be considered pressing. From this sacred pulpit I repeat: It is enough that the dialogue should be conducted "in an atmosphere of love, humility and prayer". And I add: *and in equality in truth and in sincerity.*

Biblical Precept

And so I come to the fourth and last distinctive sign of the theological dialogue, the biblical precept.

My brothers, the distinctive and characteristic fundamental signs of the theological dialogue between Orthodoxy and Roman Catholicism, indeed of all dialogue, bear the seal of God's will. God is truth, wisdom, love. And this God who was for John the Evangelist "he who is, and who was, and who is to come, the Almighty" (*Apoc.* 1:8) bids the Churches "to live in truth, wisdom and love."

Consequently, every aspect of their life and existence, their journey and their co-existence, should be inspired by these three distinctive signs.

This means that all that they preserve as elements of faith in their teaching and tradition should be possessed in truth, wisdom and love. Orthodoxy has on many occasions borne witness of this distinctive sign.

But when the moment comes to undertake an exchange of what each side preserves, this exchange too must take place in truth, wisdom and love.

In this connection the Apostle James says: "Do not boast and be false to the truth. This wisdom is not such as comes down from above, but is earthly, unspiritual, devilish. For where jealousy and selfish ambition exist, there will be disorder and every vile practice" (*James* 3:14ff). And the same Apostle adds: "But the wisdom which is from above is first pure, then peaceable, gentle, open to reason, full of mercy and good fruits, without uncertainty or insincerity" (*James* 3:17).

Completing God's command concerning this, the Apostle Paul writes to the Corinthians describing his personal experience when establishing the truth among them according to the only wisdom possible, the wisdom of God. "My speech and my message were not in plausible words of wisdom, but in demonstration of the Spirit and power, that your faith might not rest in the wisdom of men but in the power of God" (*I Cor.* 2:4-5). The meaning of these words of the Apostle is clear.

Today's homily is certainly not an admonition; it is a simple reminder of what we are bidden by the times and by the way of the Lord.

Consequently we must all be aware that "we cannot do anything against the truth, but only for the truth" (*II Cor.* 13:8) and that the participants in the dialogue, as delegates of their churches, should "each speak the truth with his neighbour, for we are members one of another" (*Eph.* 4:25).

Must we also speak further about the realm of love? Paul, like James and John, links love with truth and wisdom. The thirteenth chapter of the Apostle Paul's First Letter to the Corinthians, a hymn to love, is so well known to all of us that there is no need to speak of it here. I would prefer to point to two of the more practical precepts of the Apostle of the Nations, one addressed to his disciple Timothy, the other to the Christians at Philippi.

To the former he says: you are "not to occupy (yourselves) with myths and endless speculation rather than the divine training that is in the faith; whereas the aim of our charge is love that issues from a pure heart and a good conscience and sincere faith" (*I Tim.* 1:4-5).

In the second text he makes a recommendation that is also a plea:

"Complete my joy by being of the same mind, having the same love, being in full accord and of one mind. Do nothing from selfishness or conceit, but in humility count others better than yourselves. Let each of you look not only to his own interests but also to the interests of others. Have this mind among yourselves, which was in Christ Jesus" (*Phil.* 2:2ff).

What could any human kerygmatic reflection add to all this? It is better to be silent. Let all listen to what John the Evangelist said in the holy surroundings of the grotto of the Apocalypse: "There is no fear in love, but perfect love casts out fear. For fear has to do with punishment, but he who fears is not perfected in love" (*I John* 4:18).

Call to Courage

The dialogue has begun. All that is said and will be said in the truth, all that is maintained and will be maintained in wisdom—in the wisdom of God and the fear of God—all that is being promoted and will be promoted in love and also, let us add, in equality and sincerity, all this should be characterized by courage before God and before men, courage which has never been lacking in the Church and which was the seal of the Spirit on the teaching of the Fathers of the one and undivided Church of the first millennium.

THE CHRISTIAN TRADITIONS OF LEBANON

by Charles Frazee

Dr. Frazee is a member of the Department of History of California State University at Fullerton. This paper was given at a symposium on the Religious Traditions of Lebanon.

The land which now is called Lebanon belonged to the Roman province of Syria at the time of Jesus' birth. Centuries before, it had been ancient Phoenicia, divided among such important cities as Tyre, Sidon, Beirut and Byblos whose merchants and colonists over a period of several centuries contested the Mediterranean with the Greeks. By the first century the Phoenician population was but one of many ethnic strains to be found there: Greeks, Syrians, Romans and Jews had also come to find homes in Lebanon and to share in the prosperity which characterized the area.

Very little is known of the first Christian settlements in this part of Syria. The New Testament speaks of the Christians of Damascus and Antioch, but nothing of the port cities. When bishoprics were first established, certainly by the latter half of the first century, the Christians along the Lebanese coast must have been more numerous. With the passage of time, they increased in size and importance. They belonged to the family of Syrian churches under the Metropolitan of Antioch, the most important ecclesiastic of the orient, but no bishop of present-day Lebanon figured prominently in the early church. However, in 337 Tyre was the site of a council in which Athanasius, Metropolitan of Alexandria in Egypt, was to stand trial before his Asian opponents. The location of the council was chosen for its convenience, not because of the importance of Tyre's Christian community.

In the fifth century the people of western Syria, like all of the Christian east, became involved in the great theological debates over the exact relationship between the divine and human natures of Jesus. These disputes split the Syrian church into two factions: one, sometimes called monophysite, declared in favor of the extreme Alexandrine position, asserting that Jesus' divinity was the predominant fact of his being. The other group, the Chalcedonian, held with the council which met at Chalcedon in 451, that there was a true and complete human nature in Jesus with all of the properties which accompany manhood. Since it was the latter who had the support of Constantinople's ruler, its members were also called Melkites, from the semitic word for emperor.

For the next eighty years efforts to bring about a reconciliation between the two parties proved fruitless. Indeed, imperial favor shifted from the Melkites to the Non-Chalcedonians during this period. Then came the powerful Justinian, emperor after 527, a strong advocate of Chalcedon, who sought to impose its formula on the Syrians, no matter what the cost, and actively persecuted the Non-Chalcedonians. They lost their churches, their clergy were imprisoned or exiled, their monks and nuns were expelled from their monasteries. It appeared that their cause was doomed to extinction.

Unwittingly, however, Justinian allowed a Non-Chalcedonian bishop, Jacob Baradaeus, to reach Syria. Almost single-handedly this man travelling in a beggar's disguise restored the clergy of the Non-Chalcedonian church and confirmed the congregations of persecuted Christians in their rejection of imperial theology. By the time of Jacob's death, the Syrian church was once more flourishing and its grateful members adopted the name Jacobite after their patron so as to immortalize his contribution to their survival. The head of the Syrian Jacobites, calling himself Patriarch of Antioch, never lived in the city whose title he bore, but took up a monastic residence in the regions of eastern Syria. His followers were to be found throughout Syria, their loyalty to their cause never flagging, despite Constantinople's efforts at repression.

In the early seventh century, Syria was swept by a Persian invasion which resulted in an immense loss of life and property. The Christians, both Melkite and Jacobite, were left reeling from this blow. But the Persian advance proved temporary. The emperor Heraklios mounted a counterattack which ousted the Persians from the Mediterranean and returned Syria to Roman control. This victory however also proved transitory for the great Arab invasion was but six years away. In 636, inspired by the new faith brought to them by Muhammed, Arab armies overran Syria and brought both Melkites and Jacobites under their political control.

The Muslim leaders granted toleration to the Syrian Christians since they were "People of the Book," to whom God had once sent a sacred scripture. In the view of Islam, the Christian scriptures had been made obsolete after the revelation of the *Koran,* but no forced conversion was to be undertaken against the Christians. Certain obligations were enforced: the *Jizyah,* a poll tax, was placed upon every Christian male except the clergy and monks in lieu of military service, no converts were allowed to pass from Islam into Christianity, no new churches were to be built and, in general, Christians were forbidden to hold policy-making positions in the Muslim state. For the Jacobite cause, the immediate effect was beneficial, since the Byzantine emperor's persecution ended when the Arabs seized Syria. Quarrels among Christians were of no interest to the Muslim leaders.

The rule of Heraklios as Byzantine emperor was important for the subsequent history of Lebanon because of other events which transpired during his rule. In 636, the very same year that Syria was abandoned to the Arabs, Heraklios issued a document known as the *Ekthesis.* In it the emperor proposed a middle ground between the Non-Chalcedonian and the Chalcedonian positions. The emperor urged a doctrine of one will, the divine, in Jesus, known as the doctrine of monotheletism. It was expected that such an explanation would please both the so-called monophysites by going half-way towards their claims while retaining the allegiance of the Melkites. Apparently the Syrian Melkites were not adverse to such an explanation although the Jacobites' response was guarded. In one Melkite monastery, called Bait Maroun, "the house of Maron," the emperor received strong support. It is from this event that the Maronites, the largest Christian community in Lebanon today, have their origin.

The monastery of Bait Maroun was located on the Orontes River close to ancient Apamea. This would place it about 40 miles south and east of Antioch and inland, approximately 25 miles, from modern-day Latakia, now the major port of Syria. The monastery had been founded early in the fifth century to hold the remains of a local saint named Maron. Very little is known of Maron's life beyond a notice in a work of Theoderet of Cyrrhus, who placed Maron among the many Syrian ascetics who peopled the mountains and deserts of the country late in the fourth century. Maron may well have been the first of the *Aerikos* saints, those who rejected any type of dwelling but lived exposed to the elements day and night, summer and winter, as their particular type of austerity.

After his death in 410 Maron's disciples removed his body to the Apamea shrine and built a church and monastery dedicated to guarding his tomb and supervising the many pilgrims who frequented it in search of spiritual and material rewards. By 445 Theoderet testifies that the community had reached four hundred monks and the nearby villages had come to depend on them for their spiritual ministry. The *Higoumen,* or Abbot, of Bait Maroun became a powerful figure and a staunch supporter of Chalcedon. While many of the other monasteries were monophysite, Bait Maroun never deviated from the orthodox faith as defined at Chalcedon, and received, in return, numerous endowments from Constantinople. On the other hand, when monophysite emperors ruled, persecution of the monks broke out. A letter to Pope Hormisdas in Rome, written in 517, begs his assistance for the Syrian Melkite monasteries. The first to sign, among two hundred others, is Alexander, "Priest and Archimandrite of Blessed Maroun."

The establishment of the Umayyad caliphate in Damascus brought prosperous times to Syria. Shipyards along the coast were kept busy in building a navy to contest the east Mediterranean with the Byzantines. Many Christians took service in this force since the Arabs were too few to man the many vessels required by the caliph. The mighty cedars of Lebanon were felled to provide the wood for the fleet which attacked Constantinople in 674. After its failure, emperor Constantine IV summoned a council to meet in Constantinople to discuss monotheletism. Few supporters of the *Ekthesis* were left, except for the Patriarch of Antioch, whom Constantine subsequently forced from office.

During the latter part of the seventh century the Melkite patriarchs of Antioch lived in exile in Constantinople; in 702 the office was left vacant for forty years. During this period the Maronites became an autonomous church with all its ties to Constantinople broken. In the ninth century its *Higoumen* assumed the title to Antioch and consecrated a synod of bishops to assist him in his office. When a Melkite incumbent returned to Antioch in the mid-eighth century, the Maronites refused to give him allegiance. Now there were three Syrian churches: the Maronite, the Melkite and the Jacobite. At this time all of them, to some extent, were losing their Syriac language, adopting the Arabic of the conquerer.

Sometime in the late seventh and early eighth century the Syrian villagers settled about Bait Maroun began emigrating southward to Mount Lebanon. Accompanied by some of the monks who cared for them, they settled on the northern flanks of Mount Lebanon so as to be free of conflict and heavy taxation. In 749 the first known monastery, dedicated to St. Mammas, was founded at Idhin. The Arab historian Al-Masûdi, tells of the destruction of Bait Maroun shortly before 939; this resulted in the transfer of the patriarch and the remainder of his people to the mountain. Here he established a theocratic state with unchallenged authority both in secular and religious affairs. Tribal chieftains known as *muqaddamin* governed their own followers in his name and provided a militia, always on the alert for trouble.

Maronite isolation was broken only in 1099 when the western knights of the First Crusade appeared on the Lebanese coast on the way to Jerusalem. The Latins were delighted to discover a Christian community who shared their likes and dislikes. A natural alliance was found. Many Maronites descended from their mountain to take employment with the Franks.

In 1181 the Maronite patriarch, whose name is unrecorded, accompanied by three of his bishops, many priests and monks and an estimated forty thousand people, entered Antioch to profess their faith in the Catholic Church. He placed his hands in those of the Latin patriarch, Amaury of Limoges, and swore to recognize the Pope of Rome as his religious superior. During the remainder of the crusading period Maronites and western churchmen were on good terms despite papal chiding over some discrepancies concerning the eastern custom of conferring the sacraments. Nevertheless the papal pallium sent from Rome soon became a symbol of legitimacy for the Maronite patriarchs, proudly worn to demonstrate their alliance with the Bishop of Rome.

The crusading period affected the other Syrian churches in different ways. The western knights who came to the orient brought their own clergy with them. Eastern bishops and priests in areas which they conquered were expected to regard Latin clerics as their superiors, to commemorate the Pope in the liturgy and to bring their problems to the western ecclesiastics for solution. Since the Syrian Jacobite church tended to be made up of a rural population, heavily in debt to the monasteries in their midst, they were generally left alone by the Franks. Their bishops were allowed to function once they had agreed to commemorate the Pope in the liturgy with few questions asked concerning their "monophysitism."

On the other hand, the crusaders created serious problems for the Syrian Melkites, since they occupied the cities along with the Latins. Western bishops appeared in Tyre, Sidon, Beirut and Tripolis, wherever a Latin garrison and merchants settled. A pattern had been set by the Norman Bohemond of Taranto who ousted the Melkite patriarch of Antioch, installing in his place a Latin. So long as the crusading states lasted, the Melkite hierarchy was oppressed, forced into impotent exile or into professing a faith with which they disagreed.

When the crusader states were extinguished in the twelfth and thirteenth centuries, the Latin bishops and priests returned to Europe. The Melkite hierarchy made their way back to their former places, the Jacobites forgot whatever western contacts they may have developed. Only the Maronites, once more withdrawn to Mount Lebanon, kept their western ties.. For the next two centuries their isolation protected them, but it also meant that their union with Rome was little more than nominal. Only wandering Franciscans served to keep the Maronites reminded of their western ties. The greater exposure of the Melkites and Jacobites to Muslim administrators meant that many of their congregants passed over into Islam: after the fourteenth century, the Christians dropped below fifty percent of the population. Accelerated erosion occurred during the difficult years of the fourteenth and fifteenth centuries when the Mongols under Timur devastated the Near East.

In 1516 a new development occurred which changed the situation in Lebanon. The Ottoman Turks succeeded in winning this part of the world for their empire. All three Syrian churches now had the sultans of Istanbul as their political leaders. The Greek patriarchs of Istanbul were made responsible for all Orthodox Christians, irrespective of their ethnic or geographical position. Armenian patriarchs headed all the sultan's Non-Chalcedonian churches. No provision whatsoever was made for the Maronites.

At the time of the Turkish conquest, the Syrian Melkites were already in difficulty. Their number continued to decline; their patriarch was so poor that he often had to move about, searching for cities which had sufficient merchants to support him. Antioch, a victim of war and earthquake, had long been abandoned so that Damascus became his usual residence. Since the Turks believed in centralization, all Melkite affairs in Istanbul were taken over by the Greeks. It was the Greek patriarch's favorites who held the important positions within the Antiochene church: the term Melkite was abandoned in preference for Greek orthodox.

In the seventeenth century Latin Catholic missionaries began arriving in the orient under the protection of the French consuls who were located there. They made contact with the Syrians and encouraged a faction which resented the Greek influence on their church. One bishop, Euthimios Sayfi, made a profession of the Catholic faith and defied all Greek efforts to oust him. In 1724 when the patriarch Athanasius III died, the Damascenes chose Euthimios' nephew, Seraphim Tanas, to be patriarch. Seraphim had been educated in Rome and had been an aide to the deceased patriarch. Not to be thwarted, the Greek patriarch in Istanbul, with several representatives of the Antiochene church in attendance, nominated a Greek monk named Sylvester to be head of the Orthodox.

The Syrian church, therefore, split in two: into a Catholic half in union with Rome and the Orthodox half, led by a Greek patriarch, whose faith conformed to the patriarch of Constantinople. The

Catholics became known popularly as Greek Catholics. Since Ottoman authorities refused to admit their existence, their patriarchs until the nineteenth century lived on Mount Lebanon among the Maronites. The Orthodox claimants held the cathedral in Damascus with the support of Turkish arms and the Greek patriarch of the capital.

In 1898 the Orthodox Melkites withdrew their allegiance to the Greek patriarch and chose a native Syrian to head the church, Meletius Doumani. His successors, all natives, were troubled by constant internal divisions until the present period, both on the national and local levels in Syria and Lebanon.

The Jacobite church, smallest of all the Syrian churches, played an uneventful role during the Ottoman period. With their center in Kurdistan, the number of Jacobites in Lebanon became so few that their presence was hardly noted. Catholic and Protestant missionaries working with dispirited Jacobite members formed a Syrian Catholic as well as several Syrian Protestant churches from among their converts.

Maronite history is another story. Although the Ottomans gave no recognition to the patriarch, he was also not troubled by the Turks. The Sultans dealt with Lebanon through the Druze chieftains who had become the masters of the Maronites after the crusades. The Druzes, a heterodox Islamic sect begun in the eleventh century, had also taken refuge on Mount Lebanon to escape persecution and gradually came to dominate the Christians.

Due to improvements in communication and transportation as well as the presence of Latin friars and the Jesuits in their midst, the bonds between Rome and the Maronites were strengthened during these centuries. Admittedly there were issues which caused friction as the culture of the east did not always conform to the western missionary's expectations, but there was never any talk of the Maronites abandoning Rome. In 1584 the popes opened a Maronite college in Italy to improve the education of the clergy, and a French guarantee of protection, established in 1649, placed the Paris government in the role of Maronite champions.

In 1736 at Saiyidat Al-Luwayzah a major council of Maronite clergy and *Mouqaddamin* accepted a revision in their church's practice which advanced the latinization of the church. It was believed by the Roman Curia that the more the Maronite customs reflected Latin usage, the closer the bond between the Eastern Church and Rome would be. To be sure, there was resistance among many of the traditionalists, but Rome won the day and since this council a gradual latinization has continued within the Maronite community. French missionaries to Lebanon in the nineteenth century were anxious to make the Maronites the Frenchmen of the Orient and to a large extent Maronite Arabic culture dissolved in the schools established by French religious orders in the Orient.

In the mid-nineteenth century the Maronites were caught in the middle between the Ottoman government and the Egyptian, Muhammed Ali. By now the Maronite population was 140,000 strong while the Druze's numbers had not increased. The Maronite chieftains armed by Ibrahim Pasha, son of Muhammed Ali, refused to turn in their rifles after the Egyptian's campaign against the Sultan faltered. The alarmed Druzes, fearful that the Maronites were escaping their control, attacked the Maronites in 1841 and again in 1860, causing a great slaughter among the Christians. By the time the landing of French troops saved them, the Maronites had lost 15,000 people; 100,000 were homeless, 250 churches and 48 monasteries lay in ruins.

In June 1861 the Ottoman government, pressured by France, England and Russia, agreed to allow the Christian area of Lebanon to become autonomous, placed under a Christian governor, the *Mutesharrif*. After long centuries of subjection, the Maronites now enjoyed a favorable position within the Ottoman empire. From 1861 the Maronites had a feeling of security which brought them prosperity and a higher standard of living never before known. Many took advantage of their freedom to emigrate to Egypt, Europe and the United States, believing that the good times could not last, for they recognized that there were but a small island of Christians in a Muslim sea. Despite this emigration, which weakened the Maronite presence in Lebanon, the region was still 80% Christian in 1914.

The period from 1861 to 1914 was very important for Lebanon. The freedom enjoyed here allowed Arab nationalism to be shaped by

Lebanese intellectuals. The presence of Catholic and Protestant educators contributed to this development, for two universities were founded in Beirut, St. Joseph's by the Jesuits and the Syrian Protestant College by American Presbyterians. Both groups sponsored secondary schools and Arabic printing presses which made Lebanon the heart of intellectual and cultural life of the Near East.

The worst fears of the Syrian Christians were realized during World War I. The Armenian tragedy has been told many times. Not so well known is the disaster which struck the other Christian communities in the Near East. Jacobites, Syrian Catholics, Melkites all suffered thousands of losses. Lebanon was placed under a military government that regarded all Arab Christians as traitors. Ottoman troops swept through the Maronite villages burning them to the ground. A hundred thousand Maronites lost their lives due to disease, starvation and war—one out of every four Maronites died between 1914 to 1918.

The shattered Christian community which survived did not put much trust in Prince Faisal's government in Damascus which professed that Arab-speaking Christians would enjoy the same rights as Muslims. The Maronites, as well as most other Christians, believed they could be safe only if France became their protector. The maronite patriarch Iliyas Butrus Al-Huwayyik told President Wilson's King-Crane commission that if Lebanon was not granted independence, only France could be trusted to manage the region's affairs.

In August 1919 Patriarch Iliyas Butrus went to France and was assured by Premier Georges Clemenceau that France would rise to the occasion. In September 1920 Greater-Lebanon was created as a French mandate—it included the old region of the *Mutesharrifiya,* as well as the coastal cities, the hill country to the south and the Biqa'valley on the east. The incorporation of these new areas, mostly Non-Christian, reduced the proportion of Christians to about 50%; the Maronites were now only one-third of the total. The Sunni Muslims and many Orthodox were not at all happy with the prospect of a Maronite-French coalition administering the country and sought to find ways to circumvent the Mandate government. On 23 May 1926

Lebanon adopted a constitution which shared power among the religious factions, but French presence continued to ensure Maronite predominance in the area.

The weakening of French power in the Near East as a result of World War II caused the Christians and Muslims to declare complete independence from France on 1 January 1944. An unwritten gentlemen's agreement called the National Pact had been agreed to previously. Each religious group in the country would be represented in the National Assembly and within the government based upon the census of 1932. This showed 29% for Maronites, 9.7% for Greek Orthodox, 5.8% for Greek Catholics and 3.29% for the Armenians as the four largest Christian groups. Since this census showed a slight Christian majority, it gave the Maronites a predominant role in the new country. Lebanese emigrants, mostly Maronites, were allowed to hold citizenship, thus giving the Christians a 54,000 majority. The presidency was to be held by a Maronite, the prime minister—a Sunnite, the chief of the National Assembly—a Shi'ite. In the assembly, the number of seats were awarded in multiples of eleven: six for Christians, five for Muslims.

Political life in Lebanon after 1944 was very active. Leading families in the various regions of Lebanon gathered supporters, often tenants on their land, and formed political parties. There was no unity among the Maronite families: the Eddes, the Chamouns, the Jemayels, the Khuris. The Jemayels were sponsors of a patriotic youth group begun in 1936, called *Phalanges Libanaises.* It was strongly Maronite and its members began wearing uniforms to show its strength in the 1950's. Complicating Lebanese politics were the tens of thousands of Palestinian refugees who entered Lebanon after 1949. Christians rejected the Muslim demand that they be counted citizens.

In 1958 a revolution occurred as a result of Muslim discontent and a fervor for Abdul Gamel Nasser's plea for Arab unity among Muslims. A new census was demanded, but knowing how that would turn out, President Camille Chamoun resisted. In the rioting which followed, the Maronite patriarch held firm against Chamoun and refused to bless his call for the United States troops called in to restore order. After 1958 the clock began ticking for a new outbreak of violence as the problems of who should govern the country remained unresolved.

The present problems of Lebanon stem from the war which broke out between Christians and Palestinians in 1975. Native Muslim military units, especially those closely allied with regimes in the Arab world which were mostly anti-American, joined in on the side of the Palestinians. The Syrian army intervened to act as a buffer, but soon became embroiled in the fighting. Lebanon's central government collapsed; in its place were a dozen local chiefs with their private armies: Christian, Muslim and Druzes, some supported by Syria, some by Israel, others by Libya. Moreover, several thousand Palestine Liberation Organization fighters were also present. The last page in this conflict, after the Israeli invasion of this year, has still not been written. Casualties have reached about 100,000 people in this tragic war: physical damage is in the billions of dollars.

The new president, Amin Gemayel, who succeeded his murdered brother Bashir as president, is the son of the Phalangist founder. He must work with a chamber of deputies of 99 members which still reflects the complex religious patchwork of Lebanon. The Maronites have 30 members, Sunni Muslims 20, Shi'ite 19, Greek Orthodox 11, Druzes 6, Greek Catholics 6, Armenians 4. Others (Armenian Catholic, Jacobite, Syrian Catholic, Chaldeans, Latin Catholics and Protestants) are awarded 3 seats. The balance is 54 Christian deputies to 45 Muslims. Much more important for the nation's future than the present internal composition of the chamber will be the policy adopted towards the new government of Lebanon by Israel, the Palestinian Liberation Organization, Syria and the United States.

The Christians of Lebanon are not a unified group. Those who stem from the ancient Antiochene Patriarchate are divided among themselves. Even the Maronites have several factions. The leading families among them all have ambitions, and their followers are little given to compromise.

It was the Maronites who went to war with the Palestinians and the Lebanese Muslime; most other Christians in the country did not commit themselves. While many armed themselves to defend their "turf", they believed it was not their war. An exception was the seige of the Greek Catholics of Zahla. Traditionally, both the Orthodox and Greek Catholics have resisted the Maronite claim to represent the Christians of Lebanon. They are especially nervous about a Maronite-Israeli alliance which they feel would place Eastern Christians in jeopardy throughout the rest of the Middle East. While Maronite strength is found only in Lebanon, the other Christian groups are spread throughout the area. Most have large congregations in Syria, Israel and Jordan, and must be careful not to depart too far from the directives of Damascus of Baghdad.

What has been the Church's role in the past ten years? This is difficult to answer. The Maronite clergy have generally kept a low profile with the exception of a few individuals, principally abbots of the major monasteries. The patriarch is Anthony-Peter Khoreache, a man who prefers to use his influence with his flock in a way that seeks to lessen personal animosities and diffuse tensions. He is deeply aware of the precarious position of the Maronites. More than anyone else he represents a unifying force in the country, someone whom all Maronites and most Muslims respect. His advice and moral strength extend from the presidential palace to the most remote parish on the Mountain. His public appeals for peace are only the most visible of his activities to reconcile the factions of the country.

Patriarch Anthony-Peter must also deal with the other Eastern Catholic Patriarchs. He has an opportunity to do this at the Synod of Bishops, an assembly which meets at Rome on a regular basis to which all the oriental patriarchs are *ex officio* invited along with certain other bishops who are members of their staffs. The Latin Patriarch of Jerusalem (Giacomo Beltritti) is also in attendance. Two of the Oriental Catholic Patriarchs are also located in Lebanon: the Armenian in Bzommar (Peter Ignatius Ghedigian), the Syrian in Beirut (Anthony II Hayek). The Greek Catholic (Maximos V Hakim) lives in Damascus and Cairo, the Chaldean (Paul II Chiekho) in Baghdad. Here it is possible to discuss the political problems of their communities as well as the religious. There are also annual meetings of all the local Catholic Bishops in Lebanon.

The Greek Orthodox leader (Ignatius IV Hazim) and the Cilician

Armenian Catholicos (Karekin II-Sarkissian) who lives in Antelias are also in contact with the Maronite patriarch through visits and correspondence. Relations, which traditionally have been hostile, have improved at least formally, in the past decade.

For the Maronites the present struggle is a matter of life and death; their pro-Western bias places them in the role of beseiged crusaders in the single Middle Eastern nation which constitutinally retains a majority of Christians. They believe that their experience justifies a wary attitude towards Muslims. The other Christians, especially the Greek Orthodox, have learned to live with Islam; but they have not had the same history. The Orthodox attitude, which prefers accommodation with the Arab East rather than the West, regarded as secular and materialistic, is rejected by the Maronites as illusory.

The Maronites take seriously the views of Muammar Kaddafi, speaking in *Al safir* (August 15, 1980) "it is abnormal to be Arab and Christian; the religion of Arab nationalism is Islam . . . If the twelve million Christians of the Arab world are authentic Arabs, they must embrace the Islamic faith . . ." While everyone realizes that Kaddafi holds an extremist position, what guarantee do the Christians have that a Lebanese Kaddafi is impossible?

The Christian Traditions of Lebanon have had a long history. Many who belong to them can trace their ancestry back to the first generation of those who followed Christ. Through the centuries, amid great difficulties, Lebanese Christians have kept the faith while others, not so strong, have not persevered. The Sunday Liturgy has been their greatest source of strength and, if at present, a recourse has been made to the rifle and cannon, this cannot last. A solution to Lebanon's problems requires a return to the principles of respect for human rights taught by Jesus and Muhammed. When these are forgotten hatred and conflict appear. The many traditions that form the Christian communities of Lebanon are all needed to rebuild a Lebanon which can take its place among the nations of the world and testify to the rich heritage of the Christian Orient.

JERUSALEM AND FRATERNITY AMONG HER THREE RELIGIONS

By Stephen Bonian, S.J.

Father Bonian, a Chaldaean Catholic priest born in Iran, is currently engaged in advanced studies at The Pontifical Oriental Institute in Rome.

Jerusalem is the Royal City that has exchanged hands among many peoples and nations from ancient times until today. She has therefore become the symbol of human and inter-religious conflict and resolution, war and peace, subjection and freedom.

My aim in this paper is to see how Jerusalem has become this symbol. I will first sketch a brief history of the city from ancient times up to and including our modern times. Then I will sketch a picture of what Jerusalem means to each of the three major faiths (Judaism, Christianity, and Islam) that hold her shrines, and finally from an ecumenical perspective to see the Christian West as a transnational and transreligious actor between the Israeli Jews and the mostly Muslim Arabs. My hope is that an all-out effort from all the political and religious parties related to this situation would help to reestablish Jerusalem as a true City of Peace and a symbol of fraternal good-will among believers.

Jerusalem in History

The history of Jerusalem is over 4000 years old. The name of the city appears among the cities of Canaan in the Execration Texts of the 12th-13th Dynasties of Egypt in the early 2nd millennium B.C.[1] In the Amarna Letters, it is ruled by a satellite king named Abdu-Hebba (probably a Hittite). After the Israelite settlement the city lay in neutral territory on the boundary of Judah and Benjamin; it was occupied by the Jebusites.

The capture of the city by David is not to be placed immediately after his accession. Several motives besides the mere desire for territory seem to have been at work. David was king for all Israel in a sense in which Saul had not been; and his identification with Judah would not recommend him to the other tribes. He preferred for his royal city a community which had no tribal associations whatever. In addition Jerusalem was a stronger defensive site than any of the older Israelite cities which he might have chosen. The name "City of David" may indicate the character of the royal city; some historians have suggested that the population of the city in David's time was composed entirely of David's court, palace personnel, and personal military force.

Jerusalem suffered a number of invasions and total or partial destructions during its history. In the reign of Rehoboam it was taken by Shishak of Egypt. An invasion by Arabs and Philistines took place in the reign of Jehoram. It was taken by Jehoash of Israel in the reign of Amaziah and parts of its fortifications were dismantled. The city was invaded by the Assyrians under Sennacherib in the reign of Hezakiah. The city was taken apparently without fighting by Necho of Egypt after the death of Josiah. The city surrendered to the Babylonians under Nebuchadnezzar in 598 B.C., apparently without fighting or substantial damage; but when Nebuchadnezzar took it by storm in 587 B.C., after a siege of 18 months, the entire city was destroyed and left depopulated. It was resettled after 537 B.C.

No events are recorded during the Persian and early Greek periods; but Jerusalem was the scene of strife during the Maccabean period. The city was besieged and stormed by the Romans under Pompey in 63 B.C. It was again besieged and stormed by the Romans under Vespasian and Titus in A.D. 70 and suffered substantial destruction. This was effectively the end of Jerusalem as a Jewish center, although the city was not left uninhabited. In the insurrection of Bar Cochba (A.D. 132-135) Jerusalem was again a center of resistance and was again stormed. After its fall Hadrian forbade Jews to dwell there and founded a Roman Colony on the site with the name of Aelia Capitolia.

Over the centuries there followed other conquerors; Byzantine Christians, Arab Muslims, Latin Crusaders, Ottoman Turks, the British and today the Israelis. The present "Jerusalem problem" began with the British conquest of the city in 1917, ending four centuries of Ottoman Turkish rule in Palestine. Britain accepted the responsibility for governing Palestine under a League of Nations mandate but, from 1936 on, found itself caught between Arab and Jewish nationalists in their increasingly bloody contest for control of the area. The number of Jewish immigrants also began to increase. World War II interrupted the struggle, but after the war Britain lost both resources and will to continue governing Palestine. The question of who shall govern it was placed before the United Nations.

In November 1947 the U.N. General Assembly, acknowledging irreconcilable differences between Arabs and Jews, recommended the partition of Palestine, allowing the establishment of independent Arab and Jewish states; the city of Jerusalem was designated a "corpus separatum", to be administered under "a special international regime."

Jews and Arabs of Transjordan (later, after the annexation of the West Bank, to be called "The Hashemite Kingdom of Jordan") both stood to gain from the partition and supported it. All other Arab states stood by the Palestinians and opposed it. The Palestine Arabs of Jerusalem and the West Bank, fearing the absorption of their land by Jordan, violently opposed the plan. Events soon made the scheme politically unenforceable.

Israel declared its statehood on May 14, 1948, a day before the end of the British mandate. On May 15th the British withdrew, and a number of Arab states, including Jordan, went to war against Israel. The results of that war determined the fate of Jerusalem and Palestine for the next 20 years. Israel successfully defended the western, Jewish "New City" of Jerusalem but failed to take possession of the eastern, Arab-speaking half and lost the ancient Jewish Quarter within the walled "Old City". The political division between Arabs and Jews was physically reinforced when Jordan (which annexed East Jerusalem and the West Bank) erected barriers to prevent Jews from entering East Jerusalem to visit their former homes and holy places in the Old City. The barriers were torn down in 1967 during the Six-Day war; the victorious Israelis reunited the city under their own flag and formally annexed East Jerusalem as part of the Capital of Israel.

It should also be mentioned that during the 1948 war (after the partition of Palestine) and in the months immediately preceeding it,

Palestinian Arabs in the hundreds of thousands fled their homes in fear and panic. Following the mass exodus of Palestinian Arabs, Israel took possession of entire cities, or quarters of cities, and hundreds of villages. The farms, the factories, the animals, the shops, and most of the rich Arab citrus holdings fell into Israeli hands.[2]

To this day the vast majority of refugees have continued to live in the enormous refugee camps in the Sinai, in Syria, and in Lebanon. In addition, Israel has refused to allow some 60,000 Arabs who fled Jerusalem during the 1967 Six-Day War to return, and it has used Israeli laws to bring under Jewish ownership much property in Jerusalem that had been Arab-owned before 1967.

Since then Israel has enlarged the boundaries of Jerusalem very significantly and has annexed the whole city into Israel. Moreover, a systematic effort has been made to change the demographic character of the city by encouraging heavy Jewish settlement, and declaring Jerusalem as the Capital of Israel.[3]

In the 60-year period since 1917, neither Great Britain nor the United Nations, nor any other "outside body", has effectively mediated rival Arab and Jewish claims to Jerusalem, leaving unanswered two fundamental questions: Who has the right to rule Jerusalem and how should Jerusalem be governed?

Jerusalem for Jews

The sanctity of Jerusalem in Jewish consciousness is set forth by the themes of unity, loss, and restoration, but most of all loss. The banishment from Jerusalem upon the destruction of the temple by the Babylonians in 586 B.C. then again in 70 A.D. by Romans, instilled the feeling that Jerusalem is the city vital to Jews in the practice of their faith and necessary to their sense of solidarity as people. This essential obligation laid on every Jew to keep the memory of Jerusalem alive is immortalized in the often-quoted words of the postexilic Psalm 137: If I forget you, O Jerusalem, let my right hand wither!

The remembering of Jerusalem became ritualized into the Jewish daily living; when praying a Jew must face Jerusalem; if in Jerusalem, he should turn his heart toward the Temple. In temple days Jews were obligated to make pilgrimages to the Temple. Pilgrimages must still be made to Jerusalem, but the pilgrim is also obliged to mourn the destruction of the Temple (by rending his garment). Mourning for Jerusalem, in fact, was enjoined upon every Jew until the restoration.

The centrality of the memory of Jerusalem is also evidenced everyday in scripture, liturgy, poetry and songs, in the blessings for birth, marriage and the daily meal, and in the words said over the dead.

In Jewish tradition, the hope of restoration is conveyed in the image of children returning to their mother, as first set forth by Second Isaiah (Is. 49:15). Jerusalem, therefore, carries the meaning of "mother" in a way that parallels the designation "mater ecclesia" in Christian expression. Jerusalem is the maternal, earthly home for the Jew in which he or she is to live the life of righteousness, sanctity, and dedication.

Thus the essential meaning of restoration is that of "homecoming". One could speak of an "indissoluble bond" linking Jews together as people in and through Jerusalem and the land. Jerusalem, therefore, as the capital of Eretz Israel has instilled in Jews throughout the world a sense of solidarity, of belonging to this city as their home even if they do not in fact live in it.

A small number of ultra-Orthodox Jews living in Jerusalem reject the Zionist recognition of Jerusalem as the capital of the State of Israel. It is their belief that true Israel will come into being only with the appearance of the Messiah. Yet even they give support to the State of Israel and to a Jewish governance of Jerusalem as the indispensable means to their own communal life expression in this land.

Jerusalem for Christians

Jerusalem in the Christian tradition is built on the Jewish concept of the messianic kingdom and its restoration by Yahweh. From the time of the exilic prophets, Jerusalem had become the center of worship of Yahweh to which all nations will resort. It is the source of the river of life which flows from the temple.

For the early church, therefore, Jerusalem had become the symbol of the place of contact between God and human beings, and the point from which salvation radiates. In both Luke and Acts Jerusalem is given a central position; it is the point toward which Jesus moves throughout the Gospel, and it becomes the focus from which the preaching of the Gospel goes out to the entire world (Lk 24:47, AA1:8).

Earlier, St. Paul also makes Jerusalem the origin of his personal ministry (Rm 15:19). But it is the general refusal of Judaism to accept Christianity and the judgement which in the New Testament threatens it or has overtaken it that causes the transformation of Jerusalem into the messianic symbol which it already is in the Old Testament.

It is the Jerusalem above that is free and the mother of Christians (Gal 4:26), the heavenly Jerusalem which is the end of the pilgrimage of the Christian (Heb 12:22) and the throne of the Lamb (Apoc. 14:1). The vision of the Apocalypse culminates in the descent of the heavenly Jerusalem, which is now synonymous with the kingdom of God and the point of meeting of heaven and earth (Apc. 3:12), 21:9-22:6).

Alongside of this spiritual Jerusalem, Christians from every corner of the earth have come on pilgrimages and still come to gaze on the birth place of Jesus in neighboring Bethlehem, to make their reverent processions on the Way of the Cross to the Church of the Holy Sepulchre, to touch the sacred stone of Christ's tomb, to kiss icons, sing hymns and offer prayers in these and 50 other shrines in and around the city. It is here where a Christian's faith, and one's quest for the historical Jesus are mediated.

Here also the Church is seen at large. The priests who tend the shrines and await the pilgrims represent every branch of Christendom: Greek Orthodox, Roman Catholics, especially the Franciscans (whose duty today as during the later crusades 650 years ago is to protect Roman Catholics rights to the shrines), Armenians, Ethiopians, Copts, Syrians, Russian Orthodox, Anglicans, Lutherans and other Protestants.

Nevertheless, the dual tension between the earthly and heavenly Jerusalem among Christians still persists. While the sacred sites are associated with the life, ministry, death, and resurrection of Jesus Christ, Jesus was, after all, arrested, tried and tortured in Jerusalem. The Jewish religious establishment of Jerusalem rejected Jesus' prophetic ministry, preparing the way for his condemnation and death.

Jesus wept over the city. He prophesied the destruction of the temple, the symbol of Jerusalem's authority and greatness in Hebraic faith.

The Christians of Jerusalem today seem to worry less about who should govern the city, Jews or Arabs, than about who will protect their properties and privileges. Nevertheless there are some divisions among them of the political nature such as being pro or against the P.L.O., along with rivalry over privileges over holy places and in relation to the new Israeli administration of the city.

Thomas Idinopulos sites the example of the antagonism between the Greek Orthodox and the Roman Catholic churches in Jerusalem since the time of the Crusaders up till the present over the control of the Holy Sepulchre and Nativity churches; "The Israelis continue to seek official Vatican recognition of Israel's statehood, and they also would like expressed Vatican support for their unification of Jerusalem. So eagerly did they persue both goals that they were willing to make a deal with the Vatican at the expense of the Greek Orthodox." However, "The Vatican declined the offer, fearing the negative reaction of Arab Catholics throughout the Middle East."[4] Vatican officials have also made it clear that the ecumenical relations between the two churches had a decisive roll to play in arriving at this decision.

JERUSALEM FOR MOSLEM

There is no doubt that Islam has been influenced by its own understanding and interpretation of both Judaism and Christianity. Jerusalem (AL-Quds: The Holy) occupies a distinctive place in Muslim tradition: "O Jerusalem, the choice of Allah of all his lands!" (The Hadith of Mohammed).

Muslim tradition acknowledges a host of Hebraic and Christian personalities of Scripture as constituting one great prophetic line beginning with Adam, continuing through Abraham, Moses, David, Solomon, John the Baptist and Jesus, and reaching its final fulfillment with Mohammed.

It was in Jerusalem that Mohammed is said to have stopped on his journey to heaven to receive the final form of the truth directly from God. Muslim pilgrims journeyed to Jerusalem in great numbers after the Arab conquest of Palestine in 638 A.D. The building of the beautiful shrine of the Dome of the Rock in Jerusalem about 691 A.D. fixed the city as a central place of worship for the Muslim faithful. The shrine was built over what Hebraic tradition holds to be the cornerstone of Solomon's Temple and the site of Abraham's intended sacrifice of Isaac.

Of Jerusalem's 312,000 population, 12,000 is Arab Christian, and 68,000 Muslims. What preoccupies the Israelis, therefore, is the Muslim populations, and how to maintain an effective relationship with these Muslim Arabs who shape the culture of East Jerusalem and who have provided its political leadership for generations. It is these Arabs who prefer to remain an independent, "captive people" in spite of the efforts of the Israelis to unite them with Jews under a common political authority. They see themselves as true Palestinians and the P.L.O. as their real representative body.

Since the Israelis have risen to become the new protectors of the holy shrines in Jerusalem, a new fear has striken the Arab Muslims especially in confrontation with Jews over the Western Wall— Temple Mount area. The wall is sacred to Jews as remanent of the Sacred Temple, destroyed by Romans in 70 A.D. It is also sacred to Muslims as one of the supporters of Haram el-Sharif, the Temple Mount, on which sit two of Islam's most treasured sanctuaries, the Dome of the Rock shrine and the El-Aqsa mosque. Both Jews and Muslims claim religious rights in this area.

When the Israelis took control of East Jerusalem, they cleared an area at the Western Wall to accommodate the thousands of Jews who were expected to gather for worship at the wall or come there simply to gaze at the structure. This project entailed razing a number of Arab houses in the district known as the Mugrabi Quarter. The administration of the Temple at the present time is still with Muslim authorities but its future is still far from certain.

The Future of Jerusalem

The future of Jerusalem as a city of peace seems dependent on whether the Israelis and the Arabs there can respect each others rights, both civil and religious. An important step in this direction was taken by the peaceful initiatives of Sadat and Begin. More recent political and military events have complicated and even imperiled the process.

In any event, the process towards peace will have to address the needs of the party that has suffered most in recent history, the Palestinian refugees.

Sadat has pointed this out in his famous trip to Jerusalem, as well as in his autobiography: "I would like to ask all those who deal with the Middle East question to realize that at the very heart of it lies the Palestinian problem. Let us therefore start by solving that problem. Sinai and Golan Heights are in effect symptoms of a central malaise which is summed up in the Palestinian problem."[5]

Idinopulos also points out that the Palestinian Arabs are not engaging in pious exaggeration or nationalistic rhetoric when they speak of the centrality of Jerusalem in their lives. It is inconceivable to them that there can be a Palestinian State without East Jerusalem as its capital.

The momentum of events in the Arab World, Europe, and America is moving closer to the recognition that the Palestinian question cannot be answered without the political independence of this people in their own land. At the same time Israel will never accede to full Palestinian independence without a solution to Israel's own security problem.[6]

Due to the partial success of the American intermediacy in the peace process, and the need for more parties to be involved in the process (e.g. the P.L.O. moderate leaders), it seems to me that both America and Europe (including the Soviet Union) can play positive roles towards helping the Arabs and the Israelis reach a just and peaceful solution for all parties involved. Alongside the diplomatic level it seems to me that on the trans-religious level the Vatican, the Greek Orthodox and other Christian leaders can meet with Muslim and Jewish religious leaders to reach satisfactory solutions to make the shrines open to all.

There is no doubt that local as well as international politics, human and religious rights are all involved in the Jerusalem problem and constitute its solution. If the peace process is to succeed, then more and more relevent and responsible parties will have to be involved in it. The issue of Jerusalem has posed a strong challenge to the United Nations time and again on the subject of its own identity; as if Jerusalem is saying that its problems will be solved when those nations are truly 'united'! The solution of Jerusalem's problem also challenges the Super Powers to work together rather than against each other for the peace of the world.

It seems to me that the help of these transnational and transreligious actors will make easier the dialogue and the spirit of good will between the Israelis and the Palestinians so that they might live together in the same land in freedom and in peace (according to their own suitable forms of government).

It was never easy for Jerusalem in her history to rebuild herself into a city of peace. Yet her builders never gave up on her no matter how desperate their situation might have been. There is no reason for them to despair now either. In Jerusalem the struggle of many nations and their drive for a just peace is symbolized. Jerusalem is the religious symbol perhaps of what the United Nations is about on the secular level. To stand idle, therefore, or to give up on the problem of Jerusalem, is to give up on God's words of salvation for humanity through the prophets, Jesus, and Muhammed, echoed off the walls of this city.

Even if Jerusalem's inhabitants and their neighbours "grow weary", "tired" and despair (an attitude that is well symbolized in a devastating war) it seems that her God will never give up on her, but will continue to call all nations to meet him in Jerusalem (See especially Is. 49).

NOTES

1. In preparing these remarks, extensive use has been made of the following sources:
   John L. McKenzie, *Dictionary of the Bible* (New York: Macmillan, 1979)
   Thomas A. Idinopulos, two articles in the *Christian Century*: "Jerusalem the Blessed—The shrines of three faiths" (April 1978)
   "Jerusalem the Blessed—Religion and Politics in the Holy City" (May 1978).
2. C. Pratt, *Peace, Justice and Reconciliation in the Arab-Israeli Conflict* (New York: Friendship Press, 1978), p. 25.
3. *ibid.,* p. 33.
4. *op. cit.* (May 1978), p. 500.
5. Anwar el Sadat, *In Search of Identity* (New York: Harper Colophon, 1979), p. 297.
6. T. Idinopolis, "Politics, Theology and Folly in the New Jerusalem Law", *The Christian Century* (October 1980), p. 1008.

DOCUMENTATION

THE VISIT OF HIS HOLINESS
PATRIARCH PIMEN TO NEW YORK

The following is a summary in English of a BBC broadcast prepared by His Grace, Bishop Basil (Rodzianko) of the diocese of San Francisco and the Western United States, Orthodox Church in America.

The invitation of the Preparation Committee of the Second Special Session of the General Assembly of the UN on disarmament to the Patriarch of Moscow and All Russia, Pimen, was completely unexpected in Moscow; there were no preliminary negotiations of any kind.

The invitation was addressed to the whole Russian Orthodox Church, as one of the world religious organizations and therefore has even greater significance. Since the Russian Church within world Orthodoxy is the largest in its membership and has a history of a thousand years, the address of its Patriarch to the General Assembly of the UN can be considered as comparable to the addresses there of the Roman Popes.

His Holiness Patriarch Pimen addressed the Assembly on Thursday, June 24th. It was not reported in the press or media for security reasons. There appeared to be a tacit agreement on the part of everyone involved.

In his address, the Patriarch brought greetings from "millions of believers of the Russian Orthodox Church" and stressed the special responsibility of Christians and all believers to be genuine agents for peace.

"We are well aware that genuine peace can be brought about only as the outcome of joint efforts undertaken by statesmen and peoples and that the duty of churches and religious organizations is to educate believers for peace, to humanize international relations, to seek ways of peace and to follow them in no idle manner. This has always been the course pursued by the Russian Orthodox Church, now approaching her millennium.... Indeed our people know the price of a peaceful life, having suffered through their own tragic experience.... The greatest majority of the Russian Orthodox membership are citizens of the Soviet Union. Therefore, speaking on their behalf, I take it as my duty to present my witness from the position of the peoples of our State on the problems of war and peace."

The Patriarch then conveyed the well known political position of the Soviet State on disarmament, citing the words of the Head of the Government, Leonid Brezhnev. [In a totalitarian system, the official policy of the State always has to be taken into account by every public speaker.] The Patriarch ended his address with a pledge to "exercise our moral authority so that by the prayers of believers and through their active involvement, these resolutions may be brought to life," and his blessing: "Putting trust in the triumph of a lasting and just peace and believing in the Providential help of God to all people who long for peace, I wholeheartedly wish the special session the utmost success and invoke the blessing of the Most High Almighty Creator upon your work."

The unexpected visit of the Patriarch of Moscow and all Russia to New York—the first in history—was also a pastoral visit, with some of his flock here. The Patriarch was visiting a part of the world that for centuries has been an apostolate for Orthodoxy, since that moment when the first Russian missionaries settled in Alaska and began the teaching of Orthodoxy. Since that time the descendents of millions of Orthodox from various countries have settled throughout the whole of America and Canada and an independent Orthodox Church in America has been established. Referring back to the beginnings of Orthodoxy in America, the Patriarch said in a sermon at St. Nicholas Cathedral in New York:

> "On this blessed day, we look back to the origin of Orthodoxy on this continent in the 18th Century and with gratitude to the Lord we think about the blessed educational mission of the many dedicated workers of the Russian Orthodox Church on the soil of North America. Among these missionaries we name above all the first enlighteners of Alaska and the islands located nearby—St. Herman of Alaska and St. Innocent of Moscow and Kolomna who, bringing the light of Christ, prayed and interceded for the whole Church of Russia and for all Orthodox Christians in America.

> "It is with reverence that we recall the names of many Russian archpastors who were in charge of the American See, among them Archbishop Tikhon who later became the Patriarch of Moscow and all Russia, and many other hierarchs, clergymen and laymen who diligently spread and strengthened Holy Orthodoxy on American soil despite many difficulties which they encountered in their saving work."

Patriarch Pimen referred to these difficulties well known to him personally, at the reception arranged in his honor at the Waldorf Astoria Hotel in

New York by the Primate of the Orthodox Church in America Metropolitan
Theodosius.

> "It was the Providence of God that the tomos issued on February 10,
> 1970 by the Patriarch and the Holy Synod, which declared the autoce-
> phaly of the Russian Orthodox Greek Catholic Church in America was
> handed to you, Your Beatitude, then the Bishop of Sitka and Alaska, on
> May 18 of that year when as the head of a delegation authorized by the
> Orthodox Church in America, you came to Moscow."

In his greeting to the Patriarch, Metropolitan Theodosius thanked him
as the representative of the Russian Orthodox Church, for the gift of
independence and, recalling the Russian saints who had brought Orthodoxy
to America, said that the American Church always prays for its mother
Russian Church. Among those in attendance at the reception were Archbishop Silas of the Greek Orthodox Church in America, the Anglican Bishop
of New York Paul Moore, the deputy Permanent Observer of the Holy See
(Vatican) to the United Nations and many other distinguished guests from all
areas of church life in America. Archbishop Iakovos of the Greek Orthodox
Church also hosted a large reception for the Patriarch.

Several hours before his departure for Moscow, Patriarch Pimen gave
his blessing to the Head of the Foreign Department of the Moscow Patriarchate Metropolitan Philaret of Minsk and Byelorussia, for an interview with
Bishop Basil (Rodzianko), the only correspondent to be given a direct
interview. Bishop Basil has been a broadcaster of religious programs for the
BBC for over twenty five years. *The interview, as follows, was included in the
BBC broadcast.*

Bishop Basil: Vladyka, as we know, His Holiness Patriarch Pimen visited
    the United Nations by special invitation to the special session on disar-
    mament. How do you regard such an invitation?
Met. Philaret: We regard the visit of His Holiness the Patriarch of Moscow
    and all Russia to the second special session of the General Assembly of
    the United Nations on disarmament as a high call to our Church to the
    service of peace, of creating a peaceful society, which includes participa-
    tion in the problem of disarmament.
    The address of the Patriarch is an address from millions of believers in
    our country. Millions of parishioners of the Russian Orthodox Church
    speak in the person of Patriarch Pimen. He stated the position of the
    Russian Church, its way of serving the cause of peace. He also stated the

position of our Church with regard to the recent World Peace Conference in Moscow, "Religious Workers for the Preservation of the Sacred Gift of Life from Nuclear Catastrophe."

The Patriarch expressed the conviction that it is by spiritual means, as used by both the Eastern and Western Churches, that the main task of strengthening peace among peoples can be accomplished—that is disarmament of the heart. This is the best way to educate believers to peace; this is our general task: education for peace, in the Western and Eastern Churches, unremitting strengthening of the humanization of relations within national societies and in international relations.

That is how, in general terms, the goal and task of the Patriarch's visit can be characterized—his visit to the second special session of the General Assembly of the UN to which, I repeat, he was invited by the Preparation Committee of this Assembly.

Bishop Basil: We know from information received from Russia that Russian believers are very attached personally to the Patriarch because of his prayerful attitude to the services. What can you say, from your side Vladyka, about the Patriarch's flock?

Met. Philaret: This information is correct. The Patriarch's flock of course is not only Muscovite, but also of all Russia. And I myself can testify to this question here not as a hierarch and immediate member of the Synod, but as a close aide to His Holiness in his enormous Patriarchal work. I can witness here simply as a young Orthodox Christian, who happened to be with His Holiness when he was still the Patriarch's delegate at the Troitse—Sergieva Lavra at Zagorsk and we students would eagerly await Father Pimen at the shrine at Sunday Vespers, with the akathist to St. Sergius, to listen to his spiritual words. Then I became a sub-deacon to Vladyka Pimen, and as sub-deacon I came closer to our present Patriarch and was able to observe him in life, in prayer, in services—and it is precisely this attitude of prayer, love of the Divine Liturgy, the Church, love for his flock, that has carried His Holiness through all his service to the Church up to the present time when he now fulfills the high calling of Patriarchal service in our Church.

Bishop Basil: The visits of both Popes—Paul VI and John Paul II—and His Holiness Patriarch Pimen of Moscow and all Russia, obviously reveals enormous power of faith in the world. Millions of believers are a force which cannot be ignored by any government. What do you see, Vladyka, as the source of that force which is being so overwhelmingly used for the cause of peace, disarmament and the preservation of life?

Met. Philaret: For us Christians, the answer is simple: Christ is our Peace. This peace of Christ which we bring into ourselves, is a reconciliation with God, first of all in our soul. We must diffuse this around ourselves. This is our task. In this is our likeness to God and in this clearly is the strength of all Christian churches. It is precisely in the realization that Christ our God is the basis of our service to the cause of peace that we are fulfilling His words in the Gospel: "Blessed are the peace-makers, for they shall be called the Sons of God." In following His words in the work of creating peace among people, we are thereby participating in the building of the Kingdom of God, to the degree that it can be realized on earth. We don't speak about it being entirely realized; that would not be correct from our point of view; but to feel the Kingdom of God on earth and do something in its name here in our human environment, we must fulfill the words of the Gospel. In this sense the recent Conference in Moscow on religious affairs was very successful, formulating its own motto: "the preservation of the sacred gift of life." Life is sacramental, that is a gift of God that we cannot dispose of. It is sacred for us and we must preserve this gift of life with all the means available to us.

In this is both the strength and effectiveness of religious people and in particular, the Christians who are now organizing a general movement in defense of peace—a march of peace throughout the capitals of Europe. And the religious leaders, the church leaders, are, to their credit, in the forefront of the movement.

Bishop Basil: To what extent, practically speaking, are peace in the world and religious faith related to one another?

Met. Philaret: They are absolutely connected. There is a deep connection between us Christians as representatives of peace and the representatives of other religions on peace, life and simply the aims of people of good will who wish to build on earth a firm and just peace. But we, as the Gospel says, are the "salt of the earth" and the "light of the world." We Christians must yield this salt; we must "salt" with Christian consciousness, spiritually enlighten all the good aspirations of people toward justice and a just society.

Bishop Basil: Would you agree Vladyka, with the opinion held ever more prevalently by many people in the world, that without the active support of genuine believers all over the world, peace on earth is simply not possible?

Met. Philaret: Absolutely, Vladyka, we are of the deep conviction that a real peace can only be achieved through the combined efforts of all people of good will whom believers who are really participating in its creation, treat with understanding, and people who are not religious. Only all together can we achieve, to one degree or another, the just peace desired by all.

Commentary:

Nearly all of the words of the Patriarch, his address at the UN and the interview given by Metropolitan Philaret, are unprecedented as a direct address to the nations of the world and especially the American and Russian people, describing in purely Christian language, the position of the Russian Orthodox Church toward peace as the "peace of Christ," and explaining to the world the Church's efforts toward peace as the spreading of the Kingdom of God. This is not just an earthly peace such as the goal of the Communist Party, but heavenly peace on earth which is the peace of eternal life as taught by Christ. Metropolitan Philaret spoke significantly of the "power of faith"—the witness, mission and spreading of Christianity in the world around us, explaining it as the "salt of the earth" which is needed by those who want to create peace. Quite openly he stated that peace on earth is "simply impossible without Christians" and that, as the Patriarch said in his remarks, must include all countries and governments reconciling their differences in a Christian influenced dialogue. Peace is clearly qualified as a peace in justice, which implicitly refers to human rights and freedom of faith as well as social and international justice. The Patriarch deliberately used the Russian word "pritesnenie" which means "oppression," in his address.

Most important of all to note is that an independent invitation was issued by the UN to the entire Russian Orthodox Church, the Patriarch being its spokesman. The only other such case has been the Pope of Rome. The fact that the Russian Church and the Soviet government were not previously consulted and that the invitation came as a surprise, makes the entire Church and all believers an important factor in international relations and world peace. The Church thus has been allowed to speak in a sense, for the first time since the Revolution, from a position of strength, as is evident in the documents and interview quoted above, and of hope: "Be of good cheer, I have overcome the world."

BOOKS RECEIVED

LIFE IN THE SPIRIT AND MARY, Christopher O'Donnell (Michael Glazier, Inc., Wilmington, Delaware, 1981) pp. 126, $4.95.

FAMILY SERVICES, Alcuin Club Manual #3, Kenneth Stevenson (SPCK, Holy Trinity Church, London, England, 1981) pp. 45, $1.95.

ORTHODOX THEOLOGY AND DIAKONIA, Demetrios J. Constantelos (Hellenic College Press, Brookline, Mass., 1981) pp. 397, $17.95.

ORTHODOX SYNTHESIS The Unity of Theological Thought, Joseph J. Allen (St. Vladimir's Seminary Press, Crestwood, N.Y., 1981) pp. 231.

SYNODICA (Les Editions du Centre Orthodoxe, Geneve, Switzerland, 1981) pp. 152.

EGLISE LOCALE ET EGLISE UNIVERSELLE (Les Editions du Centre Orthodoxe, Geneve, Switzerland, 1981) pp. 359.

DIONYSIUS THE PSEUDO-AREOPAGITE, translated by Thomas L. Campbell (University Press of America, Inc., Wash., D.C., 1981) pp. 230, $10.25.

JOHN PAUL II ON ECUMENISM 1978-1980, John B. Sheerin, CSP, John F. Hotchkin (Office of Publishing Service, Wash., D.C., 1981) pp. 172.

HUMAN GROWTH AND FAITH, John T. Chirban (Univ. Press of America, Washington, D.C., 1981) pp. 211, $10.25.

CATHOLICS IN SOVIET-OCCUPIED LITHUANIA, translated from Chretiens de l'est No. 27, 1980, (Lithuanian Catholic Religious Aid, Brooklyn, N.Y.) pp. 120.

REDEMPTIVE INTIMACY, Dick Westley (Twenty-Third Publications, Mystic, Conn., 1981) pp. 176, paperback $5.95.

JOHN & CHARLES WESLEY, selected Writings & Hymns, Frank Whaling (Paulist Press, New York, 1981) pp. 412, $7.95.

GEORGE HERBERT, THE COUNTRY PARSON, THE TEMPLE, John N. Wall, Jr. (Paulist Press, New York, 1981) pp. 354, $7.95.

ALL THE FULLNESS OF GOD, T. Hopko (St. Vladimir's Sem. Press, Crestwood, N.Y., 1982) pp. 187, $6.95.

REVELATION OF LIFE ETERNAL, N. Arseniev (St. Vladimir's Sem. Press, Crestwood, N.Y., 1982) pp. 144, $5.95.

NEW & OLD IN GOD'S REVELATION, B. Engelzakis (St. Vladimir's Sem. Press, 1982) pp. 122, $12.95.

I THESSALONIANS: A COMMENTARY, Paul Nadim Tarazi (St. Vladimir's Sem. Press, 1982) pp. 190, $7.95.

THE LIGHT OF THE WORLD, Serge Verhovskoy (St. Vladimir's Sem. Press, Crestwood, N.Y., 1982) pp. 163, $6.95.

THE MESSAGE OF THE BIBLE, George Cronk (St. Vladimir's Sem. Press, 1982) pp. 293, $8.95.

THE DIARY OF A RUSSIAN PRIEST, Alexander Elchaninov (St. Vladimir's Sem. Press, 1982) pp. 255, $7.95.

THE POPE AND REVOLUTION, Quentin L. Quade (Ethics & Public Policy Center, Wash., D.C., 1982) pp. 195.

THE SPIRITUAL HERITAGE OF THE ST. THOMAS CHRISTIANS, James Aerthayil (Dharmaran Publ., Bangalore, India, 1982) pp. 241.

PRAYER WITH THE HARP OF THE SPIRIT, Vol. 1, Frances Acharya (Dharmaram Publ., Bangalore, India, 1982) pp. 241.

PRAYER WITH THE HARP OF THE SPIRIT, Vol. II, Frances Acharya (Dharmaram Publ., Bangalore, India, 1982) pp. 632.

RESURRECTION LIFE AND RENEWAL, Varghese Pathikulangara (Dharmaram Publ., Bangalore, India, 1982) pp. 501.

LETTERS FROM THE HEART, John Main (Crossroad Publishing Co., N.Y., 1982) pp. 136, paperback $5.95.

SIMPLICITY, The Heart of Prayer, Georges Lefebvre (Paulist Press, N.Y. 1982) pp. 73, paperback $2.95.

SPIRITUAL FRIEND, Tilden Edwards (Paulist Press, N.Y., 1982) pp. 264 paperback $8.95.

DIAKONIA

INDEX

1982

VOL. XVII

	No.	Page
Editorials	1	1
	2	93
	3	189

Articles and Comment

	No.	Page
BECKER, Russell, O.F.M.: Byzantine Art & Theology	3	224
BONIAN, Stephen, S.J.: *Mary and the Christian in the Mystical Poetry of St. Ephrem*	1	46
_____: *Jerusalem and Fraternity among her Three Religions*	3	265
CHRYSOSTOMOS, Metropolitan of Myra: *The Beginning of the Dialogue between Orthodox and Roman Catholics*	3	243
CLAPSIS, Rev. Emmanuel: *St. Basil's Cosmology*	3	215
DAMASKINOS, Metropolitan of Tranupoleos: *The Holy Spirit in the Church*	1	40
EMILIANOS, Metropolitan of Silibria: *Life Giving—An Interpersonal Action*	2	109
FORTINO, Eleuterio F.: *Sanctification and Deification*	3	192
FRAZEE, Charles: *The Christian Traditions of Lebanon*	3	251
KILMARTIN, Edward J., S.J.: *The Active Role of Christ and the Spirit in the Divine Liturgy*	2	95
LONG, John F., S.J.: *Reflections on the Orthodox Catholic Dialogue*	1	21
MORE, John Blake: *Problems in the Study of Early Monasticism*	3	223
MORSE, Rev. Mr. Jonathan: *Fruits of the Eucharist—Henosis and Theosis*	2	127
ORIENTAL ORTHODOX AND ROMAN CATHOLIC DIALOGUE COMMISSION: *Purpose, Scope and Method of the Dialogue*	2	168

RITCHEY, Mary Grace: *Khomiakov and His Theory of Sobornost* 1   53

SABLE, Thomas F., S.J.: *Chronicle of Events Concerning Eastern Christianity 1981* 1   63

SLESINSKI, Rev. Robert: *Contemporary Essays in Orthodox Tradition and Life* 2   151

STYLIANOPOULOS, Rev. Theodore: *Orthodox and Catholicism—A New Attempt at Dialogue* 1   4

TAFT, Robert J., S.J.: *The Question of Infant Baptism in the Byzantine Catholic Churches of the U.S.A.* 3   201

TATARYN, Rev. Myron: *Theological Anthropology of the Byzantine Rites of Christian Initiation* 2   143

Documentation

INTERNATIONAL ROMAN CATHOLIC-ORTHODOX THEOLOGICAL DIALOGUE COMMISSION: *Press Release* 2   176
Document: *The Mystery of the Church and of the Eucharist in the Light of the Mystery of the Holy Trinity* 2   178

RUSSIAN ORTHODOX-ROMAN CATHOLIC CONVERSATIONS AT ODESSA: *Communique* 1   80

VISIT TO ROME OF HIS HOLINESS, PATRIARCH-CATHOLICOS ILIA II 1   83

VISIT TO NEW YORK OF HIS HOLINESS, PATRIARCH PIMEN 3   275

DIAKONIA

Devoted to promoting a knowledge and understanding
of Eastern Christianity
edited by Rev. John F. Long, S.J.

MANAGING EDITOR
Rev. Richard d. Lee

ORTHODOX ASSOCIATE EDITORS
Dr. John E. Rexine
Bohdan Demczuk

CIRCULATION MANAGER
Mrs. Rita Ruggiero

Editorial and Business Correspondence: Manuscripts should be typed double-spaced, with footnotes separate. Authors should retain a carbon copy and enclose return stamps. All manuscripts, subscriptions and correspondence should be sent to the following address: DIAKONIA, John XXIII Center, 2502 Belmont Avenue, Bronx, N.Y. 10458.

Published by the John XXIII Center
2502 Belmont Avenue
Bronx, N.Y. 10458

Subscription price:

USA: $ 9.00
CANADA and Foreign: $10.00
Single Numbers: $ 3.00

DIAKONIA

Published by the John XXIII Center

2502 Belmont Avenue

Bronx, New York 10458